Stamp indicates date for RET... returns will be charged in accordance with the regulations.

Books required by another reader will be recalled. This also applies during vacations.

27. MAR. # 91	-2. MAR. # 95	2. MAY # 97
14. JUN # 91	15. MAY # 95	
20. DEC. # 91	29. MAY # 95	22. ??? # 99
	30. SEP. # 95	30.09.00
12. JAN. # 93	23. OCT. # 96	
	-6. MAY # 98	
24. JAN. # 94	7. NOV. # ??	
-3. ??? # 95		

£35.000

49 - 50
109 - 110
65 - 66
95 - 96
107 - 109.

SOCIAL SECURITY AND SOCIAL CONTROL

Is there any justification for the growing poverty in the western world?

Do some welfare state policies actually exacerbate poverty?

How important are questions of social discipline in shaping the relationship between poverty and welfare state policies?

Social Security and Social Control takes a fresh look at social security policy and demonstrates how the disciplinary effects of social security and relief programmes are more extensive, pervasive and subtle than is commonly supposed. Based on his academic research, drawing particularly upon the post-structuralist ideas of Foucault, and aided by twelve years' practical experience as a front-line advice worker at a centre in Brixton, South London, Hartley Dean re-interprets the historical development of the British Poor Laws and the modern social security system. Thus he provides a new context within which to analyse the latest social security reforms and the significance of poverty as a contemporary phenomenon in advanced western societies. Also included is a unique case study of the Social Security Appeal Tribunal and the development of the tribunal system is presented as a commentary upon the disciplinary mechanisms inherent within the social security system as a whole. The book concludes with a reappraisal of the most recent debates about social security policy and about alternative social security systems.

Invaluable reading for undergraduates and lecturers in social policy, welfare law, sociology, socio-legal studies, politics and social history. *Social Security and Social Control* will also be of particular interest to anyone involved in welfare rights, advice work or legal services.

The author: Hartley Dean is a Research Fellow in social policy at the University of Kent.

SOCIAL SECURITY AND SOCIAL CONTROL

HARTLEY DEAN

LONDON AND NEW YORK

First published in 1991
by Routledge
11 New Fetter Lane, London EC4P 4EE

Simultaneously published in the USA and Canada by
Routledge
a division of Routledge, Chapman and Hall, Inc.
29 West 35th Street, New York, NY 10001

© 1991 Hartley Dean

Typeset by NWL Editorial Services, Langport, Somerset TA10 9DG
Printed and bound in Great Britain by
Biddles Ltd, Guildford and King's Lynn

All rights reserved. No part of this book may be
reprinted or reproduced or utilized in any form or by any electronic,
mechanical, or other means, now known or hereafter invented,
including photocopying and recording, or in any information storage
or retrieval system, without permission
in writing from the publishers.

British Library Cataloguing in Publication Data

Dean, Hartley, 1949–
Social security and social control
1. Great Britain. Social security
I. Title
368.4

Library of Congress Cataloging in Publication Data

Dean, Hartley, 1949–
Social security and social control/Hartley Dean
p. cm.
Includes bibliographical references (p.
1. Social security – Great Britain. 2. Social security – Law and
legislation – Great Britain. 3. Social control. I. Title.
HD7165.D43   1990   90-8323
368.4'00941 – dc20   CIP
ISBN 0-415-04862-1

TO BRENDAN AND NICOLA

CONTENTS

List of illustrations	ix
Acknowledgements	x

1 SOCIAL SECURITY REFORM AND THE QUESTION OF SOCIAL CONTROL — 1
- *Some basic assumptions* — 3
- *Retrenchment as reform* — 4
- *Perspectives on change* — 7

2 CONCEPTS OF SOCIAL CONTROL — 10
- *Social control and political settlement* — 11
- *Social control and social sanctions* — 18
- *Social control and individual behaviour* — 23
- *Conclusions* — 32

3 SOCIAL CONTROL AND THE DEVELOPMENT OF THE SOCIAL SECURITY SYSTEM — 35
- *From begging bowl to social wage* — 37
- *From corporal to pecuniary sanctions* — 43
- *From repression to discipline* — 51
- *Conclusions* — 60

4 POVERTY AND PARTITIONING — 65
- *Constructing poverty* — 66
- *Partitioning the poor* — 75
- *Prevention, relief and the strategy of social control* — 85

CONTENTS

**5 THE DEVELOPMENT OF THE SOCIAL
   SECURITY APPEAL TRIBUNAL: A CASE-STUDY** — 88
   The containment of protest — 89
   The adjudication of penalties — 103
   The adjudication process: looking through the window — 115
   Conclusions — 132

**6 THE EMERGENCE OF THE DISCIPLINARY
   EXAMINATION** — 136
   The form of the tribunal — 136
   Exposure to disciplinary examination — 144
   Performance of the tribunals — 156
   Consequences of social security reform for the SSAT — 167

7 STRATEGIES FOR SOCIAL CONTROL — 175
   Reprise — 175
   The great social security debate — 179
   Social security and 'New Times' — 192
   Beyond social control — 199

References — 203

Name index — 213

Subject index — 216

ILLUSTRATIONS

FIGURES

1 Appeals activity rates (Index II only) for unemployed claimants, 1913–1983	117
2 Appeals activity rates (Indices I & II) for all claimants, 1953–1983	118
3 Appeals activity rates (Index I only) for all claimants, 1976–1985	120
4 Appeals activity rates (Index II only) for all claimants, 1976–1985	122
5 Appeals activity rates (Index II only) for retired claimants, 1953–1983	123

TABLES

1 Supplementary Benefit appeals – subjects of appeal	130
2 Attendance and representation at appeal hearings	148
3 Types of representative appearing at Supplementary Benefit appeal hearings	152

ACKNOWLEDGEMENTS

The author wishes sincerely to thank Pam Dean, Peter Taylor-Gooby, Vic George, Peter Fitzpatrick and the Brixton Advice Centre, all of whom have, in various ways, contributed to the production of this book. The views here expressed, however, are entirely those of the author, who accepts sole responsibility for all errors of fact, omission or interpretation.

Chapter One

SOCIAL SECURITY REFORM AND THE QUESTION OF SOCIAL CONTROL

After the reforms, I was left with barely enough to live on. Life became a nightmare of juggling the money about. [*Susan – a single parent receiving Income Support*]

When you are poor you have to be extra good at managing, extra good at self-discipline, extra good at economising, extra good at managing without and extra good at dealing with constant crisis, stress and frustration. [*Joan – a pensioner with a disabled grown up son*]

(Quoted in Campaign Against Poverty 1989)

There is a sense in which, although they do not rhyme (like 'love and marriage'), poverty and social security go together 'like a horse and carriage'. Not only does one drive the other, but they are formed or designed so as to fit one another. There is a peculiarly intimate relationship between the kind of poverty that is still experienced in advanced western societies and the social security systems through which we claim to relieve or prevent such poverty.

And, if the experience of claiming social security is inseparable from the experience of poverty, it is also inseparable from the experience of social control from the experience of having to be 'extra good'.

Several eminent writers on social policy, such as Peter Townsend, have observed that social security (and particularly the administration of social security benefits) appears to have as much to do with controlling behaviour as with meeting need (Townsend 1979: 823). What is more, there are aspects of the reforms made to the British social security system in the 1980s which have quite explicit consequences for the control of behaviour and, as Tony Novak has put it, have played a part in the creation of a more 'coercive' social policy (Novak 1988: 200).

The idea that social security or relief giving may be instrumental in regulating both the economic and indeed the political behaviour of the poor is hardly new. In a seminal work, written in 1970, analysing the development of public welfare programmes in the USA, Piven and Cloward (1974) argued that the chief function of such programmes was to regulate labour: they charted the cyclical nature of the development of US relief programmes and concluded that expansive relief policies were designed to mute civil disorder, and restrictive ones to reinforce work norms.

The aim of this book, however, is to do more than apply Piven and Cloward's thesis to the UK's social security reforms of the 1980s. In Chapter 2 I shall seek to enlarge the concept of 'social control' so as to encompass, not only the suppression of civil disorder and the enforcement of work norms, but also the imposition of individual self-discipline and 'extra goodness'. In Chapter 3 I shall briefly trace the history of the British social security system as a history of emerging disciplinary techniques and in Chapter 4 I shall consider the sense in which the phenomenon of modern poverty has been created or constituted through the social security system. And, to illustrate this new way of thinking about social security and social control, in Chapters 5 and 6 I present, as a case-study, an analysis of the history and the operation of social security tribunals in the UK.

Finally, in Chapter 7 I shall return to the question of the social security reforms of the 1980s and seek to reinterpret their significance as part of a broader 'strategy' of social control. I shall also consider what such an analysis might portend in terms of the 'counter strategies' of social security claimants, poverty campaigners, advice workers and welfare lawyers.

But the purpose of this introductory chapter is to set the scene, first, by setting out some of the basic assumptions of the book and second, by explaining very briefly why it is that in the UK the social security reforms of the 1980s have pushed the question of social control to the top of the political agenda.

SOME BASIC ASSUMPTIONS

The writer shares with Ian Gough (1979) and others the contention that the social security system and the welfare state are ambiguous phenomena. Their development has brought significant benefits and, in relative terms, a lasting enhancement to the quality of life in the UK; but these have not been unqualified advances. The social security system also has negative effects and these stem, not only from the chronic insufficiency of state provision and the dead bureaucratic hand by which such provision is administered, but from social security's inherent capacity for what this book will redefine as 'social control'. This book does not therefore set out to present a simple condemnation of our social security system, nor even a critique of recent reforms, but to analyse the relations of power which they both mediate and obscure.

It must also be acknowledged that changes in social policy in the UK are occurring in the context of a process of global economic restructuring. Capitalism's internal dynamic is shifting us into a new 'post-industrial' or 'post-Fordist' phase (Murray 1988). Gone is the age of homogeneous, centralised industrial production and the mass market; in has come the age of information technology, market diversity and the service sector. Gone is the age of full employment and of an identifiable proletariat or working class; in has come the age of privileged 'core' workers and a disadvantaged reserve of 'peripheral' workers, the under-employed and the non-employed. In such a scenario, the very substantial and permanent role which the social security system must now play is of crucial and growing importance. The distributive and disciplinary functions of the welfare state require a new analysis.

Finally, the persistence of poverty in the UK results not merely from the failure of the social security system but from the contradictions and structural limitations of the process of capital accumulation. Poverty, as it is understood in this book, can only be ended by a fundamental redefinition of the bases for productive human activity and for the distribution of resources to meet human need – a process which would require an end to both the wage relation and the commodity form and which is therefore ultimately unattainable under capitalist social relations, whether they be characterised in form as 'industrial', 'advanced' or 'post-Fordist'.

RETRENCHMENT AS REFORM

The so-called social security 'reforms' introduced by the governments of Margaret Thatcher during the period 1979 to 1989, represent, in fact, a significant retrenchment of the social security system. In Piven and Cloward's terms, the period could be identified as a restrictive phase or cycle, characterised by a reduction or at least a containment of public spending on social security and an explicit attempt to enhance work incentives and to promote self-reliance and independence (Piven and Cloward 1974).

The actual changes to the social security system introduced since 1979 are both legion and complex. Some specific detail is contained in later chapters, but here I shall outline what may be regarded as five major trends.

First, there have been cuts in benefit spending and a shift away from universal and social insurance based benefits towards means-tested benefits. The consequence is greater hardship for many social security claimants and/or more surveillance of claimants by state officials. By a series of measures, the government has changed the basis on which most social security benefits and pensions are periodically uprated so as to link them to price inflation, rather than to rises in earnings: the result will be that if real earnings rise no more than 1.5 per cent per year faster than prices, the relative value of the basic Retirement Pension will fall by more than a half over the next fifty years. By other measures, the government has abolished Earnings Related Supplements to National Insurance Unemployment and Sickness Benefits and halved the value of supplements under the State Earnings Related Pension Scheme. As changes such as these erode the adequacy of what remains of the UK National Insurance scheme, increasing numbers of claimants will be obliged to supplement their incomes by recourse to means-tested (i.e. social assistance) benefits, such as Income Support and Housing Benefit. What is more, since 1987 the value of non-means-tested Child Benefit has been frozen in order, it has been claimed, to switch resources into the new means-tested Family Credit scheme. These changes have been accompanied by enjoinders and incentives to workers to opt for occupational provision, private insurance and personal pension plans. For most of those without access to such forms of provision, levels of state income support have been tightened and support is now more likely to be conditional upon a means test (see Social Security Consortium 1987; CPAG 1989).

Second, the basis of the main means test has been changed. The Income Support scheme, which replaced the Supplementary Benefit scheme with effect from 1988, is officially recognised not as a 'safety net' but as the main fulcrum of a social security system which supposedly 'targets' resources to those who need them most (DHSS 1985b). Under Income Support, however, the specifically need-related benefit additions of the old Supplementary Benefit scheme have been replaced by 'client group premiums' (Social Security Act 1986 Part II). There are different premiums for families, for pensioners, for single parents, for disabled people and so on, and the accentuated differences in benefit levels for the different 'client groups' help to emphasise distinctions between the more and the less 'deserving'. Distinctions are now drawn on the basis of status, not need.

Third, the Social Security Act 1986 (Part III) also created the Social Fund, through which the special needs grants formerly available to long-term Supplementary Benefit claimants have been replaced, for the most part, with 'crisis loans' and 'budgeting loans', which claimants must repay by instalments from future weekly benefits. This change amounts to and has indeed been justified as the direct imposition of budgetary discipline upon the poor.

Fourth, there have been several measures explicitly directed against the unemployed or intended to increase work incentives. Between 1979 and 1988 there were no fewer than 38 significant changes affecting social security benefits for the unemployed (Atkinson and Micklewright 1988). Despite the fact that this was a period during which the levels of unemployment reached unprecedented levels, most of these changes have been disadvantageous to the unemployed. Most significantly, the rules in relation to disqualification for voluntary unemployment or misconduct, the administration of 'availability for work' tests and 'Restart' interviews, and contribution conditions for National Insurance Unemployment Benefit have all been tightened, signalling an altogether more punitive regime for the unemployed. At the same time, social policy in the UK has been moving quite consciously in the direction of US-style 'Workfare' systems (see Davies 1987). During the past decade, community programmes and a range of work experience and employment training schemes for the unemployed have burgeoned, whilst the government has taken powers (under Social Security Act 1988) to make participation effectively compulsory, since social security benefits may now be withheld from unemployed persons who refuse places upon such schemes.

Fifth, many of the changes to the social security system have been made to bear with particular severity upon school-leavers and young people beneath the age of 26. The intention behind this is quite clearly to make young people a charge upon their families until such time as they can be fully 'independent' (Allbeson 1985). Thus, the right of most 16 and 17-year-olds to Income Support has been removed entirely and 18 to 24-year-olds receive only a reduced level of Income Support personal allowance. Unemployed under 25-year-olds living in bed and breakfast accommodation have been dogged throughout the 1980s by an ever-changing round of social security regulations intended to limit their entitlement to assistance with their board and lodging charges and to restrict the period of time which such persons can remain in any one area, so forcing them either to return to their families, or else into a nomadic existence.

Although the government clearly intends that it should play such a role, the social security system is not a particularly effective vehicle for certain kinds of disciplinary incentive or disincentive. Evidence from the USA already suggests that 'Workfare'-type benefit systems have little effect in engendering a work ethic (Gueron 1986; Burton 1987) and Department of Employment research conducted before the withdrawal of Income Support from school-leavers showed that the vast majority of school-leavers would have preferred to work rather than to claim benefits (Banks and Ullah 1986). Changes in social security rules may therefore be more significant for their symbolism than for their relevance.

Conversely, reforms in social security policy may have important consequences which belie the rhetoric of policy-makers. For example, the government's intention to 'target' benefits upon those most in need (DHSS 1985b) has failed: by December 1988 means-tested Family Credit was reaching fewer than 40 per cent of the families for whom it was intended (CPAG 1989). The switch of priorities from a high take-up universal benefit (Child Benefit) to a low take-up means-tested benefit (Family Credit) is an extremely effective way of tightening the belts of low income families.

PERSPECTIVES ON CHANGE

Examination of the impact of the changes which they have brought about reveals that the social security reforms cannot be taken at face value. There are three distinct perspectives on such changes.

The first perspective is that presented by Margaret Thatcher's ministers. In a widely reported speech made in September 1987, John Moore, then Secretary of State for Health and Social Security, contrasted the 'dependency culture' of welfare benefit recipients with the 'enterprise culture' of those who seek to create wealth and opportunity. Aspects of the social security reforms are expressly motivated by a desire to eradicate or modify this 'dependency culture'. In this version, social controls are necessary to ensure that the experience of claiming social security does not sap individuals' capacity for independence and initiative or their inclination to engage in economic activity.

The second perspective is shared by academics, such as Dahrendorf (1987), who effectively ally to this popular notion of 'dependency culture' the idea that there is emerging in the UK an 'underclass', separated in life chances and expectations from the mass of the population. As welfare benefit levels for many groups fail to keep pace with changes in earnings, the very basis of citizenship is undergoing a radical restructuring. The social security system is the principal and most immediate means of control over this 'underclass' and, in this account, the dependent docility engendered by the process of claiming social security is a necessary means and an effective technique by which to control this 'underclass' or 'reserve army' of unproductive labour.

The third perspective is adopted by the poverty lobby (e.g. Walker and Walker 1987) and old-fashioned Fabians who point out that these changes in social security are imposing ever stricter controls on the purchasing power and opportunities of a substantial proportion of the population. This reversal in income redistribution and the new strictures on social security 'consumers' may have long-term implications for social cohesion since it undermines the integrative function of social security. According to this account, the proper purpose and the continuing potential of social security is to promote the individual's sense of identity, participation and community: the social rights and mutual interdependency which the social security system ought to underwrite are a necessary guarantee which ensures that all citizens have an opportunity to participate in social life.

For the moment, it matters little which of these perspectives is correct. It is in the telling of the different accounts that we may detect the various ways in which social security and social control can be linked. Through these competing versions of what social security is for, there runs a common strand; an unspoken consensus about the relevance of social security to issues of social dependency and social discipline.

Poverty and social security do indeed 'go' together like a horse and carriage. The thing which links them is the question of social control. A better analogy perhaps is the relationship between criminality and penal policy, since that is a relationship which is clearly founded upon issues of social control. This is a theme which will recur in future chapters, but the basic argument can be summarised as follows.

It is widely acknowledged that our prison system has never been particularly effective at reforming criminals or deterring crime. Several theorists have argued that the sub-culture, the ethos and the state of mind that we might call 'criminality' is actually perpetuated by the way in which society organises the definition, detection and punishment of crime. Objectively speaking, the preoccupations of penal policy are irrelevant to the amount of wrong-doing in society. They are however effective in identifying and marginalising criminals as a 'dangerous class'. In this way, the real disciplinary effect of the penal system has less to do with the punishment of criminals than with the way that criminals and non-criminals are made to identify themselves and each other.

In much the same way, it has been amply demonstrated that the social security system is remarkably ineffective at either relieving or preventing poverty. Whether we define poverty in terms of relative material deprivation, the enforced lack of socially perceived necessities or an imposed exclusion from social participation, such things are in fact perpetuated by the ways in which society organises income redistribution and maintenance through the tax and social security systems and by the conditions and tests which attach to the receipt of social security benefits. The preoccupations of social security policy and the rules of the social security system are quite divorced from the causes of material inequality in society, but they are highly effective in identifying and marginalising the poor so that they appear as a 'claiming class' or 'underclass'. Thus, social security has a disciplinary effect. Not only does it place constraints on claimants, but it structures the way in which claimants and non-claimants are made to identify themselves, to act and to think about each other.

It is not suggested that poverty and criminality are the same thing, only that in their contemporary forms they are each of them products of a particular kind of social organisation and policy. The social security and penal systems are in many respects fundamentally different, but they are both disciplinary: they both define a 'social problem' in terms that are 'socially manageable'. This framework furnishes an alternative view of poverty and social security to those advanced by the proponents of 'dependency culture' and 'underclass'. Such a view is capable of reinterpreting the phenomena which such terms address by identifying disciplinary mechanisms which displace the dimensions of class and culture and which strategically detach social security claimants, not only from the productive working class, but also from one another.

Some may look back on the social security reforms of the 1980s as just another 'turn of the screw'; as a particularly restrictive or repressive phase in the cycle of social security policy development. What this book will argue is that the reforms tell us more than that, not because they were unusually radical or far-reaching, but precisely because they illustrate that every social security system has its inherent and peculiar capacity for social control.

Chapter Two

CONCEPTS OF SOCIAL CONTROL

> Since capitalism is still with us, we can with impunity suppose, if we wish to, that at any time in the last three hundred years the mechanisms of social control were operating effectively.
> (Stedman-Jones 1985: 42)

Anyone intending to use the term 'social control' must distinguish his/her specific use from that of other writers, and also situate that use in relation to the plethora of other uses and abuses to which the term has been subject. As Stanley Cohen has observed, the term 'social control' has lately become something of a 'Mickey Mouse concept' (1985: 2). Its value has at times been reduced to that of a facile slogan. None the less, in spite of the diversity of the theoretical discourses in which the term has been ascribed various meanings, the notion of social control remains central to any understanding of the fact that capitalism is indeed still with us.

The many forms and mechanisms of social control may be ranged along a continuum from the coercive at one extreme to the consensual at the other. Social control may be understood as repression, as exploitation, as co-optation, as integration, as paternalism, as conformity, or even as self-determination (see Higgins 1980). At one extreme, social control represents the oppression of a ruling class; at the other, social control is the connective tissue which binds together the perfectly functioning social organism.

If social control is to be presented as a means by which capitalist society manages to perpetuate itself, then one might legitimately enquire as to who exactly is being controlled and by whom; by what means and for what purpose? (Higgins 1980; Mayer 1985). It is seldom possible to give simple or unequivocal answers to such questions, not least because of the evident lack of congruence between the apparent intentions and the actual effects of the social policies which may appear to be directed to social control.

The purpose of this chapter is to outline three general levels at which social control seems or has been presumed to operate:

1. the level of 'political settlement' at which social order is achieved through the medium of concessions granted by a ruling class or power bloc, or by the state, to a subjected class;
2. the level of coercive repression and penal sanctions at which physical force or substantive deprivation is applied in order to modify behaviour;
3. the level of the individual actor at which social institutions (such as the family), social pressures or social norms tend to shape individual conduct.

These levels of social control intersect and overlap and the analytical distinctions drawn between them are not necessarily exhaustive.

SOCIAL CONTROL AND POLITICAL SETTLEMENT

The provision by society of the so-called 'social wage' – the parcel of services and benefits provided by the modern welfare state – is often seen as having a direct effect in containing popular discontent and averting threats of social disorder. As such, the social wage can be said to make a contribution to social control. However, it is difficult to determine in whose interests the social wage is paid or indeed whether its payment is effective in guaranteeing social harmony.

The social wage as ransom

John Saville (1958) has argued that the welfare state developed through the interaction of three principal factors: the struggle of the working class against their exploitation; the requirements of industrial capital for an effective environment and a productive work-force; and the recognition by the propertied classes of the price which had to be paid to ensure political stability. Upon a simple reading of such an analysis, the social wage may be taken to be paid as a ransom by the capitalist ruling class to the working class in return for political peace and industrial productivity. At various moments during the development of the welfare state, many of the reformers who campaigned for welfare reforms and many of the politicians who conceded them were motivated by a belief that the process of reform represented an accommodation between the interests of labour and the interests of capital: for example, such an interpretation was shared at least by some members of the reforming Labour government of 1945 (see Bevan 1978).

However, whether or not such accommodations have contributed to peace and productivity, the social wage itself has not brought unqualified benefits to the working class; nor (according to some theorists) has it necessarily been paid for by capital. Governmental and academic studies alike have shown that the relative inequality in the social distribution of income and wealth has hardly been affected by the advent of the welfare state (e.g. Royal Commission on the Distribution of Income and Wealth 1976; Field 1981). Kincaid (1975), for example, has argued that the only redistribution of income which occurs through the social security and taxation system is a 'horizontal' redistribution between wage earners (or even within the life cycle of the individual wage earner). If the working class are no better off in relative terms and appear to have been paying their own social wage, the explanation for the significance of that social wage must surely be more complex than that suggested above. It is therefore necessary to consider in greater detail the role of the welfare state as paymaster of the social wage.

Keynes and Beveridge are widely accredited as the prime theoretical movers of the expansion of the welfare state after the Second World War. They are perhaps aptly characterised as 'reluctant collectivists' (George and Wilding 1985) or 'reluctant interventionists' (Taylor-Gooby and Dale 1981). They recognised the failings of capitalism in the 1930s and sought to 'mend (the) evils of our condition by reasoned experiment, within the framework of our existing system' (from an open letter by J.M.Keynes to President Roosevelt in 1933 – quoted in Taylor-Gooby and Dale 1981. 73).

From this perspective, the enhancement of the social wage was one of several measures intended to improve capital accumulation by mitigating the hazards and excesses of an unplanned free market. The social wage was to be paid, not as a ransom, nor even out of beneficence, but with a view to regulating the potential of the working and non-working population as both producers and consumers. O'Connor (1973) has argued that all state expenditure takes the form of 'social capital' or 'social expenses' or both: social capital is required for either investment (in projects such as health and education which increase the productivity of labour power) or consumption (in projects such as family allowances, food subsidies, etc. which reduce the reproduction costs of labour) to assist profitable private accumulation; social expenses represent the necessary costs of maintaining social harmony and legitimating the existing order. According to this model, the provision of the social wage is more than a simple accommodation between capital and labour: it operates for the benefit of capital.

If this approach explains who ultimately benefits from the social wage, it does not explain how it is that social control may be achieved in the process. Nor should the value or importance of the social wage to its recipients be ignored. Ian Gough (1979) calculated that in aggregate in 1975, in spite of a net flow from the personal sector to the state of some 7 per cent of total personal incomes, social services in cash and in kind amounted to almost 30 per cent of total personal incomes. Arguably, it is only through the social wage that the real as distinct from the relative living standards of substantial sections of the working class have been improved. And so Gough speaks of the welfare state as a contradictory phenomenon which

> embodies tendencies to enhance welfare, to develop the powers of individuals, to exert social control over the blind play of market forces; and tendencies to repress and control people, to adapt them to the requirements of the capitalist economy.
> (Gough 1979: 12)

Gough and others (e.g. George 1973) point out that many of the key welfare reforms between 1944 and 1948 were perceived as being in the mutual interests of capital and labour: in their final form, Butler's Education Act, Beveridge's social security scheme and the setting up of the National Health Service attracted all-party support. The social wage, even if it has not increased relative living standards, undoubtedly makes a day to day contribution to real living standards. Even if the social wage cannot be proved to operate as a guarantee of social order, it is widely seen as a significant factor – not least within the Thatcher government itself, whose 'dry' and 'wet' factions continue to debate, as Jennifer Dale has put it, 'the merits of stern monetarism, protecting profits but risking social turmoil, versus a more gradualist approach' (Taylor-Gooby and Dale 1981: 187).

However, although the Wilson/Callaghan government of 1974–1979 attempted to institute a 'social contract' with the TUC (see Townsend 1980), the social wage has never in reality been 'negotiated' between the representatives of capital and labour. It appears instead as the result of campaigns, debates and 'struggles' within the political sphere. If the social wage is anything other than a symbolic description of those services and benefits which the market itself cannot or will not provide, the link between the interests of capital and labour and the political formulation of the social wage must still be demonstrated.

This can only be done if the social wage is understood as reflecting the form of welfare state provision rather than in terms of the constituent elements of the content of such provision. Any such approach must to some extent draw upon the 'state derivation' debate (Holloway and Picciotto 1978).

The state derivation debate

The starting point of this debate is to eschew purely 'instrumentalist' (e.g. Miliband 1969) and 'structuralist' (e.g. Poulantzas 1973) notions of the state under capitalism and to 'derive' the form of the state from the 'anatomy of civil society' (Marx 1969). By reference solely to the specific stage of development of the social relations of production, the protagonists in this debate seek to explain the source or the origin of capitalist society's constituent features – first, economic relations (the processes of material production, the market, the circuits of capital); second, political relations (the state and its legislative and administrative machinery); and third, the separation and functional interrelationships between these two spheres.

To try and put this rather less abstractly; for the purposes of this book, the notion of a social wage paid outside the market place by the welfare state can only be understood by reference to the way in which our particular society organises and reproduces its means of material production. At the most schematic of levels, the capitalist mode of production is characterised by the production and exchange of commodities. Since all goods and materials must be taken and exchanged on an open market as 'commodities', the producers and owners of commodities must recognise in each other the rights of private proprietors and must relate to each other on a contractual or legal basis. In addition, the abolition of feudal land tenure meant that all forms of property entered the market as commodities and also that the labouring population was transformed into 'free' legal subjects who contract to sell their labour to the capitalist commodity producer in return for their own means of subsistence. Pashukanis (1978) has argued that human beings thus become 'legal subjects' by virtue of the same necessity which transforms the products of nature into 'commodities', and the state and its legal and political apparatus are formally separated from the source of economic interests in order to preserve in appearance the freedom of all politico-juridical subjects.

Hirsch (1978) has taken this general line of reasoning further. He suggests that the exploitation of labour by capital – the process by which commodity producers extract surplus value from work 'freely' performed by wage labourers – is dependent not upon the use of force but upon the 'dull compulsion of uncomprehended laws of reproduction'. The process by which one 'earns' one's day to day subsistence appears as 'natural' as the necessity to procure that subsistence in exchange for money and in the form of commodities. Thus the domination of capitalist producers over wage labourers is abstracted or removed from the immediate sphere of the processes of material production and constitutes a discrete political sphere, the form of which – parliamentary democracy and a 'neutral' state apparatus – is distinctively conditioned by the social relations of production. Just as the social form of exchange (based on commodities possessing purely abstract values) necessarily gives rise to legal relations (based on legal subjects possessing purely abstract rights), so the social form of exploitation (based on the wage relation and the purely 'formal' freedom of contracts entered between parties of unequal standing) necessarily gives rise to political relations (based on state power and the purely formal 'freedom' of citizens subject to that power).

This analysis of the state form dispels any idea that the welfare state and the provision of the social wage is a simple conspiracy to achieve social control. Similarly, it qualifies any functionalist conception that the state merely delivers what capital or society happens to need.

It is in this context that the application of the so-called 'fetishised' or surface category of the 'wage' to the services and benefits provided by the state becomes important. Ian Gough (1979) has demonstrated that the services which go to make up the social wage function so as to modify the reproduction of labour power and to regulate it both quantitatively and qualitatively. The wage form, derived from the direct exploitative relationship between capital and labour at the point of material production, is thus abstracted and applied to the relationship between the 'neutral' state and the 'free' politico–juridical subject. The necessity for the reproduction of the means of production also reproduces the social relations of production, and so the state itself through the provision of a 'social wage' reproduces those social (i.e. class) relations. In furnishing the social wage, the welfare state may or may not succeed in maintaining social control, but the point which is being made is that the welfare state in its inherent form constitutes a part of the relations of domination under capitalism.

Who pays?

Having situated the phenomenon of the social wage in this manner, it is possible to return to the question of who pays it and who benefits. We have already noted that, according to Kincaid and others, the social wage is paid for largely by forms of taxation upon the working class itself, but this itself raises the question of who ultimately bears the cost of taxation: is it a drain upon capital accumulation or upon the living standards of workers? Norman Ginsberg (1979) has contended that the cost of state expenditure is borne entirely by capital since the 'real' price of labour is represented by net wages (i.e. wages after stoppages for National Insurance contributions and income tax). According to Eric Shragge (1984), however, this is too simplistic. He concedes that, so long as workers can defend their post-tax and post-inflation standard of living (which has generally been the tendency since the Second World War), then the burden of taxation does fall upon capital, but he goes on to observe that increased taxation can reduce wages and that this 'will intensify workers' struggles over their living standards, posing problems for capitalists, as taxation increases have the potential of taxing some surplus value out of circulation, as well as increasing class struggle' (Shragge 1984: 15).

Shragge concludes that the limits of welfare state expansion (and therefore the substantive value of the social wage) are linked to the totality of class relations and he goes on to show that the recent economic crisis of capitalism and the resulting 'reforms' of welfare provision have resulted in an attack on working class living standards. This more complex view of 'who pays' gives a more dynamic picture of the social wage as a 'trade off', since the costs and benefits in financial terms are not static.

It is also now possible to consider more fruitfully the sense in which the payment of the social wage may do more than merely underwrite the cost to private capital of the reproduction of labour power, but might in effect 'buy' social order. We have considered in simplified form the argument that the control of labour at the point of material production (e.g. upon the factory floor) is dependent not upon force but upon a 'silent compulsion' and that the relations of domination (i.e. political struggle) have become abstracted to a separate level. Historically, this is a gross generalisation: the 'factory floor' has on occasions been the site of tyrannical discipline, whilst there have been other occasions when a burgeoning trade union movement, with effect, took 'politics' into the factory rather than to parliament. More recently, Taylorism and 'scientific management' have been deployed in order to secure conformity at work, but ultimately the managers of labour have relied upon the assumption, expressed here in the words of Sohn-Rethel, 'that the workers, while working as a combined force with their hands, in their minds remain divided in conformity with their pay packets' (Sohn-Rethel 1978: 162).

Capital maintains control through the concessions it appears or purports to make through wages – including, indirectly, of course the social wage – and so what John Lea (1979) has termed the 'monetization' of the class struggle occurs. Lea claims that the terrain upon which compliance is generated shifts outside the factory, and outside the market place, and into a 'trade off' of gains in the market, in the price of labour, in return for compliance in the labour process. 'Monetization' therefore binds the labour movement under modern capitalism to an ideology that is essentially reformist and, at the industrial level, 'it acts to transfer the struggle "peacefully" to other areas, notable among which is the state where the class struggle takes the predominant form of a political struggle for increases in the social wage' (Sohn-Rethel: 87).

The point about this level of explanation is that it does not require the social wage to be effective as a means of abating poverty, for example, in order to demonstrate its potential for what may be termed social control. This provides the sense in which the terms 'social control' and 'social wage' may be used in conjunction. The provision by the state of the social wage has the capacity to make the relationship between the individual citizen and the state appear as a matter of social policy, whereas the subjection of labour by capital cannot have that capacity. What is argued here is that it is only through the state that the domination of labour by capital may be translated into social control.

SOCIAL CONTROL AND SOCIAL SANCTIONS

The second sense in which the term 'social control' is used describes the overt measures deployed by the state to punish or reform particular forms of behaviour defined as 'deviant': if the social wage is the carrot of social control, then social sanctions are the stick.

Penal policy

The recent 'revisionist' historians of deviancy control (Rothman 1980; Ignatieff 1978; Melossi and Pavarini 1981; Thompson 1975; Foucault 1977) share the following general conclusions. During the eighteenth and nineteenth centuries an entirely new approach to criminal justice emerged and new concepts of punishment were forged. These developments were ultimately embodied in institutional form in the reformatory prison and similar forms of 'total institution' (for example, the asylum). These signalled the advent of a new source of political power and a new kind of social regulation and control.

Before the development of centralised state apparatuses, the punishment of crime tended to be arbitrary, uninstitutionalised, violent and spectacular. It took the form of retribution visited upon the body of the offender. During the seventeenth and eighteenth centuries, as the power of the sovereign and the aristocracy was gradually wrested away by an emerging landed bourgeoisie, parliament enacted statutes creating a host of capital offences against property and so generated the bloodiest penal code in Europe; the capacity of such a code to 'freeze terror of legitimate power' (Hay 1975) in the public mind was undermined by jury acquittals and the use of prerogative pardons. Thus the code came into conflict with utilitarian doctrines which insisted upon requirements of certainty and calculability. What emerged was a more centralised, generalised and pervasive state power, a more rational penal code and a form of punishment (the reformatory prison) which was discrete and institutionalised. The reformatory prison, instead of inflicting pain upon the body of the criminal as an 'outlaw', by incarcerating and controlling the body, operated upon the mind or soul of the criminal as a 'legal subject'. Indeed, the object of imprisonment was not only to inflict a determinate penalty in proportion to the 'seriousness' of the offence committed, but also to reform prisoners and, in the words of the Gladstone Report of 1895 – 'turn them out as better men and women'.

The prison remains the dominant form of punishment in spite of the fact that as a measure for controlling or reducing crime it appears to be an unmitigated failure. Prison neither reforms nor deters criminal behaviour. This has led to the limited development of alternatives to prison, although the prison population continues regardless on a 'steady upward spiral' (Cohen 1985). There has been an increasing tendency towards the 'medicalisation' of deviance (Szasz 1961); to regard wrong-doing as a manifestation of individual illness or pathology and control as a question of 'treatment' or 'therapy'. At the same time, there have been tendencies towards 'decarceration' (Scull 1977) and 'diversion' (Morris et al. 1980) and to forms of 'rehabilitation' or even 'reparation' within the community. The development of such measures and techniques, however, has always been supplementary to existing provision and have served, to use Cohen's terminology, to 'widen the net' of social control (Cohen 1985). It remains the case, however, that 'treatment' and 'rehabilitation' philosophies, when applied in practice, have not proved any more successful than conventional penal measures. This has fuelled a continuing debate (particularly with regard to the punishment/treatment of juvenile offenders) and something of a 'back-lash' in favour of stricter and more retributive punishment regimes.

In an attempt to disentangle some competing theoretical views of the 'story of correctional change', Stanley Cohen categorises three versions of that story (Cohen 1985: ch. 1). First is the conventional progressive view which sees prevailing social sanctions policy, in spite of its failings, as an advance upon previous policies in terms of its enlightenment and humanitarianism and which believes such policies may be further improved by providing 'more of the same'. The second view, attributed primarily to Rothman (1980), is that the dictates of conscience have been frustrated by the dictates of convenience and the good intentions of various reformers in history have been undermined, corrupted or subverted by the managers (the administrators and professionals) of the state system: the consequences have been disastrous but, stripped of their naive optimism and informed by the lessons of history, the original reform projects are still valid. The third view, attributed to a number of key writers (Ignatieff 1978; Melossi and Pavarini 1981; Foucault 1977), is that social sanctions are fulfilling functions other than the declared intentions of their instigators: the prison, like the social wage, forms part of the relations of domination and epitomises either the ultimate power of capital over the organisation of labour (according to Melossi and Pavarini), or the generalised techniques of power exercised throughout a 'disciplinary society' (according to Foucault).

State coercion: social discipline

The argument that the state is a 'relation of domination' (in the sense that the form of the state may be derived from the nature of the exploitation of labour by capital) was discussed in a previous section. This analysis was applied to the idea of the 'social wage'. A similar analysis may be applied to the idea of the 'social sanction'. The 'silent compulsion' (Marx 1970a) of the wage labourer's economic 'reward' (the wage which represents the means to the worker's own subsistence) is complemented by the equally silent compulsion of the sanction reserved to the capitalist of the withdrawal, withholding or 'docking' of that 'reward': physical force is not necessary to that compulsion so long as both the worker and the capitalist appear to each other to be formally free and equal subjects under the law. The use of more palpable compulsion (and particularly the use of physical force), like the provision of enhanced forms of 'wage', is reserved to the state and to the sphere of political/legal relations.

Max Weber (1949) contended that one of the constitutive characteristics of capitalism was the emergence of the state, holding a monopoly of legitimate physical violence; central to the concept of social (as opposed to economic or 'civil') sanctions is the use or the 'right' to use force in the apprehension and punishment of wrongdoers. Lenin (1965) argues that the state, exercising such a monopoly, should be regarded as no more than an instrument of class oppression. Alternatively, the state may be understood as an assemblage of apparatuses having both repressive and ideological functions (Althusser 1971).

Against such views, Nicos Poulantzas (1980) has argued that account must be taken of the 'institutional materiality' of the state, representing as it does a 'condensation' of the several class forces (and fractional forces) in play within society: the state, precisely because it inhabits a separate and relatively autonomous realm, incarnates through its institutions and apparatuses the competing demands and discourses arising out of the social relations of production. By the substantive operation of those institutions and apparatuses, it materialises and reproduces those social relations of production. If this sounds as if, according to Poulantzas, the state is both the child and the parent of class struggle, then it should be added that he none the less sees the state monopolisation of violence and the power of sanctions as underlying the capacity of the state to exercise domination: although such domination in its day to day form entails neither coercive repression nor crude ideological inculcation, but expresses the real effects of a 'complex web of class powers'.

This position, while acknowledging the repressive appearance of the state and its capacity to impose coercive social sanctions, also recognises that domination or 'social control' functions at levels which operate well beyond or even in spite of the nature of such sanctions.

The social sanctions policy, founded upon the institutional form of the reformatory prison, embodied an important new technique in punishment, intended to act continuously over time and to produce docile and useful bodies. Melossi and Pavarini (1981) have linked this development to the need of the new manufacturing industries for a skilled and ordered labour force, whilst Michel Foucault (1977) claims that it symbolised a more general shift towards a 'disciplinary society'. Of these two views of the generalised form which state administered sanctions have taken, one relies upon a relatively simplistic causative explanation, whilst the other enigmatically evades the question of whose interests are served by social sanctions (see Ignatieff 1985). None the less, as a materialist analysis of power and of what we are calling 'social sanctions', it is Foucault's account of the prison as the embodiment of disciplinary techniques which may be married to Poulantzas' highly abstract account of the state to provide a more concrete understanding of the significance of social sanctions (see Poulantzas 1980: 66).

Foucault puts it thus:

> the prison, apparently 'failing' does not miss its target, it reaches it, in so far that it gives rise to one particular form of illegality in the midst of others which it is able to isolate, to place in full light and to organise as a relatively enclosed but penetrable milieu.... This form is, strictly speaking, delinquency. One should not see in delinquency the most intense, most harmful form of illegality, the form which the penal apparatus must try to eliminate ... ; it is rather an effect of penality ... that makes it possible to differentiate, accommodate and supervise illegalities.... For the observation that prison fails to eliminate crime, one should perhaps substitute the hypothesis that prison has succeeded extremely well in producing delinquency, a specific type, a politically or economically less dangerous ... form of illegality; in producing delinquents, in an apparently marginal, but in fact centrally supervised milieu; in producing the delinquent as a pathological subject.
> (Foucault 1977: 276–7)

And according to Foucault, the reformatory prison may not merely be regarded as the site of discrete forms of social sanction, since it has refined, developed and continues to exemplify the techniques of power (such as 'surveillance' and 'normalisation') which Foucault calls the 'disciplines'. Such techniques are exercised throughout our social institutions – in factories, schools and hospitals – as mechanisms of a continuous discipline by which all individuals (whether they be delinquents, workers, pupils or patients) may be distinguished and meticulously ordered.

So, if social sanctions have an effect in the exercise of social control, it is not because they deter those who might offend or because they reform those who have already done so. Such sanctions are effective because the disciplinary techniques which they embody in generalised form are of particular application in the differentiation, accommodation and supervision of individual behaviour. Their effectiveness also lies in the fact that the state, which materialises and reproduces the social relations of production, assigns what Poulantzas (1980) describes as 'class pertinency' to those disciplinary techniques and enmeshes them within a general web of class powers. At this most conspicuous level of social control – the level of state coercion and social sanctions – we are confronted, not by a distinct phenomenon, but by the tip of a metaphorical iceberg, the submerged portion of which extends far beyond the boundaries of the penal system and into water also occupied by other less conspicuous levels of social control.

SOCIAL CONTROL AND INDIVIDUAL BEHAVIOUR

The mechanisms of social control therefore are plainly more complex than the 'sticks' and 'carrots' of state capitalism's social policy. This section will consider some of those sociological definitions of 'social control' which regard it as a process occurring independently of any enterprise in social policy.

The concept of social control was central to the classical nineteenth-century sociological tradition (Cohen and Scull 1985), in which society as a whole was the object of study and the question to be answered was that of how society could, without physical coercion, achieve the degree of organisation and regulation which was perceived to exist. Attempting to reassert that tradition, Janowitz (1975) defines social control as a 'perspective which focuses on the capacity of a social organisation to regulate itself' and, in so doing, the task is to 'clarify and explicate the content and criteria of self-regulation'. To this end, Janowitz suggests, the language of political discourse is inadequate and he urges a return to the classic macro-sociological questions of order, organisation and authority.

Macrosociological approaches

Social *order* had been the paramount concern of Durkheim, to whom 'Collective life is not born from individual life, but it is, on the contrary, the second which is born from the first' (Durkheim 1964a).

To Durkheim, society was synonymous with social control in the sense that he held the only properly observable manifestation of social reality to be 'social facts', which he defined as 'ways of acting, thinking and feeling, external to the individual and endowed with a power of coercion by reason of which they control him' (Durkheim 1964b).

Thus, the currency, the law, the division of labour, the language we grow up with are social facts which constitute the unique social reality by which no individual can avoid being constrained, as indeed are the shared values, sentiments and opinions reified by Durkheim as the 'collective conscience' and to which he attributes an autonomous existence and an independent power over the individual. So it is, according to Durkheim, that the individual is socially controlled and 'finds himself in the presence of a force which is superior to him and before which he bows' (Durkheim 1964b: 123).

Having so defined the relationship of the individual to society, the problem for Durkheim was that of how social order could be sustained in the face of the destabilising and disintegrating effects of modern industrial capitalism and the differentiation, specialisation and fragmentation which he observed it to bring at every level within society. His answer lay in his concept of 'social solidarity' as the force which binds the individual to society. In 'simple' societies solidarity is of a 'mechanical' nature, while in complex or 'advanced' societies, solidarity is 'organic'. The process of evolution from one form of society to another is reflected and can be measured in society's increasingly secular moralities, its increasingly complex and sophisticated divisions of labour and forms of co-operation and, for example, a change of emphasis from retributive law (based on repressive sanctions) to law based on principles of restitution.

A similar concern with social order is found in the cruder and more explicitly 'socially Darwinist' writings of the American social control theorists. At the turn of the present century E.A. Ross (1959) attempted to advance a theory of the ways in which society constrains the darker animal nature of 'Man' whilst developing his natural sociability and sense of justice. The system of control posited by Ross depended on persuasive or 'ethical instruments' (such as public opinion, suggestion, personal ideals, etc.) as well as upon more coercive or 'political instruments' (such as law, belief, education, etc.). This notion of social control was taken up by Park, Burgess and the Chicago sociologists and their emphasis upon 'the processes by which individuals are inducted to and are induced to co-operate in some sort of permanent corporate existence we call society' (Park and Burgess 1924: 42). It has survived, not in the forefront of sociology, but as a part of its background or 'folk-wisdom'. That sociological 'folk-wisdom' usually presents such processes by way of a three-fold typology: the first and most fundamental process is 'internalisation' or 'socialisation'; the second process is constituted by the 'informal' means of control exercised by social pressure, peer group opinion, etc.; and the third process is constituted by 'formal' means of control, namely coercive sanctions, the law, police, etc. which are depicted as external agencies of last resort which enter the picture only incidentally, when the more primary and truly 'social' means of control have failed (Cohen and Scull 1985).

The conceptions of social order with which Durkheim and the American social control theorists were preoccupied may be characterised by their parallels with biological conceptions of the integrity and self-regulation of living organisms. Only slightly different are Talcott Parsons and his followers, whose preoccupation with social *organisation* may with some justification be characterised by its parallels with the theoretical conceptions of cybernetics and the technology of electronic control systems. Parsons' theory of social control is derived from his systematic theory of deviance and he defines the process of social control as 'the obverse of the theory of deviant behaviour tendencies. It is the analysis of those processes within the social system that tend to counteract the deviant tendencies, and of the conditions under which such processes will operate' (Parsons 1951).

Implicit in Parsons' theory is that all 'social systems' (which term can be applied not only to whole societies but to the subsystems or institutions of which societies are composed) are characterised by a tendency to maintain themselves and to maintain equilibrium: social control is seen as an infinitely complex process of interactions which automatically correct or accommodate deviant behaviour and value 'patterns'.

Also within the macro-sociological tradition, but quite distinct from the above-mentioned concerns with order and organisation, is Weber's concern with the question of *authority*. Whereas none of the sociological theories outlined above will admit the idea that there have been human actors in the course of human history and none can account for the real exercise of power, Weber addressed his mind to the question of how control or domination can be substantively exercised within society. He sought, in particular, to explain what differentiated Western capitalist societies in this respect. Weber did not claim to reveal the unseen and omnipotent forces of a reified society, but to consider the meaning to the individual actor and the means employed by such actors to achieve whatever their chosen ends might be: this form of interpretive sociology or 'methodological subjectivism' was bound to produce an idealist account if not indeed an apologia for capitalism, but it at least produced an explanation rather than a mystified description of social control.

Central to Weber's theory is the concept of 'legitimation' as the underlying basis for the acceptance of authority or acquiescence to the exercise of power within society. Weber (1949) distinguished three kinds of society with reference to the type of domination exercised and the manner of its legitimation: 'traditional' societies governed by customs and conventions; 'charismatic' societies in which the rules issuing from a leader are adhered to by virtue of some inherent quality of that leader; and 'rational' societies in which rules are rationally and 'legally' constituted and are obeyed because they are rational/legal. In traditional and charismatic societies the legitimacy factor is external to the individual subject, but in rational societies, the legitimacy factor is very much internal to the individual. Weber contended that modern Western industrialised societies were characteristically and uniquely rational. He sought to define the unique characteristics of the capitalist market economy, of the liberal democratic state and of Western legal systems and he delineated the conditions which had permitted their emergence. However, Weber stopped short of enquiring how or why it is that individuals by and large accept or refrain from violating the rational legal order of modern Western societies.

Time and space would not here permit a detailed rehearsal of any substantial critique of the classical macro-sociological theorists. However, the central problem of all such approaches lies in their failure to produce a convincing explanation of how it is that society can secure the 'self-regulation' of individual behaviour.

Marxist approaches: the concept of ideology

For this reason, the argument returns to certain theories in the Marxist tradition and, specifically, to the concept of 'ideology'. The discussion earlier in this chapter of the form of the state under capitalism looked at ways in which more recent Marxist theorists have developed his conceptual framework. At this stage it is useful to distinguish the Marxist conception of ideology from the Weberian conception of legitimation by outlining the origin of the former. The seminal formulation of the concept is customarily expressed in the form of a metaphor and arises out of the relationship postulated by Marx between the economic or material 'base' and the ideological 'superstructure' of human society. According to Marx:

> In the social production of their life, men enter into definite relations that are indispensable of their will, relations of production which correspond to a definite stage of development of their material productive forces. The sum total of these relations of production constitutes the economic structure of society, the real foundation on which rises a legal and political superstructure and to which correspond definite forms of social consciousness.
>
> (Marx 1969)

Historical change occurs when the material productive forces so develop that they conflict with the existing relations of production and, as the economic 'base' is revolutionised, so too is the 'superstructure' and 'social consciousness' transformed, but

> In considering such transformations a distinction should always be made between the material transformation of the economic conditions of production, which can be determined with the precision of natural science, and the legal, political, religious, aesthetic or philosophic – in short, ideological forms in which men become conscious of this conflict and fight it out.
> (Marx 1969)

Marx, however, both in earlier and later writings, advances notions of ideology which have somewhat different emphases: ideology on the one hand is seen as a representation of dominant material relations and as denoting a quite mechanical correspondence between the ruling class and ruling ideas in society (Marx 1976); on the other hand, ideology is seen as arising from the systematic necessities of the process of capital accumulation and circulation (Marx 1970a and b). None the less, irrespective of the particular emphasis used, the concept amounts, in Marx's own work, to a demonstration of the ways in which ideas such as 'freedom' and 'equality', doctrines such as utilitarianism and mystificatory representations of economic transactions not only served the economic interests of the bourgeoisie, but were the product of specifically capitalist relations of production.

Later writers were to attribute perhaps rather greater significance and meaning to the term 'ideology' and to define a role for ideological inculcation in the process of social control. Antonio Gramsci elaborated the concept in its most extreme form and advanced a further related concept, that of 'hegemony' (Gramsci 1971). Gramsci used this latter term to describe the material nature and the specific effectivity of ideology in asserting and perpetuating the dominance of a ruling class. Within this idea lies the possibility that different and conflicting ideologies might coexist and compete for overall hegemony: and so, ideology and what Lukács (1971) defines as 'class consciousness' may become fields and objects of struggle in themselves. In a more mechanistic vein, Althusser (1971) has attempted to elaborate Marx's original 'architectonic metaphor', by suggesting, not only that the state/ideological 'superstructure' is relatively autonomous of its civil/economic 'base', but that it is composed by a range of structures or 'state apparatuses' – both repressive and ideological. The repressive apparatuses consist of the army, the police, the courts, the prisons, etc., while the ideological apparatuses, claims Althusser, include a plurality of 'private' as well as 'public' institutions, such as the church, the education system, the legal system, the communications and cultural media, the family and even trade unions and political parties.

Taken as a whole, these strains of thought posit what Stephen Lukes (1974) defines as a 'Three Dimensional Model' of power in society, in the sense that social control (as has already been argued) operates on several levels: it is not merely that one class or group can impose their will on another, nor even that some classes or groups are systematically excluded from the decision-making process. It is rather that the forces of hegemony and of the ideological apparatuses (e.g. education system, mass media, etc.) dissuade certain classes or groups from advancing their claims or prevent them even from recognising the nature of their own interests. According to this view, the great mass of individuals in society are therefore so influenced or duped and their perceptions so shaped or distorted that they want only that which is required of them, and conflict (i.e. class conflict) is averted.

The way forward, it is suggested, is to return again to the most developed (and abstract) of the formulations posited by Poulantzas (1980) in which he speaks of the 'institutional materiality' of the state and that complex 'web of class powers' over which it presides. These formulations may be concretised by drawing (as Poulantzas does himself) upon Foucault's analysis of the technology of power. It is only by marrying a sketchy, if sophisticated, development of Marxist theory (which does at least account for a source of power/domination) with a post-structuralist theory (which doesn't) that it seems we can come close to a plausible explanation of social control as a phenomenon which specifically directs individual behaviour.

Foucault: the technology of power

Foucault (1977) claims that his concept of a technology of power differs from the concept of ideology in Marxism in that the individual is not just the 'fictitious atom of an ideological representation of society', but a reality which is actually 'fabricated' by this very specific technology of power which he calls 'discipline'. The point made by Poulantzas (1980: ch.2) is that the 'ideological' process of individualisation becomes, in fact, a material process (i.e. it is real) by virtue of the very techniques which Foucault describes.

The most important of the techniques or disciplines are defined by Foucault (1977) as 'surveillance' and 'normalisation', and together they constitute a 'modality of power' in which (unlike the feudal mode of domination for example) the differences between people are relevant. Although Foucault has developed these concepts in the context of a study of the prison, he contends that they are of general application: not only does he identify similarities and continuities between the techniques employed within different institutions (see p. 23) but, by means of various analogies and metaphors, Foucault seeks to characterise the pervasive essence of 'the disciplines'.

Without doubt, the most powerful of these heuristic devices is his characterisation of the 'panopticon' as a spatial representation of his disciplinary society. The panopticon was an architectural form advanced by Jeremy Bentham in the mid-nineteenth century as the ideal design for the reformatory prison. It provided for the arrangement of prisoners in individual cells around a central observation tower, from which each prisoner could be seen, but into which the prisoners themselves could not see. The prisoners could thus be minutely ordered and individualised, while their captors and observers remained anonymous and unseen. The image or the ideal of the panopticon as a method of distributing bodies and exercising power is counterposed to the image or ideal of the theatre or circus where, in contrast, an anonymous and unsegregated crowd observe a spectacle or demonstration upon a central stage. The theatre represents the architectural model of power appropriate to feudalism, whereas its obverse, the panopticon represents a model of power under capitalism: indeed, in spite of Foucault's sometimes quite perverse posturing against Marxism, he quite explicitly states that the techniques which made possible the accumulation of capital also made possible the 'calculated technology of subjection' of which he speaks.

> ... the two processes – the accumulation of men and the accumulation of capital – cannot be separated.... Each makes the

other possible and necessary and each provides a model for the other. The disciplinary pyramid constituted the small cell of power within which the separation, co-ordination and supervision of tasks was imposed and made efficient; and analytical partitioning of time, gestures and bodily forces constituted an operational schema that could easily be transferred from the groups to be subjected to the mechanisms of production.... Let us say that discipline is the unitary technique by which the body is reduced as a 'political' force and maximised as a useful force. The growth of a capitalist economy gave rise to the specific modality of disciplinary power whose general formulas, techniques of submitting forces and bodies, in short 'political anatomy', could be operated in the most diverse political regimes, apparatuses or institutions.

(Foucault 1977: 221)

As to the techniques themselves, these represent more palpable phenomena than 'legitimation' or 'ideological inculcation'. By the term 'normalisation' for example, Foucault seeks to define a form of penality not confined to penal institutions, but which imposes a 'ladder of normalcy, the rungs of which, while indicating membership of a homogeneous social body, themselves serve to classify, hierarchise and distribute social rank'. Through a myriad of minute interventions, every day institutions exercise a system of continuous normalisation and, by thousands of tiny individualised rewards and punishments, effect the substantive control of individual behaviour.

A convincing demonstration of Foucault's approach is provided by his 'disciple' Jacques Donzelot (1980). This writer demonstrates how, since the nineteenth century, the various legal, medical, psychiatric and social policy interventions which have occurred around the family have in effect reconstituted the family as a mechanism for social control. Institutions such as the family can become the focus for mechanisms or strategies of power which are not planned by any executive committee of the ruling class, nor consciously devised by a cunning state bureaucracy. Poulantzas makes the point that such a 'strategy' cannot be known in advance and may not even be susceptible to rational formulation.

CONCLUSIONS

The argument returns to the questions posed towards the beginning of this chapter: who is controlled? by whom? for what purpose? by what means?

The first three of these questions must be answered together, since they are so interrelated that any coherent theoretical stance must logically encompass them within a single framework. Any approach which takes the purpose of social control as an a priori assumption and which analytically derives the identity or status of social actors from that assumption is rejected: this is broadly speaking the position of the functionalist sociologists (such as Durkheim, Parsons, and others) and of the more vulgarly deterministic of the Marxist theorists. Weber's interpretative approach which claims to regard the process of social control from the point of view of the social actors themselves and to derive the purpose of control from the subjective meaning it has for the actors is also unsatisfactory. This leaves the theoretical framework which has been emerging from recent Marxist debates regarding the nature of the state and the approach which this book adopts may be summarised in simplified terms as follows:

1. social control is ultimately a feature of the exploitation of labour by capital;
2. under advanced capitalism, social control is exercised through various apparatuses and mechanisms which are constituted or are supervised by the state;
3. the state is a complex political institution, formally autonomous from the economic interests of capital or labour, but representing a material 'condensation' of the social relations of production (i.e. of the class forces in play within society at any moment in time);
4. the relations of domination existing between capital and labour are therefore translated into practice (or 'incarnated') within the apparatuses and mechanisms referred to above;
5. the effect of social control through the state is to materialise and reproduce the social relations of production.

The virtue of this model is that it can account not only for historical change but for the relationship between social control and social policy at several levels. The model is useless, however, unless it can be married to an account of how social control is exercised.

In turning to the fourth and final of the above questions, therefore, it is necessary to forge an alliance between a Marxist framework and the materialist theory of power advanced by the 'idealist' Michel Foucault. Foucault, in Melossi's words, has not only 'put the concept of ideology back on its feet' but has provided a theory 'far more informative about structure and superstructure than the architectonic metaphor' (Melossi 1979: 93). On its own Foucault's theory cannot provide satisfactory answers to the first three of the questions posed above. As a student of the 'technology of power' which is specific to the capitalist mode of production, Foucault is like an engineer: he can explain how a piece of machinery works and how it has been developed and constructed, but he need not be expected satisfactorily to explain why such machinery has been developed nor how it is going to be used. None the less, the historically specific disciplinary techniques which Foucault identifies and analyses are as much a part of a mode of production as any other technology.

Finally then, what is social control? And, as a concept, does it add anything to our understanding of social policy and the welfare state? In seeking to define social control, this chapter has endeavoured to locate the elements, not of a unified or coherent design, but of a none the less palpable process of subjection occurring under capitalist social relations and penetrating every aspect of human life and existence (including, for example, the family); a process which at the various levels at which it operates, is the necessary product of such relations and the necessary condition for the reproduction of such relations. As such, the term 'social control' ought not to be treated as a global substitute for the concepts of 'class domination', 'repression', 'ideology', 'hegemony', etc. On the contrary, the value of the term is to show how these specific aspects of subjection insinuate themselves into the sphere which has come to be known as 'social policy'.

Under capitalist social relations, even when these are subject to massive regulation through the state, the idea of social policy is, strictly speaking, a contradiction in terms. The production and reproduction of such social relations are not and, in the last instance, cannot be planned or regulated 'socially', rather they are fashioned and constrained by the internal dynamic of capital itself. What therefore passes as social policy must actually embody social control; not because welfare reformers are necessarily cynical and manipulative; nor even because they are gullible and naive (although some doubtless have been); but because the fundamental terrain upon which reforms are fought for, the discourses of debate and the inherent limits to state action are all fashioned and constrained through the essential form of capitalist social relations; and because that essential form is one of exploitation, not co-operation.

The next chapter considers ways in which mechanisms of social control operate within or through a specific state institution – namely the British social security system.

Chapter Three

SOCIAL CONTROL AND THE DEVELOPMENT OF THE SOCIAL SECURITY SYSTEM

> The value of history lies in helping us to understand the nature of present structures; what imperatives lay behind their introduction? ... To interpret [the] growth [of the welfare state] as a manifestation of altruism, of a desire to remove poverty and other social evils, renders mysterious the fact that much poverty remains.... Public and official discussion of social policy has rarely been solely or even centrally about redistribution for the elimination of poverty. Equally or more important have been questions of political or social order....
>
> (Thane 1982: 2)

Chapter 2 demonstrated that the *general* form of the welfare state and of the social security system is a necessary consequence of the domination of labour by capital. This chapter considers how, at the level of discourse and practice, the *particular* form of the social security system has emerged. Having contended that the social security system is a 'vehicle' for social control and identified the motive force or 'engine' which drives that vehicle with the fundamental antagonism between capital and labour, this chapter considers the 'technology' by which that motive force is translated into social control.

The history of social security is complex and confusing and the 'progress' of social policy in this sphere has been to say the least erratic. Chapter 2 identified the three general levels at which social control operates:

1. the level of 'political settlement' and the emergence of the social wage as an individualised system of rewards;

2. the level of coercion and sanctions at which corporal forms of sanction have given way to a system of pecuniary punishments;
3. the level of the individual actor at which repression of the poor has given way to 'discipline'.

In relation to each 'level' of control, this chapter will identify a loosely related philosophy or 'discourse' and will attempt to trace the lines of continuity and intersection between such discourses (cf. Donzelot 1980). For convenience, the three discourses will be referred to as:

1. paternalistic/humanitarian/pro-populationist discourse;
2. repressive/'Malthusian'/anti-populationist discourse;
3. utilitarian/philanthropic/'self-help' discourse.

The social security system, it will be argued, has been constructed at the points at which these contradictory discourses intersect. It will be seen that the discourses themselves have each ebbed and flowed and been modified over time. At any one moment any one or other of the discourses may have attained ascendancy. While poor relief and the social security system have remained the focus of such fluid and competing discourses, the discourses themselves and the contradictions between them merely give expression to the more fundamental contradictions of capitalist social relations. It is out of such contradictions that a tangible and coherent system of rewards, of punishments and of disciplinary mechanisms has emerged.

The first of the two principal disciplinary mechanisms whose origins this chapter will follow later is the 'case-approach'; and the second, 'legalisation'. A third disciplinary mechanism – 'partitioning' – will be considered separately in Chapter 4. However, a preliminary point needs to be made with regard to the concept of disciplinary mechanisms and their relationship to social control. Such mechanisms are undeniably associated with material improvements in working-class living standards – that is to say with 'rewards' as much as with 'punishments'. To define the mechanisms as 'disciplinary' is not to deny these positive benefits. On the contrary, the argument seeks to account for the overall effect of the rewards, the punishments and the various techniques of application which operate through the social security system. It is a question of relating such mechanisms to social control and of considering them as part of a technology of power under advanced (or 'post-Fordist') capitalist relations of production.

FROM BEGGING BOWL TO SOCIAL WAGE

If the social wage is the acceptable medium by which assistance is now given to the poor, in feudal times it was the begging bowl which represented the acceptable medium for such assistance. The beggar was indeed a characteristic figure in medieval life and many who subsisted by such means – such as mendicant friars, pilgrims and scholars – enjoyed a recognised status as such (de Schweinitz 1961). There was no stigma attached to the asking and the giving of alms. Poverty represented a sanctified condition in which, in Lis and Soly's words, 'the poor were nailed to a cross at the bottom of society': the spiritual value of such a condition, however, could accrue only to the rich for whom a giving of alms constituted an 'investment in the hereafter' (Lis and Soly 1979: 22).

Gifts and rights

However, the advent of capitalist norms of bilateral exchange and interventions by the state to repress begging succeeded in stigmatising those transactions which took the form of the unilateral gift (Titmuss 1968). It was only with the coming of the 'modern' welfare state that assistance provided to the poor ceased to be received as a 'gift' and supposedly became a 'right'. The parcel of benefits and services which constitute the social wage is provided on the basis of the legal entitlement of the recipients.

The transition from 'gifts' to 'rights' for the poor can hardly be said to be complete. The rights enjoyed by social security claimants are highly conditional. Many social security benefits still carry stigma (Pinker 1971). However, some writers (for example, Marshall 1963) argue that the twentieth century, with the emergence of 'social rights', has witnessed the culmination of the development of the rights and status of citizenship. According to Marshall, civil (i.e. legal) rights were the achievement of the eighteenth century. Political rights were the achievement of the nineteenth century. Finally, by the extension of welfare state services calculated to enrich the 'concrete substance of civilised life' and to reduce risk and insecurity, social rights have at last been incorporated into the 'status of citizenship'. Social rights imply, he argues, 'the subordination of market price to social justice, the replacement of the free bargain by the declaration of rights' (Marshall 1963). This in essence was the view to which the post-Second World War Labour government subscribed and it is the same view which re-emerged in the rhetoric of politicians in the 1970s when the term 'social wage' was widely popularised. In 1975 Barbara Castle, then Secretary of State for Health & Social Services, said, 'the tax man is the Robin Hood of our time, taking from those that can afford it the means whereby we can pay every worker the wage that really matters, the social wage' (*Financial Times* 8 July 1975 – quoted in Trinder 1976).

An indication of how recent is the ascendancy of social rights and the social wage as ideological constructs is a statement dating not fifty years before the quotation above and contained in the Ministry of Health's Annual Report of 1926–27: the Ministry decisively rejected the possiblity that uniform scales governing the amount of poor relief might be set and published, since 'there is a grave danger lest the recipients may begin to regard the gift as a right' (quoted in de Schweinitz 1961: 212).

Until the advent of the 'welfare' state, the state's involvement with the provision of substantive assistance to the poor had been on the basis that it supervised the making of 'gifts'. At various times between the sixteenth and nineteenth centuries, beggars were subjected to licensing arrangements or 'badging' before being allowed to seek private charity (see Spicker 1984). Far more important than private giving, however, was state giving through the medium of poor relief, although the form and the object of such giving remained for some three hundred years the focus of several competing philosophies or discourses. This chapter is concerned with three such discourses, the first of which – the paternalistic/ humanitarian/ pro-populationist discourse – is examined in this section. The argument will trace a line of continuity between the appearance in the seventeenth century of the populationist discourse (cf Donzelot 1980: 175 et seq.) and the rhetoric which characterises the provisions of the twentieth century welfare state as constituting the social wage.

The populationist discourse

The populationist discourse is epitomised in the words of Sir Matthew Hale, who was Lord Chief Justice from 1671 to 1676:

> the more populous the state or country is, the richer or more wealthy it is. But with us in England, for want of the due regulation of things, the more populous we are, the poorer we are; so that wherein the strength and wealth of a kingdom consists, renders us the weaker and poorer.
>
> ('Discourse Touching Provision for the Poor' 1678 – quoted in de Schweinitz 1961: 49).

Hale himself envisaged an ambitious programme to regenerate the nations' population and wealth by the provision of productive work for the poor: this particular vision was never realised (except partially perhaps in the model communities of New Lanark instituted by the nineteenth-century socialist philanthropist, Robert Owen (see Thompson 1968)) but within the state's own sphere it is this philosophical strand which may be said to have justified or made credible two quite isolated but important instances within the history of social security provision.

The first of these instances was the comparatively short-lived Speenhamland system of relief. By the end of the eighteenth century, the wage labour system had become universal and the accelerated movement towards land enclosure, together with the development of power machinery and the factory system of production, had hastened the rate at which labour was being displaced from the land. At the same time, wages fell far behind prices as the war with France brought steep increases in living costs. Existing Poor Law provisions were thus exposed as conspicuously inadequate to prevent the severest of hardships and a risk of social turmoil amongst the labouring classes. It was this which, in 1795, exercised the minds of the Magistrates of Berkshire when they met at Speenhamland. They rejected the idea of imposing upon employers a minimum wage sufficient to meet the cost of living (which they would have been empowered to do under a statute of 1563). And instead they decided to draw up a 'table of universal practice' under which relief – not only to the impotent and infirm, but to working labourers as well – could be calculated in accordance with the supposed requirements of each labourer's family. The difference between a man's wages and the minimum set by the magistrates as necessary for his and his family's maintenance would be met from the poor rates and paid as a supplement to wages: the scale upon which relief was calculated was based on the cost of a gallon loaf and upon the magistrates' assumptions as to how many multiples of that sum were required to sustain a family of any given size. The system was imitated and implemented throughout the country and, after the event, was sanctioned by parliament (36 George III, ch.23, 1795).

In the following year, adopting the same reasoning as the Berkshire magistrates, parliament rejected a bill to provide for the fixing of minimum wages on the grounds that small families and labourers without children would benefit unfairly in relation to larger families. William Pitt, the Prime Minister, speaking in defence of the Speenhamland system said:

> Let us make relief in cases where there are a number of children, a matter of right, and an honour instead of a ground for opprobrium and contempt. This will make a large family a blessing, and not a curse; and this will draw a proper line of distinction between those who are able to provide for themselves by their labour, and those who after having enriched their country with a number of children, have a claim upon its assistance for support.
>
> ('The Parliamentary Register, or the History of the Proceedings of the House of Commons' Vol.XLIV, 1796, quoted in de Schweinitz 1961: 73)

It was within the populationist discourse that gifts to the poor were capable of becoming rights. The Speenhamland system was not only inimical in principal to both the utilitarian and Malthusian doctrines of the nineteenth century, but also served to depress wage levels while maintaining very substantial numbers of people on the rates – as many as six out of every seven in some parts of the country. Moreover, the population dependent on the rates was being maintained in conditions of penury as the meagre level of the allowances paid was allowed to decline (by as much as a third in some places by the 1830s) (Hammond and Hammond 1936). With the New Poor Law of 1834, the Speenhamland system was swept away in favour of renewed repressive measures, although certain features of the Speenhamland system had, of course, prefigured certain elements of the means-tested benefit schemes under our contemporary social security system. In this connection, Speenhamland is most often cited as precedent for the Family Income Supplement and Family Credit schemes of the 1970s and 1980s, but more fundamentally, it must also be regarded as precedent for the fixing of 'scale rates' or 'personal allowances' for the calculation of social assistance payments from the 1930s onwards (i.e. for Transitional Allowances, Unemployment Assistance, National Assistance, Supplementary Benefits and now Income Support).

The second instance to bear the mark of the populationist discourse is the appearance of the Family Allowance scheme in 1945. Family Allowances constituted one of the cornerstones of the Beveridge Plan and of the modern social security system. The scheme was the prescription which had flowed from a diagnosis that up to one quarter of the 'want' (i.e. poverty) demonstrated to exist 'was due to failure to relate income during earning to the size of the family' (Beveridge 1942).

In Hilary Land's detailed study of the introduction of Family Allowances (1975), the point is made that eventual governmental acceptance of the scheme was conditioned as much by Keynesian economic arguments that the payment of a universal benefit to families with children would have an anti-inflationary effect as it was by socialist or feminist arguments about redressing inequality between families or between the sexes. The payment of benefit to all families with children was justified as a means of limiting or reducing the extent to which male wages must include provision for workers' families. Although the allowances themselves were not intended to be equivalent even to the subsistence requirements of the children for whom they were paid, the introduction of Family Allowances was important symbolically as a permanent shift of responsibility away from employers and towards the state: the costs of reproducing the labour force which capital must ultimately bear were in part removed from the market place and subjected to state regulation.

In so doing, the welfare state affirmed a certain commitment to supporting the family as the place where children are reared. That commitment has been carried forward into other areas of the social security system (most notably Family Income Supplement/Family Credit). The Family Allowance scheme itself was, in 1978, extended and integrated with Child Tax Allowances to become the Child Benefit scheme (under Child Benefit Act 1975) which survives as one of the very few social security benefits which are neither means-tested nor based on the payment of insurance contributions.

The claimant as citizen

Although both means testing and social insurance spring from quite different roots, it is important at this stage to grasp the nature of the transaction by which all social security benefits pass from the state to the individual. In the case of the most important means-tested benefits, Supplementary Benefit and its successor Income Support, these have since 1966 been paid 'as of right' to claimants who satisfy the conditions of entitlement. In the case of National Insurance benefits, since their inception in 1911, these have also been paid 'as of right', subject to recipients having paid the requisite contributions under the scheme. In both cases, the benefit paid by the state is presented not as a gift, but as a right.

The transition therefore appears complete and, in the process, the relationship of donor to recipient has in a sense become inverted. The beggar was an anonymous recipient and the giving of alms was an act which enhanced the identity and social standing of the donor. The social security claimant, however, is far from anonymous, being the subject of detailed enquiries, minute investigation and ongoing case records: and it is the donor who now remains anonymous, since the state administers a fund provided by many thousands of unknown taxpayers, and even the state officials who process claims for social security benefits systematically refuse to divulge their names to claimants (see Donnison 1982).

Not only has the nameless beggar been transformed into the specific object of state inquiry and surveillance, but, by acquiring 'social rights' and the status of citizenship, s/he has also acquired correlative 'social duties'. The act of claiming social security benefits, unlike the act of begging, brings into play an intricate set of rules of entitlement which announce the duties of the claimant as a citizen and which, by the tests and obstacles so imposed upon the claimant, bear upon him/her with 'normalising' effect. The 'silent compulsion' of the wage relation is thus applied to the relief of the poor by the state: the social wage replaces the begging bowl as a calculable instrument both of relief and of discipline.

The nature of the welfare state and the impact of the social wage was not forseen by Marx and Engels when they wrote

> The Modern labourer ... sinks deeper below the conditions of his own class. He becomes a pauper, and pauperism develops more rapidly than population and wealth. And here it becomes evident that the bourgeoisie is unfit any longer to be the ruling class in society ... because it is incompetent to assure an existence to its slave within his slavery, because it cannot help letting him sink into such a state, that it has to feed him, instead of being fed by him.
>
> (Marx and Engels 1970: 26)

It is through the medium of the social wage that the ruling class might be said to have thus far succeeded in assuring an existence to its slave within his/her slavery and has managed to feed and to be fed by the working class. The ideological notion of the social wage is the culmination and the particular contribution of a populationist element within political discourse. By the social wage, not only is 'pauperism' made managable, but 'population and wealth' may continue to increase. The reproduction of labour power necessary for continued capital accumulation is made possible by welfare state intervention to regulate the cost of reproducing labour power. The pauper's begging bowl was a symbol of a failing ruling class; the social wage, however, symbolises the dominance of capital over labour.

FROM CORPORAL TO PECUNIARY SANCTIONS

The first concern of the state was not to relieve poverty, but to deter vagrancy. Edward III's Statute of Labourers of 1349 was intended to ensure that 'valiant beggars ... may be compelled to labour for their necessary living' and from that point on the state has continued by various means of repression to attempt to compel those who are capable of productive work to 'labour for their necessary living'. The history of the sanctions employed to that end is one of transition from the use of violent punishment to the use of financial disincentives: the sanctions, however, have always been repressive in the sense that they are 'negative'.

During the fourteenth and fifteenth centuries the able bodied vagrant or beggar was punished in the stocks. During the first half of the sixteenth century, however, the treatment of such persons became increasingly violent and spectacular. Henry VIII's statute of 1531, which provided for the licensing of begging, also provided that 'any beggars being strong and able in their bodies to work' should be driven through the streets whilst tied naked to the back of a cart and whipped until blood was drawn. A statute of 1536 further provided that any 'sturdy vagabond or valiant beggar' who might continue to loiter, wander or remain idle should be whipped again and the top of his right ear cut off: any person reoffending after that would be put to death as a felon! As if this were not severe enough, a statute of 1547 (1 Edward VI, ch.3) attempted to substitute provision that idlers and wanderers refusing or failing to work might be branded and enslaved (although, in the event, these provisions were repealed three years later and the preceding provisions re-enacted).

From 1563 onwards began the series of enactments which were later consolidated as the Elizabethan Poor Law. Most importantly, a statute of 1572 provided for compulsory taxation to finance poor relief and charged parish officials with a duty to put rogues and vagabonds to work. This latter duty was clarified and elaborated in a statute of 1576 which provided that parish officials should provide from local taxes a stock of materials in order that unemployed youths and 'other poor and needy persons being willing to work' could be given productive employment by the parish and so be accustomed to labour: but, the statute also provided

> If hereafter any such person able to do any such work shall refuse to work or shall go abroad begging or live idly, or taking such work shall spoil or embezzle the same, [then] in convenient apparel meet for such a body to wear [s/he] shall be received into such House of Correction there to be straightly kept, as well in diet as in work, and also punished from time to time.
>
> (18 Elizabeth, ch. 4, 1576)

At this comparatively early stage, therefore, there was a major shift away from violence to more gentle but systematised means of coercion. The parish relief system during the seventeenth century was far from being a unified or coherent state system and the Elizabethan statutes were no doubt only partially observed at best, but the emphasis was upon locally administered sanctions and upon 'corrective' forms of intervention.

The argument now turns to consider the second of the three competing philosophies or discourses referred to above: the repressive/'Malthusian'/anti-populationist discourse ('anti-populationist discourse' for short). This discourse has contributed to the emergence of the social security system no less than has the populationist discourse and it has done so by the manner in which it has justified or made credible the more explicitly repressive and disciplinary aspects of social security. The anti-populationist discourse may be identified within the creation of the workhouse as an institutional form and in the operation of the 'work-test' which constitutes a key element to the legal basis for entitlement to several contemporary social security benefits.

Anti-populationist discourse: beginnings

The anti-populationist discourse has come to be associated with the name of the Rev. T.R. Malthus, who in the late eighteenth and early nineteenth centuries was one of several proponents of the view that agriculture could not support an accelerating population and that history supposedly proved that excessive increases in population must ultimately be curtailed by either famine, war or pestilence (*Essay on Population* 1798). To avoid any of the natural disasters associated with over-population, it was considered necessary not to allow the poor to increase in number and indeed to ensure that the increase in the labouring population as a whole was, by moral if not coercive restraint, confined within the limits of the nation's productivity. Added fillip to such doctrines was later provided by a popularised version of Darwin's theory of natural selection: the Malthusian reading of Darwin's *The Origin of Species* (first published 1859) concluded that the survival and improvement of the human race depended on natural laws of competition by which the inferior (i.e. economically unproductive or unsuccessful) members of human society might properly be expected to perish.

The beginnings of the workhouse and the harsh regime associated with it actually pre-dated Malthus, but it is argued here that George I's statute of 1722 (9 George I, ch.7) bore implicitly the mark of the anti-populationist discourse. This statute permitted parishes to establish workhouses on a basis quite unlike the hospitals, almshouses and Houses of Correction which many already administered: these new workhouses could be privately run on a contractual basis and would provide for all poor persons having a claim upon the parish. Any person refusing to enter the workhouse could be legitimately refused relief. The master or proprietors of such establishments would contract in return for either a per capita or a periodic lump sum payment to provide, as cheaply as possible, food, shelter and nursing care or work as may have been appropriate for the paupers of the parish. Between 1722 and 1782 many parishes took advantage of the workhouse system in order dramatically to reduce both the cost of poor relief and the number of people claiming such relief. Conditions in the workhouses, run as they were for profit, were totally unregulated and were so unbearable as to deter all but the helpless from seeking relief, whilst those who were forced into the care of such establishments, especially children, were subject to the most alarming mortality rates. A contemporary commentator described the workhouses of that period in the following terms:

> old and young, sick and healthy are promiscuously crowded into ill-contrived compartments, not of sufficient capacity to contain with convenience half the number of miserable human beings condemned to such deplorable inhabitation, and that speedy death is almost ever to the aged and infirm, and often to the youthful and robust, the consequence of removal from more salubrious air to such mansions of putridity.
> (Scott J. *Observations on the Present State of the Parochial and Vagrant Poor* 1773 – quoted in de Schweinitz 1961: 66)

Eventually, it was the Gilbert Act of 1782 which prohibited contracting for the care of the poor and which sanctioned an expanded programme of 'outdoor relief' (whilst providing that the 'idle and dissolute' be kept at hard labour in houses of correction). The general mixed workhouse, however, was to reappear in modified form under the New Poor Law of 1834. Two things distinguished the new kind of workhouse from the old: first, the new workhouses were to be a universal form of provision directly administered by Boards of Guardians elected up and down the country by combinations or 'Unions' of parishes and these Boards of Guardians were themselves to be supervised by a central board of Commissioners; second, the guiding principle of the New Poor Law was that the able bodied and their families should without exception be admitted to the workhouse and there maintained in conditions so contrived as to be deliberately worse or 'less eligible' than those endured by even the poorest independent labourer. In effect, therefore, the new 'well regulated' workhouses (Commission of Inquiry into the Poor Laws 1834: 146–147) fulfilled in an organised and explicit way what the old workhouses had achieved on a piecemeal basis and by default.

Anti-populationist discourse and the New Poor Law

The New Poor Law and the Royal Commission of 1833–34 whose report preceded it reflected the ascendancy of the Whig oligarchy which had returned to political power in 1830 and whose position had been consolidated by the extension of the franchise by the Reform Act of 1832. In essence, the 1834 Act for all the unanimity and purpose with which it was enacted, contained not one but two discourses: a utilitarian discourse, which will be considered later, but also an anti-populationist discourse, reflected in the assumption that it was neither possible nor desirable that all members of society should enjoy comfortable subsistence and in the very nature of the workhouse as a quite indiscriminate punitive device. The severity of the New Poor Law was such that Disraeli summarised its effect by stating, 'It announces to the world that in England, poverty is a crime' (quoted in de Schweinitz 1961: 124).

The workhouse, like the reformatory prison, made incarceration rather than physical violence a normal form of punishment. The workhouse would receive under the same roof the young, the old, the able bodied, the disabled and the physically and mentally ill. But within the workhouse, families would be broken up and persons falling into different categories would be assigned to different wings or dormitories: children under seven were sent to the nursery; girls between seven and thirteen were sent to one dormitory and boys of that age to another; women and girls over thirteen were confined to one dormitory and men and boys over thirteen to another; and there were wards for the aged and infirm (in which men and women were separated, even if they were husband and wife). This regimentation, together with the most menial labour for the able bodied, a meagre diet and the strictest discipline were calculated to ensure that relief was 'so irksome and disagreeable that none would consent to receive it who could possibly do without it' (*Extracts from Information received by the Commission of Inquiry into the Poor Laws* 1833–34 – quoted in de Schweinitz 1961: 133). And because this kind of regime was conspicuously and deliberately applied to the aged and infirm as well as to the able bodied, it was designed to operate 'as an inducement to the young and healthy to provide support for their latter years or as a stimulous to them, whilst they have the means, to support their aged parents and relatives' (from *Report by the Poor Law Commissioners to the Home Secretary* 1840 – quoted in de Schweinitz 1961: 134).

The New Poor Law was concerned therefore, not only with the de-regulation of labour power (by sweeping away the Speenhamland system for subsidising wages and the legal restrictions which continued to tie labour to the parish), but also with the suppression of demand for relief. The labouring population were exhorted to productivity and independence, and also compelled to regulate their own survival. The threat of the workhouse was contrived to have the same effect upon the labouring population as do the forces of nature upon the weakest members of a biological species: that is to ensure the survival of only the fittest.

The ideal form of the new workhouse as outlined by the Commission of Inquiry, in the Act of 1834 and the first reports of the Poor Law Commissioners appointed thereunder was seldom if at all realised in practice. The prohibition upon the giving of relief outside the workhouse was not in practice absolute and during the 1840s was subject to exceptions in cases of, for example, 'sudden and urgent necessity' or 'sickness, accident or bodily or mental infirmity' (Outdoor Relief Prohibitory Order 1844). In the 1860s the sick were declared no longer to be 'proper objects' for deterrent treatment at the hands of the Poor Law Guardians and asylums and hospitals began to be administered as a separate branch of local government (see Metropolitan Poor Act 1867,

Poor Law Amendment Acts 1867 and 1868 and the Local Government Board Act 1871).

The able bodied poor, even if they could escape the workhouse, would as a condition of receiving any relief be sent to a labour yard where they would be employed picking oakum, cutting wood or breaking stone. Paupers receiving relief in their own homes remained disenfranchised and would be marked as paupers by receiving at least a part of their relief by way of goods in kind, rather than in cash.

During the 1870s, the new Local Government Board (a permanent limb of government which had, *inter alia*, subsumed responsibility for the supervision of the Poor Law) commenced a drive to reduce expenditure by local Boards of Guardians upon outdoor relief. As a result, where local Boards of Guardians 'offered' relief to applicants other than in the workhouse, it was generally at such a level that it would provide a material standard of living beneath even that of the workhouse. One chairman of a Board of Guardians is quoted in the mid-1870s as having said to a widow with two children who had appealed for the renewal of relief 'If you can't earn enough to keep you with what we give you, you must come into the workhouse, we don't profess to give you enough to keep you out of the workhouse' (recounted in *Third Annual Report of the Local Government Board* 1873–74 – quoted in de Schweinitz 1961: 157).

Work-testing

In the course of the next half-century, however, the workhouse gave way to the 'work-test' and the Poor Law gave way to the social security system. The workhouse was not finally abolished until 1930 (The Relief Regulation Order 1930), when what had been known as 'outdoor relief' became 'public assistance' (in accordance with a term advocated in both the Majority and the Minority Reports of the Royal Commission on the Poor Laws as long before as 1909). A beginning had been made with a means-tested Old Age Pension (under the Old Age Pensions Act of 1908) and with a system of social insurance (under the National Insurance Acts of 1911 and 1916, the Unemployment Insurance Act 1920 and the Widows, Orphans and Old Age Contributory Pensions Act 1925). Inherent in the development during the first part of the twentieth century of insurance benefits for sickness, unemployment, death and old age was the development of an eligibility test based on the claimant's work record.

To qualify for an insurance benefit a claimant must previously have been in work so as to have paid the necessary contributions. However, there has never been anything better than a fictitious actuarial basis for the relationship between National Insurance benefits and pensions and the amount of the contributions paid by workers to the National Insurance fund, and the effect of the scheme has been to provide a range of state benefits which are strictly 'work-tested' (see particularly Shragge 1984). Claimants who do not satisfy the work-test are thrown back onto social assistance.

What is more, since 1911 entitlement to Unemployment Benefit has been subject to an additional work-test. Upon becoming unemployed, claimants must show that, in addition to having paid the necessary contributions, they have not made themselves voluntarily unemployed and they have not become unemployed as a result of their own misconduct. Persons failing to fulfil the requirements of such a test are suspended for a period of time from receiving benefit (currently under Section 20(1) Social Security Act 1975 as amended by Section 43 Social Security Act 1986) and any such person then resorting to social assistance (the contemporary form of which is the Income Support scheme) is then further penalised by being eligible to receive only a reduced level of assistance (Regulation 22 Income Support (General) Regulations 1987).

Social insurance, as will shortly be demonstrated, is a complex phenomenon and one which, within the contemporary social security system, may be said to be of declining significance. Within and through the development of the National Insurance scheme a certain strand of anti-populationist discourse has survived even beyond the implementation of the Beveridge Plan. Those who have not worked and have not therefore contributed remain, in theory at least, subject to some specific degree of material deprivation.

As the workhouse has given way to various forms of means-tested social assistance (the Public Assistance scheme, followed by the Transitional Allowances scheme of 1931, the Unemployment Assistance scheme of 1934, the Assistance scheme of 1940, the National Assistance scheme of 1948, the Supplementary Benefits scheme of 1966, and the Income Support scheme introduced in 1988), such safety nets have been so operated as to impose an array of pecuniary punishments. Even now, under the Income Support scheme, persons required to register for employment (the able bodied unemployed) can have benefit withdrawn if they refuse or fail to take 'suitable' employment or to attend 'Restart' interviews, or if they engage in any activity deemed likely to restrict their availability for work (such as full-time education or voluntary work) (Regulation 10 Income Support (General) Regulations 1987). The able bodied poor are no longer placed in the stocks or publicly flogged, and they are no longer incarcerated in the workhouse or subject to enforced labour, but they are precariously ensnared by a welfare state safety net which so operates as to keep them in a state of continuous vulnerability and which is capable, by way of punishment, of plunging them into total deprivation.

FROM REPRESSION TO DISCIPLINE

This chapter has argued that the history of social control, the Poor Law and the social security system is a story of change from the brutal repression of the poor to gentler and more subtle forms of discipline. This section will trace the strand in that process which has culminated in the capacity of the social security system to influence and to regulate behaviour by the imposition of self discipline.

Many of the principles of Poor Law administration were reflected and often preceded by developments in Europe. In the middle of the sixteenth century, programmes for the abolition of begging and for the relief of the poor developed in some sixty towns throughout the Continent (Lis and Soly 1979). In France, a model scheme developed in Ypres, Flanders – embodied in Juan Vives' *De Subventione Pauperum* – was adopted by Emperor Charles V who, in 1531, issued an edict outlawing begging and directing each municipality to maintain its poor.

In Germany, Martin Luther urged the nobility, not only to abolish begging, but to provide for the poor and, in 1523, he published a relief scheme for Liesnig, Saxony. The scheme prohibited begging, but provided for a common chest to aid the old, the infirm and those who had 'honourably laboured at their craft or in agriculture' but who could no longer obtain the means for their

The utilitarian discourse

In the figure and in the writings of Luther we find the beginnings of the utilitarian, philanthropic or 'self-help' discourse which is the third of the philosophies or discourses which have contributed to the form of the contemporary social security system. In addressing the question of begging and the need for its abolition, Luther identified the central administrative concern of the state in the provision of poor relief:

> everybody should be prudent, and cautious in dealing with beggars, and learn that, whereas people will not give and help honest paupers and needy neighbours, as ordained by God, they give by the persuasion of the devil, and contrary to God's judgement, ten times as much to vagabonds and desparate rogues.... For this reason every town and village should know their own paupers, as written down in the Register, and assist them. But as to outlandish and strange beggars they ought not to be born with, unless they have proper letters and certificates; for all the great rogueries ... are done by these. If each town would only keep an eye upon their paupers, such knaveries would soon be at an end.
>
> (*Liber Vagatorum* 1528 – quoted in de Schweinitz 1961: 37)

And so the registration, certification and surveillance of the poor is envisaged as a means of fulfilling God's ordinances as to their relief. Essential too to Lutheran religious thought and to post-Reformation ideology in general was the individual internalisation of God's ordinances: as Marx put it,

> Luther certainly conquered servitude based on *devotion* but only by replacing it with servitude based on *conviction*.... He freed the body from its chains only by putting the heart in chains ... It was no longer a question of the layman with the priest *outside himself*, but rather of his struggle with his own *inner priest*.
>
> (Marx 1975 251–2; emphases in original)

The religious moment towards individualism, self-determination and bureaucratic rather than violent forms of state management was mirrored in a secular philosophical movement characterised as utilitarianism. Represented in its most radical form by Hobbes' vision of an absolutist state, utilitarianism was the philosophy espoused at the end of the eighteenth and beginning of the nineteenth centuries by the intellectual and political champions of the emerging English bourgeoisie, of whom the most influential was Jeremy Bentham. Hobsbawm has argued that, although utilitarianism did not monopolise middle-class liberal ideology in this period (since Locke's more metaphysical conception of the 'social contract' provided a competing discourse), it was utilitarianism which 'provided the sharpest of radical axes with which to chop down traditional institutions which could not answer the triumphant questions: is it rational? is it useful? Does it contribute to the greatest happiness of the greatest number?' (Hobsbawn 1962: 280).

The Poor Law Amendment Act of 1834 (the New Poor Law) was in essence a utilitarian measure: indeed it is described by de Schweinitz (1961) as 'a doctrine founded in statute'. The authors of the Report of the Commission of Inquiry into the Poor Laws of 1833–34 (whose recommendations the Act embodied) were Edwin Chadwick, a disciple of Bentham, and Nassau Senior, a classical economist. Chadwick went on to become the Secretary to the Poor Law Commissioners appointed under the 1834 Act. The Act was designed not only to bring administrative certainty to the operation of the Poor Laws but to sharpen the distinction between the 'deserving' and the 'undeserving' poor. Like the Elizabethan Poor Law, the intention of the New Poor Law was not to abolish poverty, on the contrary, it was merely to abolish the dependence of the poor.

In pursuit of that object, Chadwick and the Poor Law Commissioners were far less compromising than the Elizabethan legislators had been, since they reduced morality and duty to matters of rational calculation and they substituted for the ordinances of God, the ordinances of rational self-interest. The principle of 'less eligible' treatment for the poor was their particular answer to the problem which had troubled Luther some three hundred years before: the problem, that is, of the need for continuous vigilance over the poor in order to distinguish the 'afflicted' from the 'indigent'. Condemning the practice of giving outdoor relief, the Commission of Inquiry into the Poor Laws observed

> it will be seen how zealous must be the agency, and how intense the vigilance, to prevent fraudulent claims crowding in under such a system of relief. But it would require still greater vigilance to prevent the bona fide claimants degenerating into imposters; and it is an aphorism amongst the active parish officers that 'cases which are good today are bad tomorrow, unless they are incessantly watched'. A person obtains relief on the grounds of sickness; when he has become capable of returning to moderate work, he is tempted by the enjoyment [sic] of subsistence without labour, to conceal his convalescence, and fraudulently extend the period of relief. When it really depends upon the receivers whether the relief shall cease with its occasion, it is too much to expect of their virtue that they shall, in any considerable number of instances voluntarily forego the pension.
> (Commission of Inquiry into the Poor Laws 1834: 26)

The answer upon which the Commission of Inquiry settled was given in the following terms:

> However diligent an assistant overseer, or an officer for inquiry may be, there are numerous cases which will baffle his utmost diligence and sagacity; the only test of those cases is making their condition more severe than that of the lowest class of labourers who obtain their livelihood by honest industry.
> (ibid.: 27)

Hence, the workhouse! Yet the workhouse, unlike Bentham's celebrated panopticon reformatory (see Chapter 2), was not the perfect embodiment of utililitarian doctrine: the disciplinary technique which was to provide the state with an answer to this need for continuous vigilance was provided from another quarter, that of philanthropy in the style epitomised by Thomas Chalmers. Indeed, towards the end of the nineteenth century, philanthropy and utilitariansim were to become concerted in a unified discourse which, I shall argue, was decisive in shaping the social security system of the twentieth century.

The case-approach

Dr. Thomas Chalmers had been a clergyman but, like Chadwick, had been a stern critic of the systems of outdoor relief to which the Poor Law had resorted by the beginning of the nineteenth century. Between 1819 and 1823, during his ministry in one of the parishes of Glasgow, Chalmers pioneered a new approach to poor relief and charitable intervention. The principles and practice of Chalmers' social work not only prefigured many aspects of contemporary personal social services, but they embodied a disciplinary technique which has become a central element of our social security system. To Chalmers, the very existence of public and charitable relief funds posed a danger, since, 'The imagination of a mighty and inexhaustible fund is not more sure to excite the appetite, and so relax the frugal and providential habits of its receivers, than it is to relax the vigilance of its dispensers' (*The Christian and Civic Economy of Large Towns* 1821–26 – quoted in de Schweinitz 1961: 104).

Inequalities of condition in life, according to Chalmers, are 'not artificial but natural' and it was not poverty but indigence which endangered civilisation. It was for the 'upper and gentle' class, therefore, to direct the 'lower orders' along the paths to self-sufficiency, and those paths, according to Chalmers, were to be found among the 'habits and economies' of the lower orders themselves. Chalmers identified four such paths or 'fountains', by far the most important of which was 'Self-Help', whereunder the individual should be encouraged into self-reliance and the acceptance of responsibility for his/her family without any material relief. The other fountains to which the poor might be directed were the 'Help of Relatives', the 'Help of the Poor for Each Other' and, only as a last resort, 'Help from the Rich'. So Chalmers organised the deacons of his parish to administer relief to the poor in accordance with a carefully prepared 'Directory of Procedure' and under his own supervision: each deacon was assigned to a 'small and specific locality' and, upon receiving applications for relief within that locality, they were instructed to gently but firmly conduct the most thorough investigation of each application so as to determine whether and what resources (other than material relief) might be available to satisfy the applicant and his/her family's needs.

By means of a systematic acquaintance with the day to day lives of the poor, an all pervasive vigilance and, of course, 'persuasion', the most dramatic reduction in public and charitable expenditure upon the poor within Chalmers' parish was achieved. The very purpose for Chalmers, however, was not the reduction of expenditure but the management of the lower classes. When giving evidence in 1830 to a House of Commons Select Committee, he cited a case in which his 'method' had succeeded by 'right moral suasion' and only 'a trifling expenditure' in keeping an orphaned family out of the town hospital, but, he added 'the worth of such management to the habit and condition of the family cannot be estimated in gold' (quoted in de Schweinitz 1961: 111).

The technique developed during Chalmers' brief experiment went unnoticed when the Poor Law Amendment Act was passed in 1834, but by 1869 it was Chalmers' example which provided the chief source of inspiration for the Charity Organisation Society, which was founded in that year and which, together with the Police Court Missioners, has been acknowledged as one of the 'grandparents' of modern social casework (Younghusband 1964). During the recession of the 1860s there had been something of a groundswell in middle-class philanthropic activity and sympathy for the poor, but as mentioned earlier (p. 49), during the 1870s there was a backlash when the Poor Law Board tried to tighten the operation of the Poor Law: that backlash and the emergence of the Charity Organisation Society may in fact be regarded as related phenomena.

The Charity Organisation Society was founded, not as a relief agency at all, but as an organising and investigative agency: its object was to obviate the problem of indiscriminate doles and charity and to bring the disciplinary techniques devised by Chalmers to bear upon a systematic basis. Octavia Hill, one of the key figures of the new philanthropic movement, described the service provided by the Charity Organisation Society as follows:

> First, it has offered to examine, free of charge, for anyone who wants to learn about them, the circumstances and character of applicants for relief.... But the Society offers a second advantage; it will give an opinion on the case of the applicant.
> (*Our Common Land and Other Short Essays* 1877 – quoted in de Schweinitz 1961: 111)

DEVELOPMENT OF THE SOCIAL SECURITY SYSTEM

The Charity Organisation Society established a central administration and district committees throughout the country. The district committees were responsible for training and deploying paid field workers and for forging working relationships with local charities and Poor Law officials. The Society trained their workers by lectures on office management and case-work methods (i.e. how to record and present a case for a committee) and instructed them in every case to visit an applicant for relief in his/her home, to check his/her sources of income and investigate independently every aspect of his/her circumstances. The Society readily admitted that the major part of its voluntarily donated income was spent on administration and salaries and not upon relief. Where relief was given, or where Society officials recommended to Boards of Guardians or private charities that relief be given, aid would only go to the 'deserving' cases (i.e. where it could be justified as a remedial measure) and would never be given as a temporary palliative. Philanthropy took on a utilitarian face and came to regard the poor not as objects of pity, but as a pathological phenomenon which must be contained for the greater good of the greater number. And the technique to be used was one which must operate specifically at the level of the 'habits and economies' of the poor so as to address the supposed defects in the individual character of each applicant.

The force of this discourse now made its impact and the activities and the approach of the Charity Organisation Society were effectively incorporated into the workings of the state apparatus when, later in 1869 – only seven months after the Society was founded – George Goschen, President of the Poor Law Board, issued a minute directing Boards of Guardians to give recognition to the role of the new bourgeois philanthropy and to secure joint action between the apparatuses of the Poor Law and those of organised charity. This development prefigured decisively the development of systematic means testing under the social assistance schemes of the twentieth century and the consolidation of the casework method or the 'case-approach' as a refined technique of disciplinary surveillance.

Legalisation

The utilitarian/philanthropic/self-help discourse was also a central element in the development of social insurance in the twentieth century, although the discourse adapted to take account of a further disciplinary technique – 'legalisation' or the insinuation of a juridical element into the administration of relief. Jeffery Jowell has defined the term 'legalisation' to mean 'the process of subjecting official decisions to the governance of predetermined rules' (Jowell 1975: 2). The technique goes further than this, since it bears not upon decision makers, but upon the objects of decision-making; it is a technique which constitutes the individual juridical subject as a bearer of rights, as an observer of rules and as an object of adjudication.

The implementation of the first Old Age Pensions in 1908 and, in particular, the National Insurance Act of 1911 could be said to have resulted from the example of Bismarck's Germany (which had introduced compulsory social insurance against accident and sickness in 1881) or from campaigns in this country dating back to the late 1870s (such as that by Canon William Blackley), or from the recommendations of the Royal Commission on the Poor Laws of 1905–11. None of these influences, however, can be regarded as decisive, although all of them shared with Lloyd George's Liberal government a common thread: they all implicitly acknowledged that the ideal of 'self-help' could be turned into an enforcible doctrine by giving the poor the status of juridical subjects and making 'relief' an 'entitlement', subject to rules.

In an earlier phase the bourgeoisie had relied upon the concept of legal rights as a means of displacing religious authority, royal prerogative and the power of the feudal aristocracy, but that concept, as E.P. Thompson has put it 'could be turned into service as an apologia for property in the face of the propertyless' (Thompson 1975: 264). In this instance, by bestowing legal rights upon the propertyless it was possible to subject them to discipline through self-regulation. The central principle of social insurance belongs therefore within the self-help discourse, since it enforces self-reliance by requiring each individual to enter into a legal, quasi-contractual relationship with the state. Under that relationship s/he is compelled to pay out of his/her wages certain contributions (which may but need not be directly related to any benefits subsequently paid), and s/he is entitled to certain benefits, subject to rules bearing directly upon the behaviour of the individual.

The social insurance principle developed into full bloom with the Beveridge Plan of 1945 which would have made that principle the basis for the provision of all major social security benefits: this was on the grounds that, in Beveridge's own words, 'the management of one's income is an essential element of a citizen's freedom' (Beveridge 1942). The self-help discourse had thus accommodated an evolution from a doctrine for managing the lower orders to a doctrine for making the lower orders manage themselves. The problem first identified by Luther had, it seems, been solved since the burden of vigilance had been shifted and had been transformed into a 'burden of proof' now placed upon every free citizen in need of state assistance. To obtain benefit, a citizen must show that s/he has complied with the rules governing that benefit; benefit levels are predetermined and the amount of 'relief' is calculable so far as the applicant is concerned; and the participation of the individual in the state's scheme acquires the appearance of being voluntary – not because National Insurance contributions are voluntary (they are not), but because the benefits are presented as the right of a free citizen and because the rules to which the citizen is subject appear more as a correlative duty to that right and less as an authoritative imposition.

If the insurance principle bloomed in 1945, it began immediately to fade. The Beveridge Plan had been founded upon the assumption that continuous economic growth would ensure virtually full employment and that the levels of National Insurance benefits would be sufficient to meet basic subsistence requirements. In the event, neither assumption held good (Field 1981: ch. 4). Beveridge had consolidated a process begun in the 1930s whereby social assistance had been recast under the auspices of national rather than local administration, but Beveridge's social assistance scheme (the National Assistance scheme of 1948) was supposed to inherit only certain residual functions of the Poor Law and was regarded as little more than a temporary safety net. With the failure of the National Insurance scheme, however, the demand for National Assistance grew rather than contracted and it began to play a major rather than a minor part within the social security system. In the face of this, the National Assistance scheme was itself recast and under the Ministry of Social Security Act 1966 became the Supplementary Benefit scheme. The reforms so introduced were largely cosmetic and Supplementary Benefit, like all preceding variants of social assistance since 1934, continued to be a nationally administered means-tested form of relief paid in accordance with fixed scales; the difference (already alluded to in a section above), however, is that Supplementary Benefit was declared for the first time to be an entitlement or right. The citizen who satisfied the various and complex rules and requirements supposedly enjoyed an absolute right to benefit, although the Supplementary Benefits Commission and officials of the Ministry of Social Security (later the Department of Health & Social Security) could still exercise considerable discretion in the interpretation of those rules and requirements. In this manner, the technique that had ushered in social insurance was now applied to social assistance. The process was carried further in 1980 when the Supplementary Benefit scheme underwent a further reform which purported to abolish the wide discretionary powers of DHSS officials and replace them by a voluminous and byzantinely complex set of legal regulations. As Carol Harlow has observed, the actual effect of such reform 'is that discretion has not been controlled, it has merely been transferred from the bottom to the top of the departmental hierarchy, being vested now in those who promulgate or draft regulations' (Harlow 1981: 549).

The self-help discourse none the less left its mark upon the Supplementary Benefit scheme (and so in turn upon the Income Support scheme) and, from the repressive institutions of the Poor Law there has been forged the more pervasive disciplinary apparatus of the social security system, based upon highly refined processes of means testing and a disembodied framework of legal rights which can systematically constrain the behaviour of the poor.

CONCLUSIONS

The historical process outlined in this chapter is centred upon the emergence of administrative power in place of absolute power; upon the emergence of legally circumscribed rights and benefits in place of arbitrarily bestowed privileges or gratuities.

The object has been to tease out from that historical process the ways in which the exercise and the techniques of power have developed. This 'revisionist' historical account has been presented in order to distinguish the theoretical framework being used here from that of the 'progressive' school on the one hand, and the Fabian/Social Democratic school upon the other. The 'progressive' view would treat the story of Britain's social security system as one of continuous progress towards 'freedom with security' (the expression being that of de Schweinitz (1961) upon whose work I have none the less relied quite heavily for reference material). The Fabian/Social Democratic school of thought, typified by the discourse of the poverty lobby and certain Labour politicians is more critical of the social security system and its failure to abolish poverty, and yet believes it to be capable of further reform in order to achieve that end.

The most conspicuous feature of the social security story outlined is the growth since the fifteenth century of a centralised and powerful state apparatus. The first point to be made is that that apparatus is oppressive, not simply because the intentions of welfare reforms have been 'subverted' by the self-interest of an unaccountable bureaucracy or by the effects of professionalisation (see Taylor 1981; and cf. Rothman 1980), but because the essential form of the state is itself derived from the capital/labour relation, as argued in Chapter 2.

The state has progressively entered into the sphere of reproduction and, as Norman Ginsberg has put it, 'The social security system assists in the exchange of labour power, ensuring that it is available as an exchange value' (Ginsberg 1979: 37).

In attempting this feat, however, the state has not followed a simple rationality. The state's entry into this sphere has been conditioned by contradictory discourses: on the one hand a humanitarian pro-populationist discourse and on the other a repressive anti-populationist discourse. The source of this confusion with regard to population (or, rather, the question of 'relative surplus population' (Marx 1970a: ch. XXV)) provides a key to understanding the erratic and untheorised development of the social security system as a vehicle of social control. Chapter 2 considered how the wage labourer is disciplined by the 'silent compulsion' of abstract laws of social reproduction or how, as Marx put it, 'The Roman slave was held by fetters: the wage labourer is bound to his owner by invisible threads' (ibid.: 574).

Marx went on, however, to show that because the continual accumulation of capital requires a continuous and cyclical change in the proportion of its constant and variable components (that is to say between real estate, machinery, etc. on the one hand and labour power on the other), the capitalist mode of production is uniquely capable of producing a surplus of population above the requirements of the technical means of production. If capital accumulation is to be sustained, such a mode of production is at the same time uniquely dependent upon the existence of that surplus population. The surplus population therefore 'forms a disposable industrial reserve army, that belongs to capital quite as absolutely as if the latter had been bred at its own cost' (Marx 1970a: 632).

Not only is the 'reserve army' available to be tapped during the booms of industrial production, but depending on the size and conditions of existence of this 'reserve army', its very existence may have a significant impact upon the degree of competition between wage labourers and upon the price of labour itself. It may therefore seem perfectly rational that the capitalist state should seek to regulate the conditions of existence of this reserve army, but if the members of that army 'belong' to capital as surely as does the wage labourer, how is it that they can be bound to their true owner? Functionality does not itself provide an explanation for the disciplinary mechanisms which can be observed within the development of social security. It is now possible to see how, at the level of ideology, the problems of poverty and of population became conflated and how the techniques of punishment and relief became entwined.

The pro- and anti-populationist discourses have never resolved their mutual conflict, but their intersection with a third discourse, the self-help discourse, has none the less materialised a strategy of power: the form of the state manifested in the social security system is both derived and reproduces the capital/labour relation in the sense that the domination by the state of each individual member of the relative surplus population now appears in like form to the domination by capital of the individual wage labourer. The pervasive investigative vigilance of the state redefines the human individual in terms of his/her capacity or potential as a 'worker' (see Melossi 1979), while the imposition of a disembodied framework of juridical rules exerts the same 'silent compulsion' as the abstract market forces which govern the wage labourer. Just as the 'fetishised' concept of the 'wage' (representing the price of labour) conceals the value of labour power, so also the fetishised concept of the social security 'benefit' (representing the cost of subsistence) conceals the cost of social reproduction. Correspondingly, the relationship between the relative surplus population (to which every worker may belong during periods of unemployment, during childhood or old age, when rearing children or should s/he be sick or disabled) and the rest of the working class is also obscured.

This chapter has identified the phenomena of the 'case-approach' and 'legalisation' as disciplinary techniques that are in a sense refinements or specific manifestations of Foucault's more generalised 'disciplines'. The social security system also, of course, provides a very general mechanism of 'surveillance' under which every citizen is known and recorded for the purpose of making social insurance contributions and for the purposes of administering benefits when claims are made. The administration by the Department of Social Security of its records may in reality be far less efficient than is popularly believed, but this in no way impairs the effect upon the individual who must assume that s/he is the subject of a more or less detailed official record (just as the prisoner in the panopticon reformatory must assume that s/he is being continuously observed). The poor are identified as such to the 'system' at the moment they submit to test in order to claim benefit: they are already known to the system by their individual insurance numbers or case paper references, but the system presents to the claimant an impersonal exterior, concealing a complex and informed bureaucracy. In the case of means-tested benefits, the poverty of the claimant is subject to a continuous process of definition, assessment and reassessment. What is more, the extent of computerisation currently being implemented or planned within the DSS will clearly serve to enhance, not only the accuracy of record keeping and assessment procedures, but the efficiency and reach of the Department's surveillance capacity (DHSS 1985b: para. 12.5; Campbell and Connor 1987: ch. 4).

Social security also 'normalises' claimants through a system of rules (cf. Foucault 1977); a system so arcane and complex that it cannot be completely understood by any individual claimant (nor even by any individual social security official) but which still has far-reaching effects in the myriads of rewards and punishments (additions and reductions to benefit) which it governs. This is the basis of the discrete and continuous power by which the state isolates, individuates, observes and controls the behaviour of the poor.

It is revealing that in 1985, when defining the role of the Police, the then Metropolitan Police Commissioner, Sir Kenneth Newman, situated that role on a par with that of other state agencies, including (specifically) the DHSS, as 'merely a sub-system of the total system of social control' (quoted in Campbell and Connor 1987: 190). Newman's terminology and sociological insights are unlikely to coincide with those of this book, but clearly he was giving expression to a perception which is commonly held as much within 'official' as within 'popular' thinking.

The conclusion to this chapter has treated social security claimants and 'the poor' as if they are a homogeneous group, which of course they are not. The interests of the unemployed, the elderly, single parents, the chronically sick and disabled are not all of a piece, not least because the social security system in fact classifies and treats them in quite different ways. One of the most important of the disciplinary mechanisms still emerging within the operation of the social security system has to do with the distinctions drawn between the various groups: this will be the subject of the next chapter.

Chapter Four

POVERTY AND PARTITIONING

> The effort and ingenuity that have gone into ensuring the survival of poverty are one of the wonders of the modern world; of a piece, in their way, with splitting the atom or walking on the moon.
>
> (Seabrook 1985: 12)

This chapter considers the phenomenon of 'modern' poverty. It argues that there is a sense in which such poverty is the creation of the capitalist welfare state; in which it is the social security system itself which defines or constitutes the modern poor, both as the object of social control and as a target for a particular disciplinary technique which is here called 'partitioning'.

Social security and the control of the poor are inseparable issues. Peter Townsend, in his mammoth study of poverty in Britain, reached the following conclusion about the nature of the means-tested social security benefits upon which the poor depend:

> Although, in principle, benefits are dependent primarily on test of means, in practice they have to be governed by other considerations as well, whether someone is genuinely sick or seeking work, whether a woman is genuinely supporting children on her own and whether an elderly person is or is not the householder. This is because the act of making up income without strings would come into open conflict with the other values upon which all societies are built – for example, that incomes are earned by work, that men living as husbands with women should support them, that children living with their parents should be supported by them, and so on. For the sake of

preserving its order and cohesion, society insists that these values are upheld. In different ways, benefits under means-tested schemes have to be conditional on behaviour and upon the readiness of potential recipients to submit themselves to test. The function of the schemes is as much to control behaviour as to meet need.

(Townsend 1979: 823)

CONSTRUCTING POVERTY

Within the last two decades, several writers have addressed themselves to the fact that, in spite of the social security system and in spite of the relative affluence and rise in living standards which have accompanied the growth of the economy since the Second World War, poverty as a 'social problem' has survived (e.g. Coates and Silburn 1970; Field 1975 and 1981; Holman 1978). The economic recession of the 1970s and early 1980s brought poverty back onto the political agenda. Joanna Mack and Stewart Lansley (1985) estimated that in 1983 around 14 per cent of Britain's population were suffering from 'an enforced lack of socially perceived necessities' (i.e. were poor); they further estimated that, in order to achieve a reduction in this figure, to say 3 per cent, minimum income levels would need to be raised to a level equivalent to 150 per cent of that which parliament acknowledged as sufficient for basic subsistence (i.e. the then current Supplementary Benefit scale rates).

However, in a speech in May 1989 entitled 'The End of the Line for Poverty', Social Services Secretary, John Moore, accused the poverty lobby and the academic establishment of 'manipulating statistics'. In a bid to defend his government's social policy record, he sought to prove that, because living standards generally have risen, poverty no longer exists. The debate about poverty has largely concentrated upon how to define and measure the phenomenon; and prescriptions for 'curing' the problem have been largely confined to proposals for change within the welfare state or to justifications or critiques of the existing social security and tax systems.

'Absolute' definitions of poverty, which seek to measure the incidence of poverty with reference to some standard for a minimum means of subsistence, have in more recent times been challenged by 'relative' definitions of poverty, which use as their bench-mark some standard for a minimum means of social participation. The approaches of earlier researchers such as Booth (1888) and Rowntree (1902, 1918 and 1937) to the quantification of the minimum level of income necessary for bare subsistence have hitherto been more or less directly applied in determining benefit levels within the social security system. But Townsend (1979), Mack and Lansley (1985) and Donnison (1982), for example, now argue that poverty should in essence be regarded as 'a standard of living so low that it excludes people from the community in which they live' (Donnison 1982: 7). The welfare state must ensure that every citizen is capable, not of subsistence alone, but of participation as a 'free' politico–juridical subject within the workings of advanced capitalist society. Either way, poverty is a problem for the welfare state which, depending on the point of view adopted, must do one of two things. The state must either administer minimal relief to society's 'failures' and 'casualties'; or else it must mitigate any excessive inequality caused by our socio-economic system by underwriting the capacity of every individual to participate in the life of society and to be a useful citizen.

Poverty is thus regarded as the principal measure of the success or failure of social policy, and consideration of the *form* which social policy intervention takes has by and large been either incidental or else has been subordinated to concerns about the *substance* of such policy and the extent to which it ameliorates or perpetuates relative deprivation. On this basis, we would have to conclude in view of the persistence and the growing incidence of poverty that our social security system is an abject failure. Why it is that, as Kincaid puts it, 'only by extraordinary ingenuity ... first Beveridge, and then successive post-war governments, have prevented social security from exercising a considerable influence in levelling post tax incomes' (Kincaid 1975: 219)?

Policy, poverty and criminality

Taking public expenditure upon social services as a whole, Le Grand (1982) has argued that, not only does it fail to redress inequality, but expenditure in areas such as health, education, housing and transport has tended to contribute to inequalities since they have benefited higher or middle income groups more than lower income groups. This is not to say that social security expenditure in particular does not have some redistributive effect, but even a commentator like O'Higgins who has argued that state welfare plays 'a valuable, if limited, role in increasing the share of resources going to lower income groups' (O'Higgins 1983: 181), also acknowledges that such expenditure alone cannot eliminate inequality so long as the market remains the principal determinant of income distribution. And what is clear is that the redistributive impact of the social security system has not over time reduced the gap between rich and poor (Royal Commission on the Distribution of Income and Wealth 1976; Field 1975). While higher income groups may look to occupational and fiscal systems of welfare, the poor must look to a social security system which is increasingly reliant upon selective benefits and means tests. The social security system of the 1980s thus created,

> a special economy for a very large number of people ... an economy in which rewards were meagre but in which a special pattern of incentives operated ... an ecomomy unknown to the luckier half [sic] of the population with higher incomes ... a separate world both of economic prospects and of social institutions.
>
> (Bosanquet 1983)

As a mechanism for the control of poverty, the social security system has been no more successful than the reformatory prison and the penal system have been in controlling crime (see Chapter 2). Like the prison, the social security system does not 'miss its target' since, as Townsend correctly observed, the function, or rather the effect, of schemes such as the Supplementary Benefit scheme can only be understood when account is taken of their capacity for the control of individual behaviour. Poverty, like criminality, can be understood as the creation of a technology of power: just as crime has been 'socially problematised' by the inception and growth of a formal state penal system, so poverty has been socially problematised through the inception and growth of a formal state social security system. Poverty in feudal society was not a 'social problem' in so far that it was an ascribed status to which the greater part of the population was born and from which it could neither in theory nor practice escape. With the collapse of feudalism and the development of capitalism in its various stages, poverty as a 'problem' emerged, representing on the one hand the failure of the labouring classes to give full effect to their economic emancipation, or on the other hand the failure of the market economy to ensure the efficient (and/or 'humane') reproduction of labour power.

As a contemporary 'social problem', poverty takes on 'an apolitical and technical appearance' (Haines 1979: 123) and the very definition of the problem has become the preserve of social policy itself. Recent writers, such as Nick Manning (1985), have therefore asked why such policy continues to have legitimacy when it is, as we have seen, such a remarkable failure. Manning himself suggests we should look more closely at the way problems and policies are perceived – professionally, publicly and academically. And, to the extent that professional, popular and academic discourse has constituted the 'problem' of modern poverty, he is right. Poverty *is* a discursively constituted phenomenon, but the knowledge and the logic behind our perceptions of poverty are rooted in historically specific relations of power. Chapter 3 shows how social policy was transformed during the transition from the nineteenth century era of free market capitalism and *laissez-faire* individualism to the twentieth-century era of monopoly capital and the interventionist state. But, not only was social policy transformed, but poverty and the poor were reconstituted as targets for more refined and more penetrating forms of institutional practice and disciplinary technique.

It was in this transition that what Garland has chosen to call 'The Birth of the Welfare Sanction' (1981) can be seen. Garland argues that the diverse economic and political developments between the eras identified above

> came to imply ... a fundamental displacement of certain social regulatory functions from the realm of civil society to the realm of the State. On the one hand the 'automatic' and unorganised market distribution of resources ... was no longer politically possible.... On the other hand, this displacement implied a disciplinary problem in that the modification of the market mechanisms not only undermined the social control inherent in unemployment, poverty, debt and so on, but also destroyed

the rationale of the market's back up institutions – the prison and the poor law.

(Garland 1981: 35)

And so a 'new strategy of social politics' emerged, based on a series of welfare and assistantial mechanisms for the positive administration, segregation and normalisation of large sections of the population. Garland claims that the transformations which first opened up the 'logic of coercive assistance' may be found within the penal reforms of the early twentieth century, and whether or not this contention is sustainable, it is important that the link is made between new forms of penality and the emergence of 'welfare'. What criminality and poverty have in common is that each is a creation of a technology of power. Such links provide a key to an understanding of the new apparatuses of knowledge upon which the interventionist state was founded (see Smart 1983). Pasquino (1980) argues that, within classical penal theory, there was no conception of the criminal as an individual, only a supposition of 'free will' and the capacity of all to choose whether or not to commit crime. The science of criminology, however, constructed a conception of 'homo criminalis', signifying a new rationality and a new logic to penal practices. Similarly, we may argue, classical poverty theory recognised not poverty but indigence and supposed that all subjects were free to choose whether or how to obtain the means of subsistence. Social policy has implicitly constucted a conception of 'homo pauperis', signifying the rationality and logic of welfare and assistantial institutions. Welfare state personnel relate to criminals and to the poor, not on the basis of an assumed equality of status, but as expert benefactors ministering to clients. As Garland puts it 'The relationship between the State and the individual, like the act of punishment itself, is fundamentally depoliticised – referenced in terms of welfare instead of power' (Garland 1981: 43).

Importantly, however, the 'problem' of poverty and of 'homo pauperis' as an object of regulation has its existence in popular discourse as much as within the discourse of state professionals and social policy academics. Whilst it may only be the poor who inhabit the realm of Bosanquet's 'special economy', and whilst social policy may claim increasingly to be concerned primarily with the materially deprived, welfare expenditure and the social security system touch in some measure and at some time upon the lives of everyone, whether they be poor or not. Regardless of questions as to the nature of its empirical existence, poverty as a discursive construct provides the logic and the rationale for the intervention of the state into the sphere of the workplace and into the family – to collect contributions and taxes and to pay allowances, benefits and pensions. It is through the very conception of poverty that each citizen of the welfare state is constituted; not as a formally free and anonymous member of society at large, but as a specific entity with a specific and governable susceptibility to poverty – and indeed to criminality or even, for that matter, to sexuality.

Poverty and sexuality

Poverty is analogous to sexuality as well as criminality. Foucault (1981b), in his study of the history of sexuality, endeavoured to focus upon sex 'as the pivot of two axes, of the disciplines of the body and of the regulation of the population, along which the technology of power over life is exercised' (a paraphrase by Smart 1983: 78).

Sexuality, according to Foucault, may be seen as a creation of various forms of discourse concerned with life, death, health and issues of population and population management: issues which were or which rather became matters for government and for 'state science'.

Sex, crime and material deprivation as potential objects of social regulation need none of them be inherently problematic. Yet the discursively constituted phenomena of sexuality, criminality and poverty are all especially problematic, since they all identify the individual both as the involuntary subject and as an object of domination. It is through the creation of sexuality, criminality and poverty that sexual activity, socially embargoed forms of behaviour (i.e. crime) and material inequality (i.e. poverty) may be brought within specific relations of power. In this way issues of social policy, become in fact issues of social control.

Poverty as subjection

Poverty cannot be defined with reference to an absolute or even a relative 'bench-mark'. In the specific context of welfare state capitalism, it is a process of subjection – not direct subjection by forces within civil society (the market), but subjection by forces organised through the state apparatus (the social security system). Poverty must be located specifically within capitalist social relations. No one can quibble with the use of the term 'poverty' in relation to the standards of living once endured by feudal serfs or, for that matter, those at present endured by the victims of famine in the Third World. Poverty in economically developed Western societies is a different phenomenon, situated in relation to the unique nature of developed capitalist social relations – social relations of production under which, not only is the mass of people alienated from the means of obtaining their own subsistence, but under which a highly developed state apparatus plays a crucial role in the reproduction of such social relations.

The (mal)distribution of income and property may be governed more or less directly by the relations of material production, but modern poverty is a product of the state and of social policy; it is a particular form of deprivation which the Poor Law and social security system have been able 'to isolate, to place in full light and to organise as a relatively enclosed but penetrable milieu'. The form of deprivation, called poverty, which exists under welfare state capitalism is a 'manageable' form of poverty: the modern poor – consisting largely of the unemployed, the elderly, single parents and the chronically sick and disabled – can be safely differentiated, accommodated and supervised within the margins of civil society.

Both 'social control' and 'poverty' should be regarded as palpable processes of subjection, the form of which is a necessary consequence of the domination of labour by capital. The social security system, appearing in the guise of 'social policy', embodies a strategy for domination: as such it is, as it were, only a substitute for social policy and represents in reality a vehicle for social control. Social control is instanced within the social security system at several overlapping levels and the argument so far has identified several of the disciplinary techniques which are unique to capitalist relations of production as they develop over time. What has been missed from the account so far, however, is an analysis of how poverty itself has been refashioned through the process of social control.

There is a view of poverty shared by writers as diverse as Illich (1973) and Marcuse (1964) which is based on a critique of mass consumer culture. According to such a view 'modernised poverty' (Illich 1973) arises out of capitalism's failure to satisfy the 'false needs' which it has itself created. The very plasticity of human need becomes the source of capitalism's regenerative power, and human 'need' is thus expropriated and fashioned by capital:

> Poverty and illusions of scarcity are ideologically indispensible to capitalism; for without them all the desperate energy and striving in the search for growth and expansion and accumulation would be undermined; and indeed, there might be a serious danger that its inner dynamic would simply exhaust itself.
> (Seabrook 1985: 12)

Seabrook, drawing on E.P. Thompson's (1968) notion of the 'making' of the working-class (during capitalism's most formative years at the end of the eighteenth and beginning of the nineteenth centuries), suggests that the working class and the working class 'psyche' have been 'reconstructed' as a result of the new forms of consumption and dependency generated by capitalism in the last half of the twentieth century. This view of poverty fails, however, to detect the development of tangible disciplinary mechanisms associated with the 'new' form of poverty and it identifies the oppression of poverty merely in terms of the effects of internalised bourgeois individualism and of false or imagined needs. This is strangely at odds with the powerful insights of writers like Seabrook into the very concrete effects of the 'new' poverty: he quotes, for example, a young Turkish single parent living on social security on a large North London housing estate

> Poverty here is different from poverty in Turkey. It's easy to say there's no real poverty here; but it's a different sort of poverty. There's hunger in Turkey; here, there's despair, there's loneliness, there are all sorts of reasons why people can't cope.
> (Seabrook 1985: 22)

The way in which such substantial numbers of people manage and are managed by means of the social security system must surely indicate, not that the working class has been 'reconstructed' to accommodate the requirements of capital, but that it has been or is in the process of being fragmented, dismantled or disabled.

Another writer who starts out from E.P. Thompson's particular historical conception of working-class consciousness is Bill Jordan. Jordan has argued that those who are made dependent upon the social security system are assigned by the state to a newly created class or underclass of their own and, by juggling to keep domestic consumption up (including consumption by social security recipients), the ruling class has succeeded in playing off the working class against the 'claiming class' (1973): here Jordan in fact anticipates by more than a decade the analysis advanced in the 1980s by Dahrendorf and others (see Chapter 1). Whether or not we accept this characterisation of the poor as a 'class' in its own right, the analysis does point to the way in which a substantial and growing minority within the working class has become marginalised – not merely from the relations of production, but from the working class itself. In a more recent work (1981), Jordan has provided an account of the way in which the growth of the 'new' poverty and the formation of his 'claiming' class are related, not to some cunning conspiracy by state planners, but to the internal dynamic of capital itself.

Two diametrically opposed political economists – Ricardo and Marx – have both from within their own perspectives predicted the limits of the process of capital accumulation and the extent to which such limits may be outstripped by the pace of technological development: continued economic growth is dependent, not only upon continually expanding capital formation and technological development to improve the methods and the 'productivity' of production, but also upon a perfectly elastic supply of labour at (or at near to) subsistence level wages and a highly elastic demand for manufactured goods at home and abroad. The expanding equilibrium of capital accumulation will be disturbed if capital investment in new technology merely replaces labour without also increasing output, and unemployment and falling wages will result. Cyclical booms and slumps are thus an inevitable feature of the process, but the system will tend to heal its own short-term wounds as long as it can sustain growth in the long term. However, in Britain in particular there has since the 1960s been a growing trend to 'deindustrialisation' and, in spite of various efforts on the part of diverse governments to stimulate capital formation, capital has proceeded to deploy new technology so as to displace labour without expanding output.

Britain, having been the first country to industrialise, remains the most industrialised country if only in the sense that it has a lower proportion of agricultural employment in relation to industrial employment than any other country in the world. In effect, however, this means that Britain and some of the other 'older' Western European economies have long since exhausted that supply of labour at subsistence level wages which had resulted from the displacement of rural population and, since the 1960s, it is industrial workers who have been displaced – out of primary and manufacturing industry and either into low paid 'tertiary' or 'service' industries, or else of course into long-term unemployment. From an analysis at this general level, Jordan (1981) argues that technological unemployment in Britain (and eventually in other 'developed' nations as well) is not a temporary phenomenon and neither monetarist nor Keynesian economic solutions can provide a lasting cure.

This trend, when coupled with underlying demographic changes in the population, now means that the state and the social security system are permanently and irretrievably involved in the maintenance of a claiming class. This book argues that these structural and demographic factors have been accompanied by a sharpening of certain of the disciplinary techniques fashioned during the social security system's earlier development.

PARTITIONING THE POOR

The most important of those techniques is 'partitioning'. Jordan's 'claiming class' is separated or marginalised from the 'working class' as a result of prejudice and stigma as much as the substantive effects of low income. The so-called claiming class is also partitioned – *from other classes and within itself* – by a far more subtle yet palpable mechanism. What distinguishes and 'marginalises' the members of Jordan's claiming class is not the mere fact of their exclusion from 'work' or from productive relations, but the effects of a disciplinary mechanism within the social security system itself: a mechanism which assigns a particular pertinence to the basis for each person's exclusion from productive relations. Retirement pensioners, for example, are treated quite differently from the unemployed or from single parents – and all these categories of claimant are partitioned and sub-partitioned with reference to criteria relating to the grounds for their exclusion from productive relations.

It is necessary, to draw a distinction between 'work', as purposeful and useful activity, and 'employment', which is paid work (but which need not be purposeful or useful!). Feminist and other commentators have observed that capital and society as a whole are served, not only by work within the formal economy, but also by the vital work performed within the domestic household and in the bringing up of children, and by that immense variety of useful work which is performed every day on a creative, voluntary, neighbourly or informal basis. Some Marxists claim that 'work' (as the transformation of nature through conscious action) is the human being's unique distinguishing characteristic, from which, through the distortions of capitalist social relations, we become alienated (Fischer 1963). The work from which social security claimants are excluded is not 'work' in any of these broader senses, but 'employment': their exclusion is not from the working class (as Jordan suggests) but from the immediate and specific sphere of the wage relation. It is through the social security system that the domination of labour by capital may be extended or perpetuated beyond the wage relation; and the principal technique by which this is achieved is the systematic partitioning of the 'non-working' population.

The origin of the term 'partitioning' lies with Foucault, who claimed that all mechanisms of power disposed around the 'abnormal' individual are composed or distantly derived from two forms: the techniques once deployed in response to the threat of leprosy and by which lepers were systematically excluded from the 'pure' community; and the techniques once deployed in response to the threat of the plague and by which entire towns or districts were quarantined, partitioned and minutely supervised in order to contain the disease (Foucault 1977).

During the nineteenth century, says Foucault, these general techniques were brought slowly together and the techniques symbolic of plague containment ('disciplinary partitioning') were applied to the symbolic lepers ('beggars, vagabonds, madmen and the disorderly'): the task of the emerging institutional state apparatuses ('the psychiatric asylum, the penitentiary, the reformatory, the approved school and, to some extent, the hospital') was to 'individualise the excluded, but [to] use procedures of individualisation to mark exclusion'.

In essence disciplinary partitioning became a double process, involving 'binary division and branding (mad/sane; dangerous/harmless; normal/abnormal)' and 'coercive assignment ... (who he is; where he must be; how he is to be characterised ...)' (Foucault 1977: 199).

Disciplinary partitioning as applied to the poor had its origins in the workhouse, but, in its mature form, the partitions erected between the poor (the 'claiming class') and the working class and those between the various categories of social security claimant are not architectural or physical. The partitions are none the less real and are constituted through the effects of the framework of social rights fabricated by the state. The poor's struggle for survival has been transformed (or reduced) to questions of legal definition or status: is the claimant genuinely sick or disabled? is the claimant genuinely available for work? is the claimant genuinely bringing up children on her/his own? is the claimant past the prescribed age for retirement? The status of claimants is assessed and categorised and the emerging public consensus is that, whatever else, social security provision needs to be directed, or 'targeted' towards specific groups within the population and that the 'right' to benefit should be conditional upon an individual's specific status – for example, as an old-age pensioner, an unemployed person, a single parent, a disabled person, etc. Having particular regard to the substantial 'reforms' to the social security system embodied in the Social Security Act 1986, this is now the direction in which the social security system continues to move and to which, in spite of hard fought disagreements as to benefit levels and various matters of design and detail, neither the labour movement nor the welfare rights 'lobby' would seem fundamentally to object. It is important, therefore, to trace, not only the development of the partitioning technique, but the origins of the consensus which enables it in its mature form to work.

Utilitarian discourse and partitioning

In common with two of the writers mentioned earlier (Seabrook and Jordan), this section will take as its springboard the historical insights of E.P. Thompson (1968) as contained in his epic book on working-class consciousness in the period 1780 to 1832. This does not imply that we need accept Thompson's descriptive approach to class composition in preference to perhaps a more rigorous analytical approach, but his work undeniably provides a rich seam of material pointing to a significant historical disjuncture coinciding with the Reform Act of 1832 and, of course, the Poor Law Amendment Act of 1834. Thompson's claim is that, by the 1830s, the formation of a self-conscious working class was more or less complete and that the political and social 'apartheid' of working people during the wars with France, coinciding as it did with more transparent forms of exploitation at home, actually contributed to the social and cultural cohesion of the exploited. It is argued here that 1834 and the New Poor Law marked the beginning of a phase in which that process of 'apartheid' – the partitioning of working and, particularly, non-working people – was developed as a technique which served to undermine that social and cultural cohesion. What is more, Thompson's work illustrates how the basis for driving a partition between various categories of poor persons already existed within the ideology and discourse of working-class reformers themselves: Thompson cites a sermon preached from the text – 'The poor ye always have with you' – by the leading Chartist reformer (and one of the leaders of the Plug Riots), Ben Rushton:

> The poor he divided into three classes: the halt and the blind who were 'God's poor': the idle and the reckless, who deserved to be left to look after themselves: then thirdly, there were the poor who had striven and worked hard all their lives, but who had been made poor, or kept poor by the wrong doing and oppression of others.
>
> (quoted in Thompson 1968: 439)

Ironically, it was distinctions of this very nature which, stripped of moral judgement and political censure, were written into the strictly utilitarian framework of the Poor Law Amendment Act of

1834. The Benthamite principle of 'less eligibility' was disciplinary rather than merely punitive; paupers were consigned to the workhouse, not because it was their just desert, but in accordance with what Foucault has defined as the 'dualistic mechanisms' of individual control; the principle was a classic manifestation of 'binary division and branding' whereby the poor were marked off from the independent and consigned by category into their own separate spaces. The institution of the workhouse – and the walls between the separate wards within the workhouse – gave physical expression to the disciplinary partitioning mechanism, but they were not and are not essential to that mechanism. Commenting with approval upon the old practice of 'badging' under the Elizabethan Poor Law, Bentham himself drew this telling distinction:

> The badge marks the class in which it finds him [i.e. the pauper]: and there it leaves him. Degradation changes the class; badging *indicates* it only [emphasis added].... If the mark for a pauper were the same as for a felon, then indeed the affixing of it would be stamping infamy upon what would oftentimes be mere misfortune; then indeed it would be confounding innocence with guilt. The mark branded upon the body of a felon certifies him to be a delinquent.... The Mark termed a Badge and locked to the garment of a pauper does not certify him to be a delinquent in any shape. What it does certify is that he is poor, and so he is: that he is a burthen upon others; and so he is.
> (quoted in Spicker 1984: 12)

As noted in Chapter 3, Chadwick, the chief architect of the New Poor Law, was directly influenced by Bentham and, indeed, the 'lesser eligibility' principle was applied in a form – the 'workhouse test' – that was to survive for a century. When Disraeli condemned the Poor Law Amendment Act for announcing that 'poverty is a crime' (see Chapter 3), he was reflecting accurately upon the Act's immediate effect, but he had none the less totally misconstrued the nature of the disciplinary mechanism which constituted the Act's central underpinning (and the very precise distinction it intended to draw between paupers and criminals). What is more, when the National Assistance Act of 1948 and later the Ministry of Social Security Act of 1966 were hailed in parliament as final 'nails in the coffin' of the Poor Law, they did not in fact signal the death of the fundamental disciplinary technique which lay behind the 'lesser eligibility' principle: on the contrary, that technique had come of age, since the partitions by which the poor were divided and categorised had long since ceased to depend on bricks and mortar, or even the symbolism of badges, but now rested on a foundation of 'social rights' and legally defined statuses.

If, as Thompson claims, the 1830s marked a formative point of disjuncture between bourgeois and proletarian consciousness in England, then the attainment of 'social rights' claimed by Marshall (1963) to have occurred in the twentieth century would seem to represent a consolidation of such consciousnesses; a point at which working-class consciousness lost a measure of the separate identity attributed to it by Thompson; and a point at which disciplinary partitioning could truly take root.

The Poor Law Amendment Act of 1834 had given expression to the ascendancy of the utilitarian state and, indeed, Thompson does not refrain from commenting upon the irony 'that the main protagonists of the State, in its political and administrative authority, were the middle-class Utilitarians, on the other side of whose Statist banner was inscribed the economic doctrines of laissez faire' (Thompson 1968: 90).

The coming of exchange relations based on market principles 'problemetised' not only poverty but also the simple yet brutal reciprocity which once existed between what we might now call 'social rights' on the one hand and 'property rights' on the other. Eighteenth-century thinkers such as Thomas Paine (1915) thus speculated that the 'Rights of Man' must be presumed to have a priori or 'natural' existence and to be subject to new and imminent dangers of infringement: such Rights, thus elevated to metaphysical proportions, became the common currency of all Radical discourse, but were capable of assuming quite different significance once such discourse progressed and diversified beyond its essentially Jacobinite origins. The utilitarian discourse which characterised the New Poor Law of 1834 brought the Rights of Man to earth and grounded them in rigorous (i.e. 'disciplined') individualism; the agrarian socialists, Owenites and Chartists, who condemned the New Poor Law, romanticised the supposed 'birth rights' of the free Englishmen and accused their rulers of cheating them of such rights:

Among these rights was, the right to live in the country of our birth; the right to have a living out of the land of our birth in exchange for labour duly and honestly performed; the right, in case we fell into distress, to have our wants sufficiently relieved out of the produce of the land, whether that distress arose from sickness, from decrepitude, from old age, or from inability to find employment ...

> (Cobbett W. *Tour of Scotland* 1833 –
> quoted in Thompson 1968: 836)

This assertion by the political reformist and journalist, William Cobbett, while based upon nothing more than historical illusion, none the less represented a powerful article of faith which, in Thompson's words, was 'to preserve the Radicals and Chartists from becoming the camp followers of the Utilitarians or of Anti-Corn Law League' (1968: 837). There was, however, a strand of Radical opinion which did become a camp follower to the utilitarians and that strand is represented in the figure of Francis Place, famous for his campaign to repeal anti-trade union laws, but who was also a disciple of Bentham and is described by Thompson as the 'founding father of the Fabian tradition' (Thompson 1968: 846). The following section will consider how the Fabian tradition developed and how, as the dominant voice of the trade union and labour movement on matters of social policy during the twentieth century, it was to exert some measure of influence in the form which the modern welfare state was eventually to assume: the Fabian tradition was to furnish the terrain for a synthesis between the technique of disciplinary partitioning and the demand for 'social rights'.

To return for a moment, however, to the nineteenth century workhouse, it is important to reiterate that it did not perfectly reflect the utilitarian principle which claimed to have given birth to it, since many conspicuously punitive practices were associated with its operation. Anti-populationist discourse intersected with utilitarian discourse in order to produce the most odious effects. Chadwick had not envisaged the workhouse as 'an object of wholesome horror'. On the contrary, he anticipated that its food would be nutritious and that its standards of accommodation and hygiene would in all probability be vastly superior to that of the 'lowest class of independent labourer': the lesser eligibility principle would be applied through the medium of the workhouse's disciplinary regime (Spicker 1984). Moreover, Chadwick and the Commission of Inquiry in 1834 had proposed the strict classification of workhouse inmates into four main categories – first, the aged and really impotent (whom Ben Rushton had categorised as 'God's poor'!); second, the children; third, the able-bodied females; fourth, the able-bodied males – and had suggested that separate buildings with differing regimes be provided for each category (see de Schweinitz 1961).

In practice, most workhouses were indeed to become 'objects of wholesome horror' since their physical conditions as much as their disciplinary regimes were often made as 'irksome and disagreeable' as ingenuity could contrive. Additionally, no attempt was made to provide separate buildings for the separate categories of the poor: certainly, separate wings and wards were maintained within the workhouse, but the partitioning of the inmates conflated punishment (the breaking-up of families) and discipline (the operation of 'binary division and branding').

As capitalism advanced into its classical imperialist phase, the workhouse system discredited itself by its own severity and, as we have seen in Chapter 3, responsibility for various categories of the poor – the sick and the elderly – was by stages removed from the auspices of the Poor Law. During the first half of the twentieth century, the beginnings of the 'welfare state' emerged, consisting of specialised 'services' (for health, social insurance, social assistance, etc.). Each service had the power to define the citizen as 'client'/'patient'/'claimant' and to categorise him/her with reference – not to expressed wants or needs – but with reference to the 'benefits' which the state itself sought to deliver. Such benefits were intended in each case for certain categories of person and, rather than coercively assigning paupers to their designated wards or wings within the workhouse, partitions of entitlement were now constructed, and clients/patients/claimants were required to accommodate themselves within appropriate categorised boundaries; to join the right queue; to submit for examination or test to establish whether their 'cases' fitted into designated categories. Disciplinary partitioning was gradually insinuated into the discourse of claims associated with notions of social rights and social justice.

The Fabian tradition

The direction and momentum for such change had in some degree already been established by the time of the Royal Commission on the Poor Laws of 1905–1909 and, even the more 'radical' Minority Report (Webb and Webb 1909) (written substantially by Sidney and Beatrice Webb) reflected in its general direction developments that were ultimately inevitable, if indeed they were not at that time already afoot. It has been said of the Minority Report that 'it has exercised more influence over social policy courses than over social policy' (Taylor-Gooby and Dale 1981: 19). However uncharitable, this charge is understandable in so far that the Webbs did little more than give voice to a Fabian tradition whose discourse subsequently came to dominate social policy debate. That discourse, however, is as crucial as the three discourses delineated in Chapter 3 so far as any understanding of social security is concerned.

The Webbs wanted all forms of social service to be brought under democratic control; they wanted specialised departments and committees to deal with children, the sick, the mentally defective, the old, etc.; they wanted Unemployment Insurance and Labour Exchanges (and detention camps for those requiring reformatory measures!). The essence of their vision was that of a highly coordinated, highly specialised state apparatus capable of a far higher degree of efficiency and precision in categorising need than was the Poor Law and, thereby, of much greater penetration into the 'habits and economies' of the poor:

> ... when the cost of providing for the several members of the family when destitute fall upon the [proposed] committees which have, as part of their ordinary duty and machinery, the periodical visitation of the home, *irrespective of destitution*, these committees will have the families continuously under observation. Is the child unfed at school? A member of the Children's Care Committee calls to ascertain the cause. At every birth, at every death, at every occurrence of notifiable disease, the officer of the Health Committee becomes acquainted with the circumstances of the household. Thus the several Committees of the Town Council ... will be perpetually doing whatever may be necessary to maintain the family intact, to *encourage* those

members of it who are striving to keep the home together, and forcibly to *restrain* any member whose conduct is threatening it with ruin.

(Webb and Webb 1909; emphases added)

If this was but an imprecise vision of things to come, it is possible none the less to detect that the techniques of surveillance, intervention and the 'case-approach' derived from the utilitarian/philanthropic discourse (and pioneered by Chalmers) have become concerted with the techniques of specialisation, categorisation and partitioning. The Fabian discourse of social justice, as a corollary to the strictly utilitarian notion of individual freedom (i.e. a qualified freedom guaranteed by the state), intersected with the utilitarian/philanthropic discourse to provide a terrain on which disciplinary state power could grow. Additionally, the Fabian tradition as it has gathered momentum during the twentieth century and sought the application of an increasing proportion of national income to social welfare goals has intersected (if it has not actually incorporated) the paternalist/humanitarian/populationist discourse. One Fabian theorist and politician, Tony Crosland (1956), even argued that it was humanitarianism and not egalitarianism which constituted the main driving force behind the efforts of the Labour movement to create a welfare state. But the point upon which (as George and Wilding have put it) 'all Fabians will agree' was made by Tawney – that 'The mother of liberty has, in fact, been law' (George and Wilding 1985: 74).

In Chapter 3 we argued that 'legalisation' (the bringing of legal rights and legal framework to social security) constituted, not a guarantee of liberty, but a disciplinary technique by which the discourse of self-help and self-regulation could permeate to the level of the individual claimant as a legal subject. That technique and the technique of partitioning have, to their mutual enhancement, been effectively welded together in the social security system to evince a most subtle and complex strategy of power. As the social security system has been brought progressively further and further within a framework of legal regulation and entitlement (a process which has continued into the 1980s) it has imposed upon claimants requirements of self-partitioning: an individual legal subject's claim upon the state is determined by questions of legal status and the legal definition of the subject's situation within the social relations of production.

By the extension of the law, so too has partitioning and the 'binary division and branding' of subjects been extended. Minute degrees of discrimination can be exerted so as to distinguish between contributor/non-contributor, retired/non-retired, sick/healthy, employed/unemployed, dependent/non-dependent, disabled/able-bodied, householder/non-householder; single/ cohabiting; etc., etc. And such statuses depend upon the extraordinary and convoluted definitions applied to purely legal concepts of, for example, 'availability/unavailability', 'capacity/incapacity', 'ability/inability', etc., etc.. There is of course no legal definition of 'poverty': but the process of subjection that *is* poverty derives from the legal definition of individual legal subjects in accordance with a technique of disciplinary partitioning. There are no badges and no workhouse walls to distinguish the pauper: there are only legal distinctions to which the pauper-subject must aspire and 'voluntarily' submit. Poverty is both the object and the subject of social control.

PREVENTION, RELIEF AND THE STRATEGY OF SOCIAL CONTROL

The final part of this chapter rounds off the first four chapters with a brief discussion of the underlying strategy of the social security system. It has been argued that the form of the welfare state has been fashioned and constrained by the form of capitalist social relations and the fundamental antagonism between capital and labour. It is not therefore possible to accept Foucault's contention that 'there is no binary and all encompassing opposition ... at the root of power relations' (Foucault 1981b: 94). It is possible, however, to go along with Foucault when he insists that such power relations should be examined for their inherent logic: 'not because they are the effect of another instance which "explains" them, but rather because they are imbued through and through, with calculation' (ibid.: 95). There is, it will be argued, a strategy of power which, while it is enmeshed within a web of class forces, is the unique preserve of the social security system.

Neither charity, the poor laws, nor the modern social security system have been successful in preventing or relieving poverty. Yet in spite of this, the rationale of each of these historical modes of intervention has been either the prevention of poverty, the relief of poverty, or both.

A conventional or 'progressive' (cf. Cohen 1985) view might be that the *ad hoc* and indiscriminate relief of poverty by the giving of alms represented a low point in the history of the poverty business, whilst the modern social security system, calculated to secure 'freedom from want' (Beveridge 1942) for all citizens, represents a high point. In this light, the efforts of the Thatcher governments to redefine the objectives of social security in terms of the relief rather than the prevention of poverty may be seen as regressive (see Bennet 1985). The alternative 'revisionist' (cf. Cohen and Scull 1985) view is that the logic of prevention and relief have each contributed to a developing strategy of social control, targeted against the poor.

It has been demonstrated earlier that poverty as a modern social phenomenon has been effectively constituted through social policy interventions calculated to relieve or prevent it. But the concern of this section is with the logic rather than the outcome of such calculation.

It was shown in Chapter 3 that the transition from charity to social security represented an inversion of the relationship between the poor and the source of poor 'relief': whilst once anonymous beggars received charity dispensed by a conspicuous and elevated donor, now the individually named and documented social security claimant receives benefit adminstered by anonymous officials on behalf of a vast and unknown body of tax-payers. There has therefore been a clear development in the logic of poverty relief which has made possible and contributed to the tactical deployment of various discplinary techniques.

Similarly, there have been developments in the logic of poverty prevention. It is the logic of poverty prevention which first constituted the necessary process of social redistribution as one of 'public spending' upon individuals, thus constructing the basis for the modern state/claimant relationship. Earlier discussion in this chapter illustrated that the 'high point' of preventative policy development amounted to an endorsement of the Fabian thesis and of what Thane has called the 'efficacy of the expert' (1982): the logic of poverty prevention thus constituted poverty as a specialised field of knowledge and constructed the social security claimant as the object of such knowledge.

By such means, the logic of prevention and the logic of relief together define a strategic objective which, while not independent of class interests, policy aims or political discourse, is inherent to the social security system itself. Social policies directed to the prevention and/or relief of poverty are thus incorporated within a strategy of social control: the meeting of needs becomes the exercise of discipline and, in so far that the elimination of need would deny the opportunity of meeting it, then the logic of prevention and relief appear as accretions to the self-perpetuating rationale of the social security system. It will be argued in chapter 7 that, far from undermining the underlying strategic objectives of the social security system, the new priorities which the Social Security Act 1986 imposed have sustained or strengthened such objectives.

First, however, the next two chapters discuss the role which social security tribunals play as a strategic element within the social security system. They are concerned with the tribunals because of what tribunals can tell us about the social security system as a whole and about the disciplinary mechanisms which function through and within it. It will also become clear that tribunals have an importance of their own as a part of a network of social control because they are themselves invested with a powerful disciplinary technique.

Chapter Five

THE DEVELOPMENT OF THE SOCIAL SECURITY APPEAL TRIBUNAL: A CASE-STUDY

> Most claimants at the time of their appeal will be too troubled and hassled by the more practical day-to-day problems of their plight ever to have the emotional energy to study the nuts and bolts of the machinery by which their appeal will be processed.
> (H.H. Judge Byrt, President of the Social Security Appeal Tribunal in DHSS 1985a: vii).

The Social Security Appeal Tribunal (the 'SSAT') is in some ways quite peripheral to the operation of the social security system. The great majority of social security claimants never appeal and do not therefore encounter the tribunals; and, even for the claimants who do appear before such tribunals, the tribunal does not constitute a part of their day-to-day experience of the social security system. What is more, the authority of the SSAT has been shown to be virtually incidental in so far that the effects of tribunal decisions which offend against the intentions of government policy can be swiftly negated by fresh legislation (Prosser 1983).

Tribunals have none the less become an integral part of the social security system (Bell 1982) and a part which functions, as will be seen, with remarkable consistency. The concrete existence of the tribunal and the abstract existence of the claimant's right of appeal have together provided an orientating factor within the functioning of the social security system, while the performance of the tribunal itself has a predictability which represents a guarantee to the continued authority of the system as a whole.

A tribunal hearing represents a controlled confrontation between the individual and the state; it is the occasion for a ritualised adjudication of an individual claim and the ritualised application of the prevailing distributive policy of the state. The tribunal, whether or not it is in reality independent, appears in the form of a 'third element' (cf. Foucault 1981a: 8) interposing itself between the social security claimant and the state agency responsible for the administration of benefits. That third element, insinuated at the interface between the individual and the state, whilst regulating the confrontation between them, also renders it visible: it provides a commentary and a window upon the relations of power which are mediated through the social security system.

This chapter considers the emergence of tribunals within the social security system and relates this to the three levels of social control already outlined:

1. the level of 'political settlement' and the containment of protest;
2. the level of sanctions and the adjudication of pecuniary penalties;
3. the level of individualised disciplinary techniques and the adjudication process.

THE CONTAINMENT OF PROTEST

There is a well argued strand of opinion which holds that the right of appeal attaching to the award or refusal of social security benefits has a certain social control effect, in so far that it channels individual and collective dissatisfaction with the social security system away from political protest (Prosser 1977; Harris 1983).

The unique form of the modern SSAT can be traced back to 1911 and, since then, much has been said and written about the proliferation and development of administrative tribunals in general and, in particular, about the constitutional issues which have surrounded their introduction (e.g. Bell 1969). The growth of the state and of public administration during the nineteenth century and the advent of the welfare state in the twentieth century have self-evidently 'greatly increased the potential area of dispute between government and citizen' (Street 1975: 1). The debate about the role of administrative tribunals has thus largely been seen as a question of 'finding a right relationship between authority and the individual' (Franks 1957: para. 6). The introduction of formal adjudicative arrangements within the social security system is attributable, in part, to a largely paternalistic or humanitarian philosophical discourse which accepts that disputes between people and the state ought to be justiciable as well as political.

Although, under the English Poor Law of 1834, a person aggrieved by a refusal of relief, or the amount or kind of relief given, might appeal to the Relief Committee of the Board of Guardians, this did not constitute a statutory right and it amounted to no more than a plea directly to the very authority responsible for the decision complained of.

The justiciability of claims for Poor Relief was not recognised in England until the 1930s, when Poor Relief evolved into 'social assistance', but, in the mean time, with the introduction of social insurance in the early twentieth century, the state was obliged to acknowledge that disputed claims for insurance benefits were justiciable and that adjudicative machinery should be provided. In the case of the Unemployment Insurance scheme created under Part II of the National Insurance Act 1911, Lloyd George's Liberal government quite deliberately set up specialised adjudicative arrangements, entirely separate from the ordinary courts: this amounted to a precedent to which the modern SSAT owes its origins.

The Courts of Referees

In so doing, the government was motivated by several factors. First, the unwelcome tide of expensive and contentious civil litigation which had resulted from the Workmen's Compensation Act of 1897 had persuaded the government that the ordinary courts were ill-suited to the task of adjudicating disputes involving the working classes (Abel-Smith and Stevens 1967). Second, the government, in seeking to 'thrust a big slice of Bismarckianism over the whole underside of our industrial system' (Winston Churchill – quoted in Gilbert 1966) sought to build upon the German model of social insurance. Third, the government was acutely conscious of the growing strength of the labour and trade union movement and saw a need to incorporate them, institutionally, into the arrangements for social insurance (Hay 1978).

This is not to say that the government responded in any consistent way to such factors. When framing the Old Age Pensions

Act of 1908 – which provided means-tested pensions to the over 70s – the only right of appeal provided was an internal appeal to the local authorities' Pensions Committees and thereafter to the Local Government Board. And when framing Part I of the National Insurance Act 1911 – which provided a limited health insurance scheme – the government bowed to pressure from the friendly societies and the commercial insurance companies for them to be incorporated into the administration of the scheme and this restricted the scope for an appeals mechanism, such that the only right of appeal lay to the Insurance Commissioners responsible for the overall administration of the scheme (and thereafter, in certain cases, to the ordinary courts).

Only in the case of Unemployment Insurance was the way clear to adopt what was at the time a radical new approach and to provide for disputed claims to benefit to be adjudicated by local 'Courts of Referees' appointed by the Board of Trade. The Courts of Referees were tribunals each consisting of three people: a workpeople's representative, an employers' representative and a chairperson (usually a lawyer). A further right of appeal lay from the Courts of Referees to an 'Umpire', a national appellate authority appointed by the Crown.

Such unemployment insurance schemes as existed elsewhere in Europe (including Germany) were at that time only voluntary and parochial (Cohen 1921), and Britain was the first developed country to legislate for a compulsory national scheme which extended specifically to cover the risk of unemployment. The principle of compulsory contributions was thought likely to generate resentment amongst workers but, in the event, the trade unions and the new parliamentary Labour Party supported the scheme in principle. The provision of a right of appeal to a Court of Referees and the inclusion of workpeople as members of such tribunals amounted, in part at least, to a concession that was contrived, proffered, and indeed accepted, as a mitigating factor to be weighed against the unprecedented element of compulsion which attached to the payment of unemployment insurance contributions.

The Court of Referees provided a model which has endured and has ultimately been adopted for all forms of social security adjudication. However, before examining the ways in which it has been refined and developed, it is worth considering the significance of its particular form as opposed to the other means of adjudication with which the early twentieth-century state administrators experimented.

Chapter 2 argued that the political form of the welfare state may be derived from the social form of exploitation and that there is a sense in which the struggle between capital and labour, at the point of material production, is transmuted into a political struggle over the value of the 'social wage'. The beginning of the twentieth century marked the crucial early stages in the development of imperialism or monopoly capitalism, when capital became increasingly concentrated and the general scale of organisation, both economic and political, grew. Foster (1976) claims that it was at this time that 'Lloyd Georgism and welfare' began a switch from bribery in the market to bribery through institutions. It is argued here that the Courts of Referees – as one such institution – directly reflected a 'bargain' struck with or rather imposed upon labour on behalf of capital.

The issues to be adjudicated by Courts of Referees were not justiciable in the sense provided for and understood within the 'high bourgeois legality' (Bankowski and Mungham 1976) of the ordinary courts; they were matters to be settled in accordance with certain rules of 'fair play' and hence the sporting nomenclature of 'referees' and 'umpires'. The 'courts' themselves were composed with equally balanced representation from labour (from a panel of workpeople directly elected from within the trades then covered by the new scheme) and capital (from a panel of local employers drawn up by the Board of Trade) and were presided over by a supposedly neutral and impartial chairperson.

Supporters of administrative tribunals claim that the prototype tribunals (the Courts of Referees) worked well and that 'once an administrative tribunal is set up, it appears to give such satisfaction that it is never replaced by the ordinary courts' (Street 1975: 10).

Whether social security tribunals can be said to have given 'satisfaction' to social security claimants, rather than to governments, is arguable, but what is undeniable is that the tribunal form, once established, took root. The virtues claimed for the tribunal system were 'speed, cheapness and efficiency' in adjudication, when their performance was compared with that of the ordinary courts (Street 1975: 5). Such virtues, however, would hardly make the tribunal system 'popular', since working-class claimants had no experience of the courts by which to make such comparisons. What the tribunal system did was to *take* adjudication *to* the insured section of the working class (a trend which has been described as 'legal informalism' by Abel 1983). What is more, the Court of Referees did not provide an opportunity for conventional litigation, but a highly specialised form of adjudication and one which, as volumes of case-law were promulgated by the Umpire, became increasingly technical and esoteric.

When social insurance provision was extended in 1925 to cover claims for widows, orphans and contributory old age pensions, the tribunal system was not correspondingly extended to receive appeals by the new classes of claimants; instead, single referees (lawyers appointed by the Minister of Health upon the Attorney General's recommendation) would sit individually to hear such appeals. It may be that the tribunal die was not yet so strongly cast as to represent an inevitable corollary to the introduction of new state benefits for the working-class, or it may be that the choice of adjudicative arrangements was influenced by the lack of political muscle possessed by widows, orphans and old age pensioners as compared with that possessed by the able bodied unemployed!

The UAT

In 1934, however, the virtual collapse of Unemployment Insurance and of the locally administered Transitional Allowances scheme (Gilbert 1970) forced upon the government the introduction of the nationally administered Unemployment Assistance scheme and a new three-person tribunal, the Unemployment Assistance Tribunal (the 'UAT'), was created to hear appeals by claimants against the decisions of the Unemployment Assistance Board. Tony Lynes (1975), in his study of the political background to the Unemployment Assistance Act of 1934, has observed that the intended function of the UAT was to protect the Minister from parliamentary and public criticism over the Unemployment Assistance Board's scale rates of assistance, which in many parts of the country compared most unfavourably with the rates of assistance formerly paid under the Transitional Allowances scheme. Thus Lynes describes the government's underlying motives in the following terms: 'The creation of the UATs was thus a deliberate political act, aimed at making an inherently unpopular reform more acceptable. It had little to do with any abstract ideas of justice or legal rights.' (Lynes 1975: 7)

The introduction of UATs in 1934 made quite explicit what had been implicit in the 1911 move to introduce the Courts of Referees. The right of appeal to an independently constituted tribunal was regarded by legislators as a quid pro quo (or, more crudely, a bribe) to compensate claimants for some other imposition or loss.

The Unemployment Assistance Board, in its first Annual Report was able to announce

> There is little doubt that [the UATs] play a real part in spreading confidence in the Board's administration among applicants. Many District Officers report that while relatively small use may be made of the tribunal system, the knowledge that it is available is widespread, and this knowledge acts as a safety valve among aggrieved applicants.
>
> (UAB 1935: 51)

The accounts of individual District Officers contained in the Board's Report generally indicate that claimants were encouraged to use the tribunals, and one District Officer expressly described them as 'an outlet for dissatisfaction' (UAB 1935: 95). In the event, the introduction of tribunals failed to divert protest at the broad political level, but the tribunals themselves were evidently still thought to be of value as a 'safety valve' at the level of the individual claimant.

The form chosen for the UAT was no doubt influenced by the 'success' since 1911 of the Courts of Referees, but by this time, as Prosser has put it, 'The choice was never between appeal to tribunals and appeal to the [ordinary] courts, but between appeals to tribunals and no appeal' (Prosser 1977). However, the UAT differed from the Court of Referees in two significant respects: first, in the details of its composition; and second (and more importantly), in the qualitative nature of the adjudicative task assigned to them.

In its constitution the UAT made less pretence to 'impartiality' than the Court of Referees. Certainly, there was a workpeople's representative on each tribunal, but s/he was appointed by the Board itself from a panel of trade union nominees drawn up by the Minister of Labour; in place of an employers' representative was a representative not only appointed by the Board but who was, at that time appointed expressly to represent the Board's interests; and the chairpersons of such tribunals, who would *not* usually be lawyers, were appointed directly by the Minister of Labour. The Unemployment Assistance Board, as the governmental body responsible for the administration of means-tested allowances, therefore exercised considerable control over the functioning of the UATs.

Circulars issued by the Board emphasised that the main function of the tribunals was 'administrative' rather than 'judicial' and that the subject matter upon which they would adjudicate had to do with 'determinations of need' rather than the interpretation of rules of entitlement (Lynes 1975). It will be seen shortly to what extent this injunction was taken to heart by the UAT and its successors.

Separate development

The Courts of Referees and the UATs each developed their own style and tradition of adjudication as their respective fields of jurisdiction were extended so as severally to cover the full range of social security benefits.

In 1936, the Courts of Referees were renamed the Unemployment Insurance Tribunals and these in turn became the National Insurance Local Tribunals ('NILTs'), under the National Insurance Act of 1946, with jurisdiction to hear appeals relating to the full range of National Insurance benefits under that Act. The NILTs retained the machinery of the Courts of Referees, since this had been adopted without criticism or comment in the Beveridge Report as a suitable model for appeals adjudication under the new National Insurance scheme. The NILT's jurisdiction was further extended in 1959 to include appeals relating to the non-means-tested Family Allowances scheme (now Child Benefit) and, in 1966, to include appeals relating to the Industrial Injuries scheme (which from 1946 to 1966 had had its own separate tribunal).

On the social assistance side, in 1940, the UATs became the Assistance Tribunals with jurisdiction to hear appeals in respect of newly introduced means-tested old age and widows' pensions schemes and these tribunals in turn became the National Assistance Tribunals ('NATs'), under the National Assistance Act 1948, with jurisdiction to hear appeals relating to a new comprehensive means-tested benefit called National Assistance which was intended at the time to serve as a residual 'safety net'. In 1966, when the National Assistance scheme was revamped, to become the Supplementary Benefit scheme, the NAT became the Supplementary Benefit Appeal Tribunal (the 'SBAT') and finally, in 1970, the SBAT's jurisdiction was extended to include appeals under the means-tested Family Income Supplement scheme.

The development of social security tribunals during this period proceeded with comparatively little political or public controversy and little is known about the views of the claimants who resorted to such tribunals during their early years of operation. It is interesting, however, that the Unemployment Assistance Board would appear to have been anxious to distinguish the UAT from the Court of Referees on the grounds that the *latter* was thought to be regarded by many claimants with suspicion (UAB 1935: 95).

In 1955, the Franks Committee on Administrative Tribunals and Enquiries was appointed with broad terms of reference to enquire, *inter alia*, into 'the constitution and working of tribunals other than the ordinary courts of law'. The Franks Committee's approach to the question of tribunals was fundamentally legalistic and the reforms which they recommended were calculated to ensure three characteristics of sound adjudication: 'openess', 'fairness' and 'impartiality' (Franks 1957). As a result of these recommendations, both the NILT (the Court of Referee's successor) and the NAT (the UAT's successor and the SBAT's predecessor) came notionally under the supervision of the Council of Tribunals, created under the Tribunals and Inquiries Act 1958. The chairpersons of these social security tribunals, while still appointed by the relevant Minister, had now to be chosen from a panel drawn up by the Lord Chancellor (in Scotland, by the Lord President), although this did not in practice guarantee that NAT chairpersons would be legally qualified as the Franks Committee had clearly wished.

Franks made little adverse comment upon the functioning of the NILT, but the Committee regarded the NAT as a different and indeed a special case:

> Although in form these tribunals hear and determine appeals against decisions of local officers of the National Assistance

Board and, therefore exercise adjudicating functions, in practice their task much resembles that of an assessment or case committee, taking a further look at the facts and in some cases arriving at a fresh decision on the extent of need.

(Franks 1957: para. 182).

This characterisation of the NAT formed a basis for exempting the NAT (and, effectively, therefore the SBAT which succeeded it) from certain of the fundamental requirements which Franks thought necessary in respect of other tribunals – including the NILT. In particular, the NATs were excused from holding their hearings in public and they continued not to be subject to any further right of appeal – whether upon a point of law or otherwise – to a higher appellate body or court.

The essential character of the two distinct types of social security tribunal was therefore preserved until, during the late 1960s and 1970s, there arose some fomentation for reform. Upon the one hand, a new breed of welfare rights activists, welfare lawyers and Fabian politicians began to consolidate a small but increasingly vocal 'welfare rights lobby', which condemned the 'injustices' perpetrated by social security tribunals (but most particularly SBATs). Upon the other hand, academics such as Kathleen Bell began to study the operation of the tribunals and advanced quite specific criticisms and proposals for reform. However, the attention which the tribunals themselves attracted was ultimately, perhaps, quite secondary to a campaign by the welfare rights lobby, through pressure groups such as Child Poverty Action Group, for a more 'rights'-oriented approach and for a Supplementary Benefit scheme based less on discretionary decision making and more upon legal entitlement. Criticism of the tribunals related more to the quality of adjudication than to the role of the tribunals within the social security system. The debate over 'discretion vs entitlement' and the discourse that demanded 'proper' justice represent phenomenona which will be examined later, but what is of particular interest here is the emergence of another less conspicuous discourse; a discourse within the paternalistic/humanitarian/pro-populationist tradition which was identified in Chapter 3; a discourse for 'citizen participation' and for a non-adversarial style of tribunal.

Bell's analysis: the seeds of reform

It is Bell's findings which would seem to have been substantially accepted or incorporated into the eventual reform of the social security tribunal system, and her studies of both the NILT and the SBAT would appear to have been informed by a common objective. Bell was fairly complimentary about the performance of the NILT (Bell *et al.* 1974 and 1975), but devastatingly critical of the amateurish approach of the SBAT (Bell 1975). She also identified issues of common concern to both tribunals.

Although NILTs were theoretically dealing with insurance benefit claims governed by strict eligibility criteria, Bell and her research team found that the tribunals exercised more judicial discretion than was commonly supposed and, in so far that they were engaged in 'an exercise which is not confined to the application of objective rules and standards' (Bell *et al.* 1974: 289), that NILTs had much in common with SBATs. Bell recommended that more advisory services and more representation should be made available for NILT appellants and that the tribunals should be 'strengthened' by means of improved training, etc. to ensure, in particular, a greater degree of participation in decision-making on the part of tribunal members. What was advocated, therefore, was a 'participatory model' which, while not neglecting the 'judicial element' to the tribunal's function, would enable appellants both to better put their own cases and to have their cases better examined by the tribunal. It is significant that, in her report, Bell counselled caution with regard to the extension of legal rights to welfare and emphasised, for example, that appellants' advisers and representatives should share in the 'enabling' process rather than monopolise the conduct of appellants' cases as advocates: the object of her participatory ideal was to 'ensure a better fit between people's roles as clients of the social services and as mature citizens of the welfare state' (Bell 1973: 20). Having turned her attention to SBATs, Bell observed

> Generally speaking, problems were encountered in the SBAT field in a more acute form, but it appears the same kind of help likely to be most valuable in meeting the needs of NILT

appellants would also be most appropriate for those involving SBAT adjudication.

(Bell 1975: 5)

Bell's substantive criticisms of the SBAT were essentially similar to those of other researchers in the 1970s (Herman 1972; Lister 1974; Fulbrook 1975; Adler *et al.* 1975; Milton 1975; Frost and Howard 1977) – the most outspoken of whom, incidentally, had already described the SBAT as 'the slum of the English tribunal system' (Rose 1975: 150) – although Bell's recommendations were perhaps more detailed and specific, and certainly more influential. Bell made similar recommendations to those she had made for NILTs, but also proposed that ultimately all tribunal chairpersons should be legally qualified, that a right of appeal to a higher appellate authority (and a system of binding precedent) should be established, and that the appeal structures of all social security benefits should eventually be integrated.

In arguing that both SBATs and NILTs should conform to the same 'participatory' model, Bell was quite explicitly seeking a compromise between 'adversarial' and 'inquisitorial' models of adjudicative process (see Bell 1970). The adversarial model, being founded upon the essentially English tradition in judicial procedure, supposedly dates from the days of trial by combat in which the adjudicator(s) did not enter the field of combat, but would merely enforce the rules as between the disputants' respective 'champions' or advocates and, at the end, declare which combatant had won. Before a social security tribunal, however, while the government department concerned will always have its 'champion' at the hearing (in the form of an experienced Presenting Officer), only a minority of appellants will come with an advocate to fight their cause. The inquisitorial model, upon the other hand, is founded upon Continental judicial custom, in which the court itself undertakes responsibility for investigating accusations, interrogating the parties and witnesses and establishing the truth. The procedural dilemma, however, is concisely expressed by Ganz:

> It is clear, therefore, that tribunals though they step into the arena much more than ordinary courts are still very much influenced by the adversary model of procedure. If they were

better equipped and more prepared to find out the facts for themselves the unrepresented party would be less at a disadvantage. But nothing would be gained if for an unequal contest there were substituted an accusatorial inquisition.

(Ganz 1974: 35)

The humanitarian compromise – the 'participatory' model – can, of course, have another effect; that of denying or minimising the extent of the actual conflicts of interest existing between the parties (cf. Lister 1974). It is within this perception of the tribunal process that tribunals can assume their greatest depoliticising effect since, notwithstanding the strictly defined limits to its jurisdiction, the tribunal is presented as the 'appellant's friend'. The tendency had in many ways already been present amongst tribunals and particularly amongst the 'case committee'-oriented SBATs, of which one tribunal member in the mid-1970s was quoted by Lister as saying 'the essence of the tribunal is a group of local citizens who sit down with you and say "what's the trouble chum?" and do something about it if they can' (Lister 1974: 29).

The reforms to the Supplementary Benefit scheme introduced in 1980 inevitably affected the role played by the SBAT, since these reforms removed most of the discretionary or policy determined elements of the old scheme and replaced them with explicit criteria governed by statutory regulation. As will be seen, this did not have quite the impact which might have been supposed. Concern about the growing number of appeals to the SBAT had been one of the government's considerations (see Allbeson and Smith 1984), although the new regulation-bound scheme continued in practice to give rise to a considerable and growing volume of appeals. Whereas the nature of the new benefits scheme meant that the task of adjudication by the SBAT should have become more akin to that of the NILT, it rapidly became apparent that many SBAT members were on the one hand reluctant to relinquish their 'case committee' tradition while, on the other hand, were confused and even embarrassed by their lack of understanding of the new regulations. For the first time, the decisions of SBATs themselves could be appealed to a specialist higher appellate body – the Social Security Commissioners (formerly the National Insurance Commissioners, who had succeeded the Umpires as the higher appellate authority under the National

Insurance scheme and whose jurisdiction was now extended). This exposed the SBATs, not only to the principles of legal precedent and a burgeoning body of case law, but also to a quite unfamiliar degree of procedural scrutiny and constraint.

The creation of the SSAT

It was therefore more or less inevitable that in 1984, under the Health and Social Services and Social Security Adjudication Act 1983, the SBATs and NILTs were merged to become the SSAT, and that they were encompassed under the supervision of a new Presidential system. It is important at this stage to note three essential elements to the changes brought about. First, the appointment of a President and Regional Chairpersons to oversee and supervise the SSATs ensured for the SSAT, in appearance at least, a far greater degree of independence from the DHSS and the Secretary of State than either the NILT or the SBAT had had, especially since the appointment of tribunal members and chairpersons and the assigning of tribunal clerks now falls to the President and his Regional Chairpersons. Second, the provision that all tribunal chairpersons should be legally qualified and for the enhancement of training for all tribunal members was intended to improve the quality and consistency of adjudication and to safeguard the 'judicial element' to the tribunal's function. Third, the abolition of the dual panel system for the appointment of tribunal wing members and the creation of a single panel of 'persons appearing to the President to have knowledge or experience of conditions in the area and to be representative of persons living or working in the area' (para. 1(2) Sch.10 Social Security Act 1975 as amended), has swept away the symbolic representation within the tribunal process of the interests of labour and capital.

The SSAT, therefore, is a more formally 'judicialised' tribunal than either of its immediate predecessors, but, it will be argued, it retains within its procedural discourse and daily practice the evidence of its pedigree. What is quite clear is that the traditions of the old tribunals have not merely been assimilated, but they are undergoing a process of synthesis as the disciplinary techniques of the social security system itself are refined.

The merger of the tribunals into a single system represents the extension of a single 'net of social control' (cf. Cohen 1985), within which the various categories of appellant may be comprehensively and coherently ordered, segregated and examined. Elements of a paternalistic/humanitarian/pro-populationist discourse remain integrated within the concerted workings of the tribunal system as is best evidenced by the extent to which what Bell defined as a 'participatory' model continues to inform the official guide to tribunal procedure (published by the DHSS and endorsed by the President of the SSAT) (DHSS 1985a). The guide cites Bell's recommendations as authority for urging lay tribunal members to 'play an active and enabling role towards the claimant by showing sympathetic understanding of his [sic] problem, by listening, asking relevant questions, drawing him out and generally helping him to sort out his case' (DHSS 1985a: para. 14). In short, an attempt is still made to portray the tribunal as the 'appellant's friend'. The guide expressly states that the tribunal's proceedings are not adversarial and that the tribunal has an inquisitorial function. In this context, it is declared that the Adjudication Officer (i.e. the departmental 'Presenting Officer' appearing before the tribunal) 'does not act in the capacity of an advocate nor should he [sic] adopt a defensive role in respect of any decision the subject of an appeal' (DHSS 1985a: para. 36). In the foreword to the guide, the President, Judge Byrt, plainly envisages that even an appellant's representative should be regarded more as an 'amicus curiae' (or friend of the court) than as an advocate.

The reality of tribunal hearings may be somewhat different from the picture painted by the guide, but the paternalistic emphasis remains an unmistakable strand within that continuing tradition of the tribunal which addresses itself to the containment and diversion of disaffection and protest. The extent to which the SSAT may be seen or can effectively portray itself as the 'appellant's friend' is conditional, however, upon other factors. As Martin Partington has observed

> it is conceivable that if the substance of social security law became so hostile to the interests of claimants that tribunals could never, in law, overturn a departmental decision and decide a case in a claimant's favour, then whatever claims for independence were made by those within the tribunal system, such

claims would contain no credibility to those outside the system. But this position has not yet been reached.

(Partington 1986a: 175)

Whether or not there are grounds for Partington's apparent optimism remains to be seen, but his point is well made in so far that the SSAT as the 'policeman' of the 'social wage' will be able to police 'by consent', as it were, only so long as the social wage itself retains both inherent and perceived benefits for social security claimants. For the SSAT to continue to exercise or to make a contribution towards social control at a time when social security law is indeed becoming increasingly hostile to the interests of claimants, it must also be capable of functioning at other levels.

THE ADJUDICATION OF PENALTIES

It was observed in Chapter 3 that there are areas of social security law which embody a policy of sanctions and which are therefore quite explicitly 'hostile' to claimants. Since their inception, it has fallen to social security tribunals, as a part of their function, to adjudicate, should claimants seek to challenge the imposition of such sanctions or penalties. In such situations, the idea of the tribunal as the 'appellant's friend' becomes hard to sustain because the tribunal has power to confirm as well as to set aside certain punishments, and because the investigative role of the tribunal is eclipsed by the self-evidently adversarial nature of the (unequal) contest between the appellant on the one hand and the state as the 'appellant's opponent' upon the other.

If the 'participatory' ideal espoused by Bell and alluded to in the SSAT's procedural guide is evidence of a compromise in the humanitarian/paternalistic/pro-populationist tradition, then the capacity of the tribunal to adopt the role of trial judge and to dispense punitive justice is evidence of a tendency within the repressive/Malthusian/anti-populationist tradition identified in Chapter 3. It has been argued that the social security system can be rendered intelligible by identifying and tracing the contradictory and competing discourses though which it has been constituted. Social security claimants and the 'modern poor' have been constituted and 'problematised' as much by the urge to repress those who stand at the margins of productive processes as by any urge to incorporate them into such processes. Tribunals, inevitably, reflect this.

To trace the history of the penalties upon which social security tribunals have adjudicated is therefore to trace one element in the history of the social security system itself. However, it is important to grasp, not merely that the operation of social security tribunals has a 'dark side' (Squires 1985), but that their jurisdiction over the administration of penalties has made the tribunals an integral part of a wider project of repression.

Work-testing and social insurance

The forms of 'work-testing' introduced with the beginnings of social insurance created a very particular role for the social security system in the field of labour discipline. Three of the key principles enshrined in the Unemployment Insurance scheme of 1911 have survived to this day, having been 'policed' by the social security tribunals since the first days of the Courts of Referees. The principles relate first to persons dismissed from employment through misconduct, second to persons who leave employment 'without just cause' and third, to persons involved in trade disputes, all of whom are subject to penalties through the social security system. The National Insurance Act of 1911 provided that persons dismissed for misconduct, or leaving their employment voluntarily, should be suspended from receiving unemployment benefit for up to six weeks (an arbitrary period which was supposed to reflect the time within which a worker could expect to find alternative employment and after which his/her own culpability could no longer be regarded as the primary reason for his/her continued unemployment). During 1986, this maximum period of disqualification was extended to thirteen weeks and in 1988 it was further extended to six months. Similarly, persons losing employment by reason of a stoppage at work due to a trade dispute were disqualified from benefit for so long as the stoppage continued.

Claimants aggrieved by a decision to suspend or to disqualify them from unemployment benefit could appeal to the Court of Referees whose task it was to ensure that penalties were 'fairly' administered under the rules of the insurance scheme. From the outset, therefore, the Courts of Referees were required to adjudicate upon matters of dispute which lay not only between claimants and state officials, but between employees and employers. 'Misconduct' in this context came to be interpreted as anything which a reasonable employer would regard as sufficient to justify dismissal. The definition of misconduct was thus effectively delegated to employers and made subject to variations in prevailing industrial practice, whilst the burden of proving whether or not the claimant was 'guilty' of such misconduct fell, in practice, upon the claimant him/herself since the employers were not formally parties to the appeal proceedings.

This bizarre state of affairs could be justified on the grounds that the rules which the Courts of Referees were required to administer were governed by the 'insurance principle'. The unemployment insurance fund, it was said, is to be safeguarded from claims by any insured persons who have brought the risk of unemployment upon themselves or who, by their conduct, have shown themselves to be unsuitable for employment (Ogus and Barendt 1978: ch. 3). The argument, of course, is inherently specious since an insurance principle need not exclude the risk of negligence or even recklessness on the part of an insured person, nor should it exclude from benefit, on the grounds of alleged unsuitability, any person or class of persons whom the scheme has already admitted and has compelled to pay contributions.

The rules which the Courts of Referees and their successors have been required 'fairly' to administer have little, therefore, to do with principles of insurance, but with a scheme which operates so as to inflict a double punishment. A person who is dismissed for an 'offence' at work is punished, not only by dismissal, but by a suspension of social security benefit and his/her right to challenge this second punishment lies before a disciplinary tribunal that is not only removed from the place of work, but which is insulated from the criteria by which a worker might judge the 'fairness' of his/her own fate. Tribunals may uphold suspensions of benefit for dismissal for alleged 'misconduct' in situations where claimants have been dismissed for acquiring criminal convictions quite unrelated to their employment (see National Insurance Commissioner's decision ref.: R(U)1/71 and R(U)2/77); in situations where claimants have been dismissed for alleged criminal offences of which they have in fact been acquitted before the ordinary courts (see R(U)8/57); and even in situations in which an Industrial

Tribunal has found that the claimant was 'unfairly dismissed' (see National Insurance Commissioner's decision ref.: R(U)2/74).

Similarly, it fell to the Courts of Referees and their successors to adjudicate upon whether unemployed claimants had left their employment 'without just cause'. Once again, the onus of proof fell on the claimant and the curious concept of 'justice' which was forged for the purpose, is quite distinct from other concepts of either individual or social justice and must be seen to derive from what is essentially an anti-populationist discourse. This is best expressed in the judgement of the Court of Appeal which, in 1982, heard an appeal against the Social Security Commissioner from a decision upholding the ruling of a NILT that a teacher, who had taken early retirement, should be suspended from Unemployment Benefit. The teacher had retired, not only in his own interests, but to make way for younger teachers and thereby to benefit his profession and the school where he had worked. But the Court of Appeal, summarising and interpreting a long tradition of decisions dating back to the Courts of Referees, held

> A person seeking to show that he voluntarily left his employment with just cause must show not only that on leaving he acted reasonably in his own interests, but in circumstances which made it just that he should be cast on the National Insurance Fund. 'Just cause' therefore means right and reasonable in the context of the risk of unemployment. It is not established by looking to the position as between employer and employee. Nor is just cause defined by reference to the rights of the rest of the community, except in its capacity as underwriter of the unemployment benefit scheme.
>
> (Crewe vs Social Security Commissioner [1982] 2AllER 745)

This discourse, which also makes its appeal to the insurance principle, is restating, in modified form, a demand for the 'survival of the fittest': regardless of their own or anyone else's interests, an insured person should work and compete for so long as they are able, or suffer some penalty if they should ever stand aside.

Perhaps the most contentious area in which the 1911 Act required the Courts of Referees to adjudicate, and in which social security tribunals have continued to be involved, relates to trade disputes and appeals against disqualification from benefit by those affected, whether as participants, or because they are 'laid off' or 'locked out'. The indiscriminate effect of this penalty was tempered in 1924 to exempt from disqualification any person who could prove that they were not participating or 'directly interested' in the trade dispute in question. But it was the words 'directly interested' which would thereafter inevitably exercise the minds of social security tribunals and bring them into intimate contact with the sphere of labour relations. This was because the nature and extent of a claimant's interest in a trade dispute and its eventual outcome must depend, in the absence of direct participation by the claimant, upon the existence of collective agreements and/or established industrial customs and practices which might tie the claimant in to a dispute (see Presho vs the Insurance Officer, House of Lords, *The Times* 16.12.83). The onus of proof is upon the claimant and the focus of the tribunal's attention is not the cause or the 'jus-tice' of the dispute, but the directness of the claimant's association with it.

The claim by legislators that this limitation of the tribunal's jurisdiction is commensurate with its 'neutrality' (Ogus and Barendt 1978: ch. 3) is as bogus as any of the justifications given with reference to the mythical insurance principle, since in cases regarding dismissal for alleged misconduct the tribunal plainly can and does 'take sides' with either the employee or (more usually) the employer. In any event, the power of the tribunal is such that it can only penalise employees and never employers in any trade dispute. Beneath the illogical discourses by which the role of the tribunal and of the unemployment insurance scheme are justified, lies a more coherent and repressive discourse.

Work-testing and social assistance

The 'tests' introduced under the original unemployment insurance scheme and 'policed' by the Courts of Referees (later the NILTs and now the SSAT), have not been confined to the sphere of social insurance. Ever since means-tested social assistance for the unemployed was first introduced, it too has been subject to penalties in respect of unemployment arising through 'misconduct', without 'just cause' or by reason of trade disputes, and it has been so in accordance with the same criteria as under the insurance schemes. In the case of social assistance schemes, however, justifications pertaining to the 'insurance principle' were inappropriate. The social assistance tribunals (i.e. the UAT, the Assistance Tribunal, the NAT and the SBAT) were actually prevented from examining the 'justice' of appellants' claims in cases involving dismissal for misconduct and unemployment without just cause. Under the Unemployment Assistance scheme, the Assistance scheme, the National Assistance scheme and both the 1966 and 1980 Supplementary Benefit schemes, claimants would be penalised (by a temporary reduction in benefit) if they had *either* already applied for and been suspended from insurance benefit, *or* if, had they so applied and otherwise been entitled to receive insurance benefit, they would have been so suspended. In this way, the determination of the basic issue was left with the National Insurance authorities – and, on appeal, the NILT – and was placed beyond the jurisdiction of social assistance tribunals. The same penalty has been incorporated within the Income Support scheme under Social Security Act 1986 and, now that the NILTs and SBATs have been merged, we have the spectacle of the SSAT being called upon to adjudicate certain social assistance questions in accordance with social insurance principles in order to preserve fictional justifications for punitive practices.

In the case of the disqualifications arising from involvement in trade disputes, the social assistance tribunals were obliged from the outset to adjudicate upon the same kinds of questions as had the social insurance tribunals. The Social Security (No. 2) Act 1980 imposed, in addition to strikers' disqualification from Supplementary Benefit, a reduction in the benefit payable for their dependants and this provision has also been carried forward into the Income Support scheme: in consequence, the adjudication of social assistance appeals in this area has in fact now assumed greater significance than the adjudication of social insurance appeals.

The argument now shifts to a slightly different issue upon which social security tribunals adjudicate. Unemployment insurance, ever since 1911, has imposed yet a further test upon claimants, since to receive benefit they have had to show that they are capable of and available for work (and, under Social Security Act 1989, they must additionally show that they are 'actively seeking work'). The Courts of Referees received numbers of appeals from claimants refused benefit on such grounds, but what is of particular interest is the situation which arose with the introduction of Unemployment Assistance in 1934. The Unemployment

Assistance scheme was intended only for those classes of workers who, had they an opportunity of employment, would have come within the terms of the insurance scheme: the 'residuum' – those who had no 'normal occupation', or who were 'incapable of work' through sickness, disability or old age, or who were 'not available' for work because of idleness, drunkenness or some other circumstance – remained the responsibility of the local authority Public Assistance Committees under the Poor Law. Where a claimant was ruled by the Unemployment Assistance Board to be outside the scope of the Unemployment Assistance scheme, it was open to the claimant or the local authority to appeal to the UAT, where the matter would be determined (by a chairperson sitting alone) (Lynes 1975; Gilbert 1970).

Although these 'scope appeals', as they were called, have no modern equivalent, they are significant because of the disciplinary and adjudicative techniques which they developed. The scope appeals were informed by a clearly anti-populationist discourse, in as much as their object was to ensure that those who were not able and willing to work should be cast back onto the Poor Law. Now, of course, SSATs are still called upon to make the same sort of distinctions – with regard to capacity/incapacity and availability/unavailability for work – but the project is no longer merely exclusionary in nature, but is part of what we have here defined as a 'partitioning' technique: it is far more a question of determining to which category a claimant properly belongs and which class of entitlements s/he may properly pursue. The origins of the technique, none the less, owe something to a repressive/anti-populationist discursive tradition.

The enforcement of family dependency

The types of appeal for which the UAT was perhaps most notable during its brief lifespan were the so-called 'leaving home' cases. The Unemployment Assistance scheme operated a 'household' means test. In calculating the amount of benefit payable, the UAB would take into account the resources of all members of a claimant's household, regardless of whether or not the household's members were, in practice, mutually inter-dependent. A young unemployed man living with his parents could therefore be refused benefit on the grounds that his father's wages were sufficient to maintain him; conversely, if the young man was working and his father was unemployed, the father might be refused benefit. In order to prevent families from circumventing this provision by collusively expelling their grown-up offspring to live in lodgings, the UAB invented the concept of the 'constructive household'. In this manner the Board contrived to treat many young people who had left home as if they were still members of their parents' households and, inevitably this gave rise to a number of appeals to the UAT. The 'constructive household' concept was a creation of policy not statute, but, as Lynes has shown, the UAB went to considerable lengths to advocate its acceptance by the UAT (Lynes 1975: 21).

In this way, the anti-populationist tendency towards the enforcement of family dependency and self-regulation (which had most clearly expressed itself in aspects of the workhouse test under the 1834 Poor Law) found new expression as the UAT was called upon to police family dependency amongst Unemployment Assistance claimants. Although the 'household' means test was replaced in 1941 by a 'personal' means test, all subsequent social assistance schemes (and the Housing Benefit scheme first introduced by the Social Security and Housing Benefits Act 1982) have, none the less, regarded non-dependent members of a claimant's household as notional contributors to the claimant's housing costs and have reduced the benefits payable accordingly. More recent developments, such as the 1985 Supplementary Benefit board and lodging regulations in respect of persons under 25 years of age (Cohen and Lakhani 1986) and several of the provisions with regard to young people, contained in the Social Security Acts of 1986 and 1988, would seem to indicate a resurgence of attempts to enforce family dependency (Alcock 1985). As in the field of labour discipline, the social security system, and with it the social security tribunals, have thus been insinuated into a wider project of repression.

One expressly penal sanction which, since 1948, has been entrusted to social assistance tribunals is that of confirming 'directions', requiring claimants, upon pain of losing their benefit, to attend state-run re-establishment centres (or their later variants – training centres or rehabilitation centres). This penalty was reserved for persons deemed guilty of refusing or neglecting to maintain themselves or their dependants. Under the National Assistance Act 1948, such directions could only be given when a report had been considered by the NAT, whilst under the Supplementary Benefit schemes, the direction could be given by the Supplementary Benefits Commission or (after 1980) the DHSS but was subject to a right of appeal to the SBAT (or subsequently, the SSAT). This provision has been substantially supplanted by the expansion of the Youth Training Scheme and the Employment Training Scheme (administered principally by private employers, rather than by the state). School leavers refusing YTS places are now excluded from Income Support (except in limited circumstances) and, although none of the present ET schemes have yet been 'approved' for the purposes of Social Security Act 1988, the government has taken powers to withhold Income Support from those who refuse places on schemes which are so 'approved': in the event, there would be a right of appeal to the SSAT.

The justification for sanctions of this nature may be found in the Beveridge Report, which said:

> At the basis of any scheme of social security ... there must be provision for a limited class of men and women who through weakness or badness of character fail to comply. In the last resort, the man who fails to comply with the conditions of obtaining benefit or assistance and leaves his family without resources must be subject to penal treatment.
>
> (Beveridge 1942: para. 373)

As an ultimate sanction, the National Assistance Act 1948 therefore created criminal offences relating to 'failure to maintain' and empowered the NAB to prosecute such offences in the ordinary courts (the provisions still exist under Section 26 Social Security Act 1986 and the prosecuting authority is now the DSS). However, in view of the non-judicial role envisaged for the NAT, it is highly significant that the 1948 Act also provided a form of penal treatment (the re-establishment centre) over which the NAT rather than the courts would have jurisdiction: even then, the tribunals had come to be seen as rather more than a mere 'safety valve'.

Deterrence: the dark side of the tribunal system

Beyond the roles assigned to social security tribunals in the fields of labour discipline, the policing of family dependency and enforcing the duty to maintain, the other penal sanction capable of becoming the subject of appeal has arisen in relation to the recovery of alleged overpayments of social security benefit. Under social insurance schemes, any benefits overpaid, for want of 'due care and diligence' on the claimant's part when claiming or receiving such benefits, have been recoverable from the claimant; and, under social assistance schemes, any benefits overpaid in consequence of a claimant's 'misrepresentation' or 'failure to disclose' material information have similarly been recoverable (even though any misrepresentation or failure may on the claimant's part have been entirely innocent). Since 1986, however, the stricter 'misrepresentation or failure to disclose' test has been applied to insurance and assistance benefits alike (Section 53 Social Security Act 1986).

In cases where sufficient evidence exists to satisfy the burden of proof required for a criminal prosecution, overpaid claimants deemed guilty of fraudulent intent have been brought before the ordinary courts; but, in other cases, the relevant state agencies have been empowered to recover sums overpaid to claimants without recourse to the courts and, if necessary, by making deductions from any benefit currently in payment to that claimant. The only safeguard for the claimant has been a right of appeal to the relevant social security tribunal. Where the overpayments in question may run into thousands of pounds, and the evidence as to whether or not the blame for this lies with the claimant may be tenuous, the power that is vested in social security tribunals is enormous.

There can be little doubt from the criticisms of social security tribunals, advanced during the last twenty years, that they have never been equipped to conduct far-reaching investigative reviews of the nature which might be required to reveal whether a government department itself might be administratively to blame for an overpayment of benefit. The tribunals are not bound by the rules of evidence which would normally apply in strictly adversarial proceedings (DHSS 1985a: para. 58). A party having the resources of a government department must therefore have an absurd advantage over any appellant in such proceedings. It is hardly surprising that the relevant state agencies have made comparatively little use of the ordinary courts to prosecute allegedly fraudulent claimants, but have preferred, in the vast majority of cases, to recover overpayments administratively (Squires 1985). The only forum before which the state agency's own actions can be reviewed is that of a social security tribunal. The tribunals have therefore been a convenient substitute to the courts and, by default, have enhanced the directly repressive power of state agencies.

Against this view it will be said that the repayment requirement imposed upon claimants who have been overpaid is no more than a matter of restitution and that it ought not to be regarded as a penalty. In reply, it must first be pointed out that anything which may reduce a claimant's level of income beneath the acknowledged subsistence level can only be experienced as a punishment. Where prolonged material deprivation may result from a requirement to make good an overpayment of social security benefit, even though this is capable of being objectively regarded as a matter of reparation, it will inevitably take on the subjective character of retribution simply because the consequences for individual and state are entirely disproportionate. Second, the issue of claimants' liability to repay has been very much at the centre of a certain preoccupation with 'non-disclosure', 'abuse' and 'fraud': a preoccupation that is, it will be argued, within the repressive/ anti-populationist tradition which we have sought to describe.

Peter Squires (1985) has argued that these preoccupations and the emphasis since the 1970s on 'claims control' procedures within the social security system have together laid the basis for a new 'strategy of disentitlement' and a new deterrent organisation in social security. While this book does not fully adopt Squire's argument, elements of it are undoubtedly important. His basic premise is 'that the foundation of any social security system in a capitalist society must be an essentially coercive form of discipline' (ibid.: 465).

Squires has traced certain shifts within official discourse since the Second World War and he has identified a trend by which the problems of 'voluntary unemployment', 'failure to maintain', etc. have become subtly redefined as problems of 'abuse' and 'fraud'. The key to the process behind this trend is the notion of the 'false statement': the long-term unemployed remained a focus of attention, no longer because they might require retraining or work experience, but because they might have undisclosed earnings; and single parents remained a focus of attention, no longer because of their vulnerability or special needs, but because they might be failing to disclose cohabitation. In this way the administration of benefits shifted its axis and, where it had once investigated in order to assess claimants' circumstances, it now did so in order to corroborate claimants' statements.

As the 1960s and 1970s saw the introduction of specialist Liable Relative Officers, Unemployment Review Officers and Special Investigators, there also occurred a transition from behavioural controls to entitlement controls and a manipulation of the imagery of abuse and fraud. By 1980, when the government launched a Campaign Against Fraud and Abuse, of the extra 1,050 staff assigned to the DHSS, a substantial majority were deployed, not to investigate 'fraud' within the legal definition of the word, but in established areas of work – such as Liable Relative and Unemployment Review work – which had by then assumed a special significance. The direction in which the social security system as a whole would appear to be have been moving in the late 1980s will be considered later, but here Squires' account of the post-Second World War social security system has been presented to illustrate the impact of a repressive/anti-populationist discourse: a discourse which, particularly through appeals in 'overpayments cases', undoubtedly invaded social security tribunal hearing rooms.

The extent to which, by the early 1970s, even Supplementary Benefit appeals were being regarded by participants as adversarial proceedings and not as 'case assessments' is reflected in the words of a lawyer at that time, who said 'As a matter of observable fact, many claimants and their advisers now see the system as one of contending parties.... It is notable that employees of the [Supplementary Benefits] Commission see it as a hostile act to appeal against a determination' (White 1973: 27).

Several researchers and welfare rights activists in this period complained about the conduct at tribunal hearings of SBC Presenting Officers. In style, the Presenting Officers' conduct would resemble that of prosecutors, but their lack of training in advocacy and their evident preoccupation with winning was such that principles of fairness and objectivity were frequently neglected. So, for example, irrelevant and prejudicial remarks about the appellant would sometimes be systematically interjected during the proceedings, or else appellants would be taken by surprise with allegations or arguments for which they had been given no chance to prepare (Herman 1972; Fulbrook 1975). The flagrant hostility once exhibited by some Presenting Officers has now been largely eradicated, but, for example, a survey on Supplementary Benefit Appeal presentation undertaken by the DHSS in 1984/85 would seem to suggest there is a continuing sense of suspicion or resentment harboured by at least some Presenting Officers, if not towards appellants themselves, then towards the welfare rights workers who may appear as representatives upon their behalf (CAO 1985: Appendix A).

Hostility, however, is not only manifest between state agencies and the claimant, but also in the punitive attitudes known to be held by some tribunal members. Ruth Lister, in her survey of SBAT tribunal members (1974), found that more than half those questioned regarded social security abuse as a significant problem and one tribunal member is quoted as praising the SBC for the 'excellent job it does sorting out the wheat from the chaff' (i.e. the 'genuine' from the 'fraudulent' claimant). There was a tendency amongst all tribunal members to regard some appellants as being 'too well informed', which was synonymous with 'trying to pull a fast one'. These findings by Lister square with Squires' thesis about the preoccupation with fraud and abuse which began to assert itself during the 1960s and 1970s. Lister herself went so far as to observe 'where the appellant was thought undeserving, the comments of some members suggest they [i.e. the tribunal members] regarded themselves as being in an adversary situation with the appellant' (Lister 1974: 27).

Social security tribunals, therefore, are not merely a sop which the system has offered to disgruntled claimants. The tribunals also have a capacity for social control through certain quite specific powers to punish claimants and through the facility they afford to the social security system as a whole for the promulgation and legitimation of a discourse of deterrence.

THE ADJUDICATION PROCESS: LOOKING THROUGH THE WINDOW

Any study of the role which tribunals play within the social security system, requires an analysis of the numbers of appeals which such tribunals hear and of the types of social security claims and claimants to which such appeals relate.

Appeals activity rates

Measures of the frequency with which claimants appeal may be based either on the numbers of cases heard by tribunals in any one year as a percentage of the number of benefit claims made in that year ('Index I'), or on the number of cases heard as a percentage of the number of claimants in receipt of benefit as at a particular date or week in that year ('Index II'). These indices will produce different results when comparing short-term with long-term benefits. With short-term benefits (e.g. National Insurance Unemployment Benefit) the number of claims lodged in a year might be large, whereas the numbers of claimants in receipt of benefit at any one time will be relatively small; conversely with long-term benefits (e.g. Retirement Pensions) the number of claims in a year might be relatively small, while the numbers of claimants in continuous receipt of benefit will be large. The task of constructing a reliable index of appeals activity is further complicated by inadequacies and inconsistencies in the available data, by the expansion of the jurisdiction of the tribunals over time and, for example, by the fact that a certain number of the cases recorded as having been heard by tribunals have not been appeals instigated by claimants, but references to the tribunal instigated by the relevant state departmental officials. Outline conclusions may none the less be drawn (Dean 1988: Appendix A and ch. 5).

Social insurance tribunals effectively began in 1913 (being the first full year of operation of the Court of Referees) and social assistance tribunals began in 1935 (with the Unemployment Assistance Tribunal). It was not until the 1940s, however, that either kind of tribunal became concerned with claimants other than the unemployed and it is notable that, however measured, the rate of appeals activity prior to the Beveridge era was significantly higher than it has been since. This is illustrated by Figure 1. This feature must be explained with reference to underlying changes in the appeals activity of unemployed claimants (which we shall consider shortly) rather than to the general pattern of appeals activity which developed in the wake of the full introduction of the Beveridge scheme.

One feature of social security appeals activity since the 1950s is striking: while the rates of appeal activity, so far as social

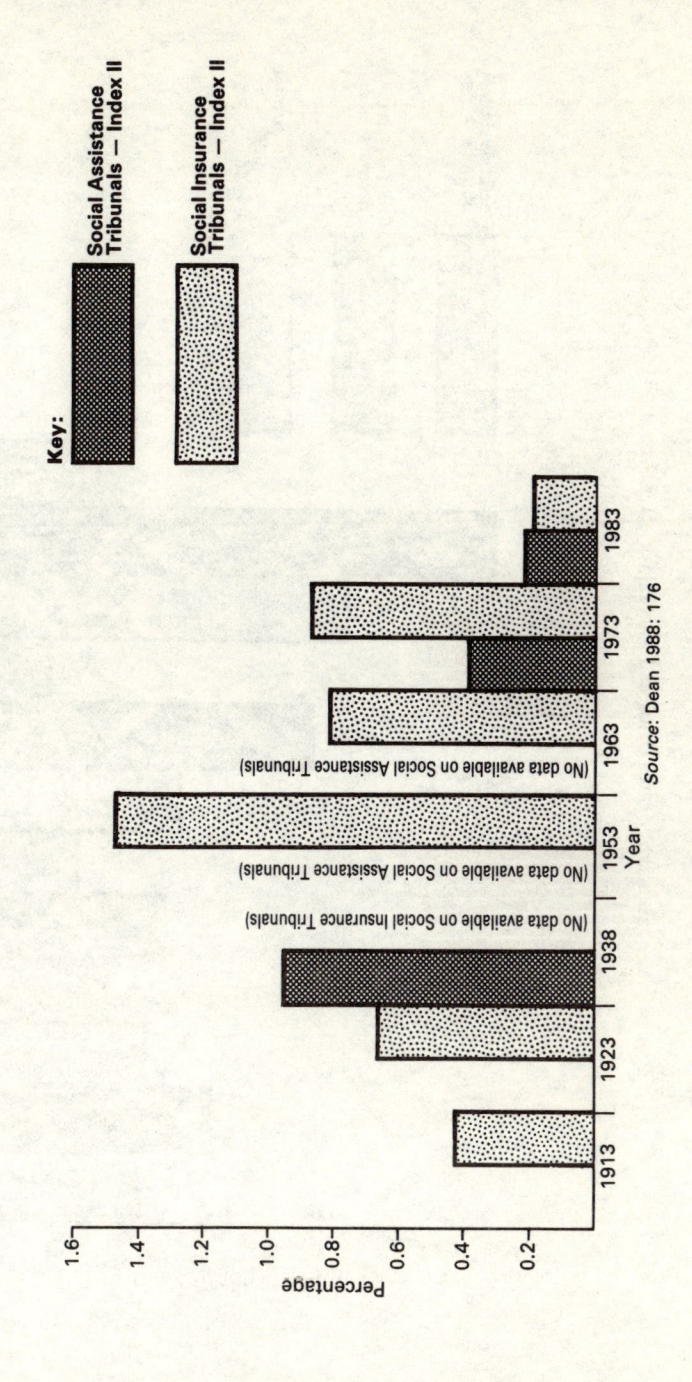

Figure 1 Appeals activity rates (Index II only) for unemployed claimants, 1913–1983

Source: Dean 1988: 176

Figure 2 Appeals activity rates (Indices I and II) for all claimants, 1953–1983

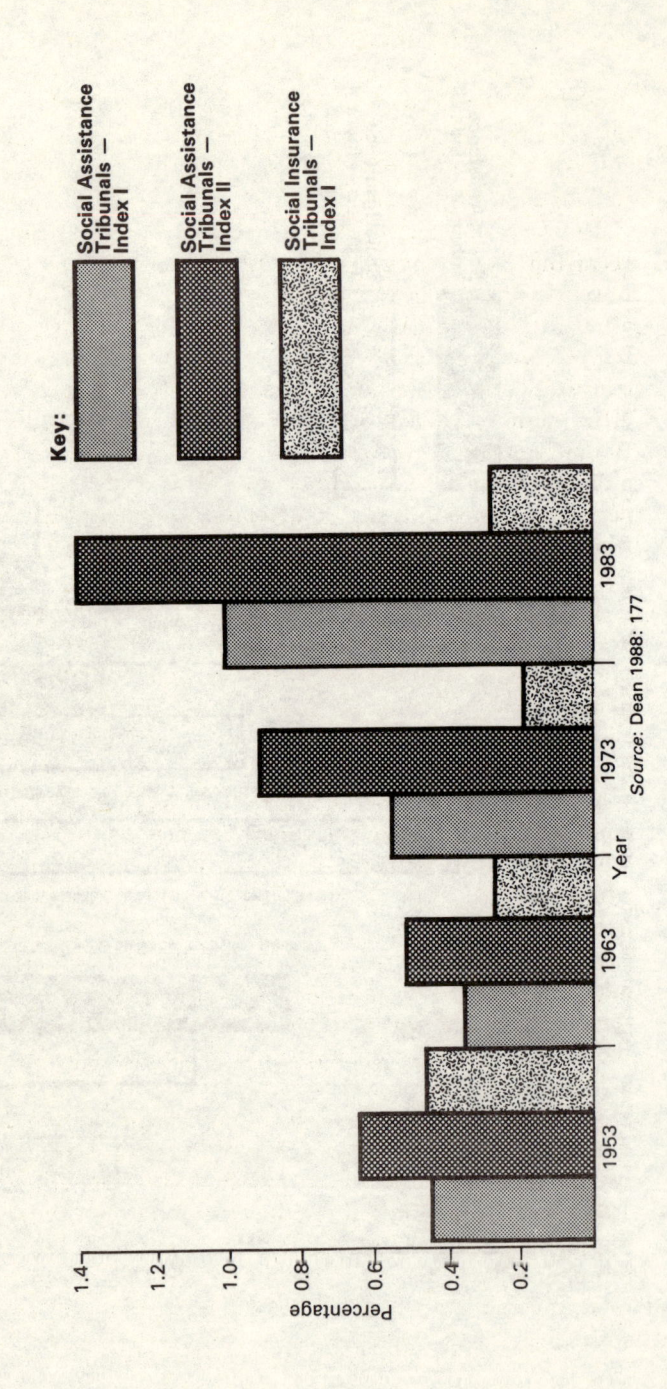

Source: Dean 1988: 177

assistance tribunals are concerned, have increased, the corresponding rates of appeals activity for social insurance tribunals have (in spite of a more recent upswing) in relative terms declined. This may be seen from Figure 2.

Between 1953 and 1983 the numbers of people claiming/receiving Supplementary Benefit more than doubled, but the numbers of appeals heard each year by the NAT/SBAT increased almost sixfold. In the same period, the numbers of people claiming/receiving National Insurance benefits remained relatively consistent, while the number of appeals heard each year by the NILT almost halved. In 1983, twice as many Supplementary Benefit appeals were heard as were National Insurance Appeals, although twice as many claims were made for National Insurance benefits as for Supplementary Benefit, and there were nearly five times as many National Insurance benefit recipients as there were Supplementary Benefit recipients.

Clearly, therefore, social assistance appeals have become invested with some particular significance. To keep the matter in perspective, it must still be remembered that in 1983 the number of appeals heard by the SBAT amounted to only 1 per cent of the claims for Supplementary Benefit processed in that year.

The relative intensity of appeals activity in the social assistance sphere, compared with that of social insurance, might itself have come as little surprise at a time when the main social assistance scheme was supposed to have a substantial discretionary element, whilst social insurance schemes were supposed to be strictly rule-bound. What is striking, however, is that during the 1950s and early 1960s the rates of appeals activity, in respect of social assistance and social insurance appeals, were broadly comparable and the divergence in appeals activity rates appears to date only from the late 1960s onwards. During the 1970s, indeed, there occurred a very marked increase in the appeals activity rates of the SBAT.

This increase, having reached its peak in 1978, was reversed during 1979/80 but then continued, in spite of the introduction of the strictly rule-bound Supplementary Benefit Scheme of 1980 (see Figure 3). It is important to note that the decrease in Supplementary Benefit appeals activity in 1978/79 (for which the Supplementary Benefit Commission was, at the time, unable to offer any explanation (SBC 1979)) preceded rather than coincided with the introduction of the 1980 Supplementary Benefit

Figure 3 Appeals activity rates (Index I only) for all claimants, 1976–1985

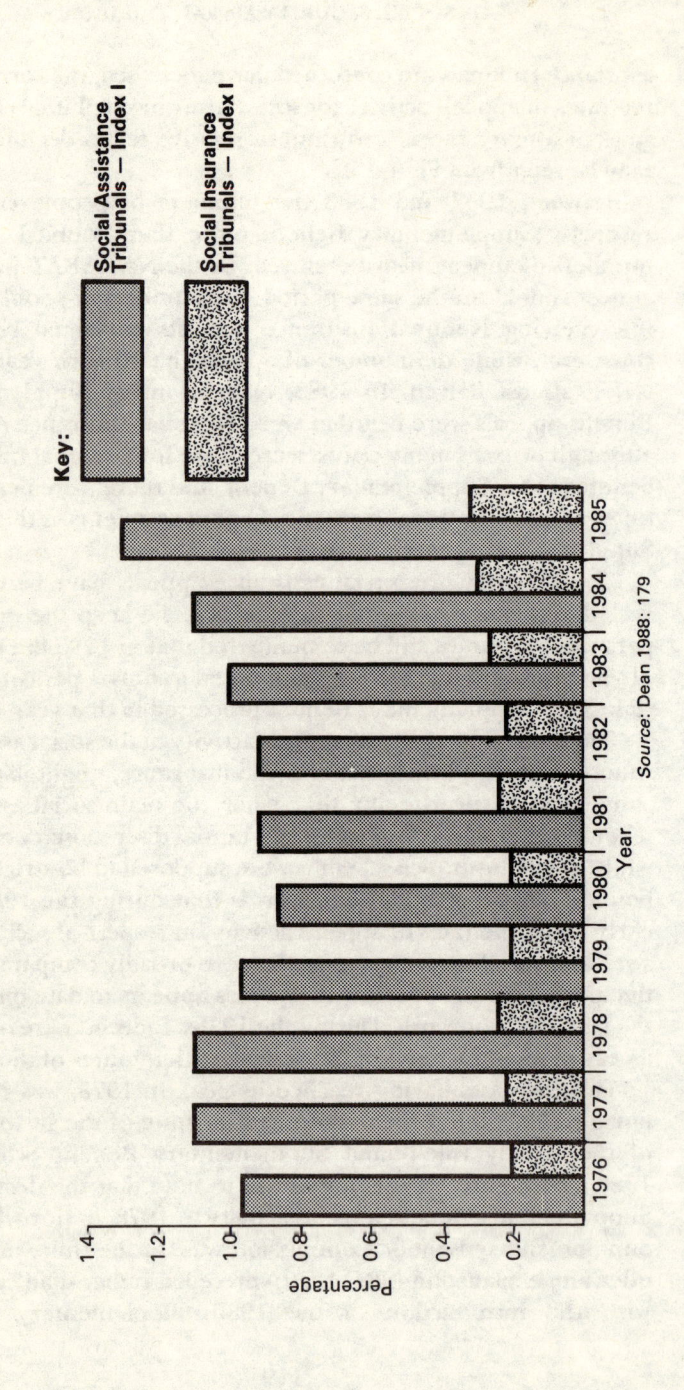

Key:
- Social Assistance Tribunals — Index I
- Social Insurance Tribunals — Index I

Source: Dean 1988: 179

'reforms' and that, indeed, a quite different level of explanation is required. It was as if, having found its trajectory, the tribunal system and its appellants held their breath in anticipation; as if their momentum was checked pending an inevitable but uncertain change of gear. Certainly, 1979 happened to be the year of Margaret Thatcher's first General Election victory, founded as it was on a manifesto which promised a change of gear. It might be argued that the maturity of the disciplinary techniques which now underpinned the social security system (and of which the growing incidence of social security appeals might be taken as a barometer) already posed an incipient demand for reforms in the structure of the system – and reforms there have been!

What is also clear is that, following the introduction of the 'unified' SSAT in 1984, the overall level of appeals activity continued significantly to rise. By 1985, the number of Supplementary Benefit appeals heard by the SSAT, in place of the SBAT, had risen to 1.3 per cent of the number of claims for Supplementary Benefit processed in that year (an increase of almost one third since 1983) and a smaller, but still significant, increase in appeals activity rate may be noted in respect of National Insurance appeals. Figures 3 and 4 cover the whole of the ten-year period from 1976 to 1985.

Different types of claimant

The general trends in the overall rates of appeals activity conceal important differences between the rates applicable to different types of claimant. The claimants of National Insurance Unemployment Benefit and unemployed persons claiming social assistance are (more or less!) 'short-term' or temporary claimants, whereas Retirement Pensioners and retired persons claiming social assistance are of course 'long-term' or permanent claimants. Also, the numbers of unemployed claimants at any one time will be determined by economic factors, whereas the numbers of retired claimants will be determined by demographic factors. Predictably, therefore, the numbers of unemployed claimants have fluctuated over time (but with a continuous upward trend between the 1960s and the late 1980s), whilst the numbers of retired claimants have been gradually but steadily increasing. These important factors, however, do not in themselves account for the substantially different appeal rate patterns of unemployed and retired claimants.

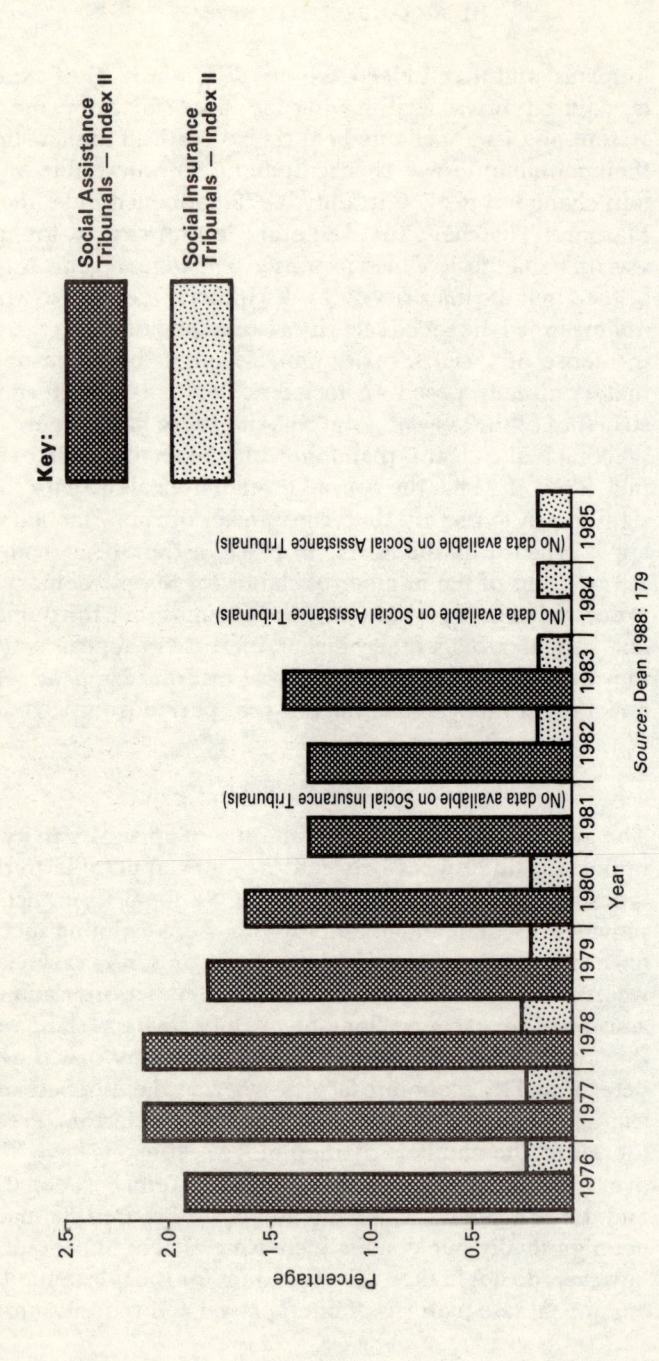

Figure 4 Appeals activity rates (Index II only) for all claimants, 1976–1985

Source: Dean 1988: 179

Figure 5 Appeals activity rates (Index II only) for retired claimants, 1953–1983

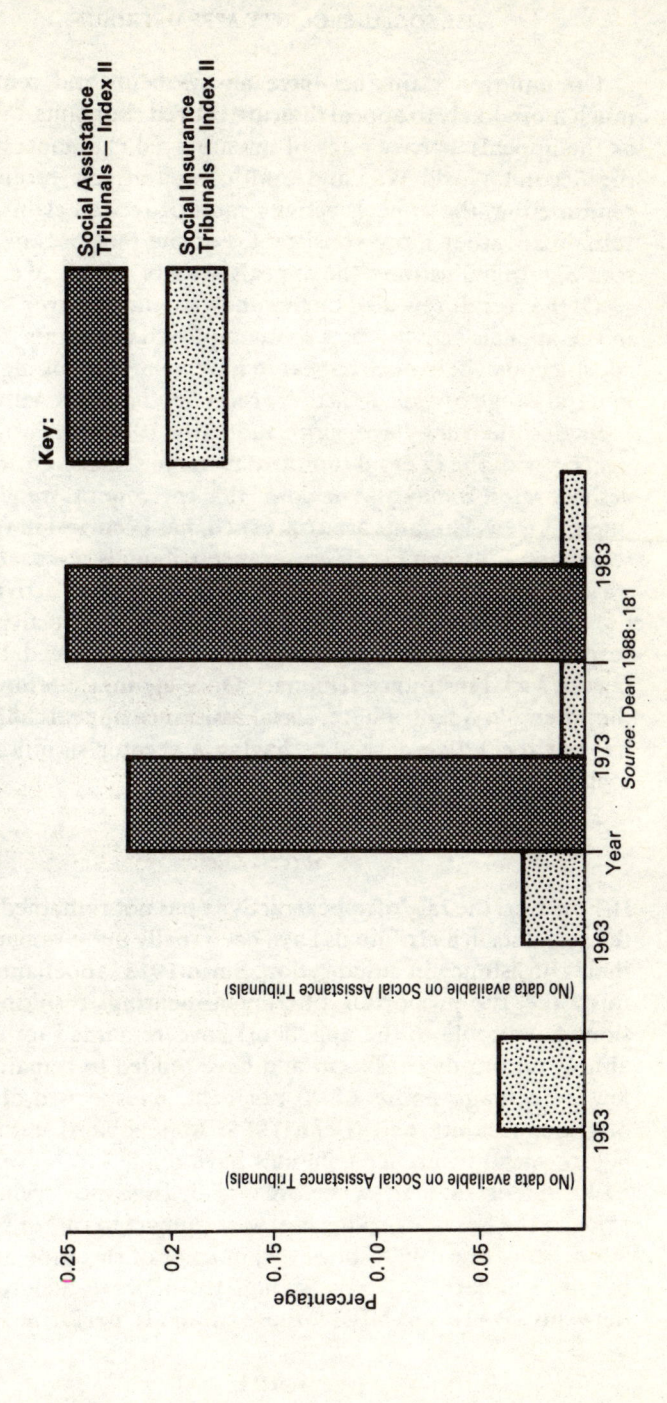

Source: Dean 1988: 181

Key:
- Social Assistance Tribunals — Index II
- Social Insurance Tribunals — Index II

Unemployed claimants have always been and remain very much more likely to appeal than are retired claimants, but, whereas the appeals activity rates of unemployed claimants had, since the Second World War and until comparatively recently, been plummeting, the appeals activity rates of retired claimants have remained rather more consistent. For the purposes of comparison, Figure 5 illustrates the appeals activity of retired claimants.

Of the trends revealed by this analysis, the fall over forty years in the appeals activity rates of unemployed claimants is the most conspicuous: these rates appear to have been converging upon the general range of appeals activity rates but, having finally arrested their decline, they have, since the early 1980s, been moving in concert with the general (upward) trend in social security appeals activity rates. It may also be noted that the general trend, so far as unemployed claimants are concerned, has occurred in relation to social assistance and social insurance tribunals alike, although it was only after the surge in social assistance appeals activity during the 1970s that the unemployed claimants' appeals activity rate, in respect of social assistance tribunals, began to exceed that in respect of social insurance tribunals. Once again, therefore, even in the unemployment sphere, social assistance appeals adjudication has but recently emerged as having a greater significance than social insurance appeals adjudication.

Success rates

If, however, the rate of appeals activity has not remained constant, the social security tribunals have been really quite remarkable for their consistency in adjudication. Since 1913, appellants' 'success rates' (i.e. the proportion of tribunal hearings resulting in decisions favourable to the appellant) have remained on the whole almost uncannily consistent and have tended to remain within a few percentage points of 20 per cent, irrespective of the type of tribunal concerned (Dean 1988: Appendix A). Success rates before social insurance tribunals have tended to be very marginally higher than those before social assistance tribunals and, prior to the post-Beveridge era, were subject to rather more variation. Since the 1960s, however, in spite of the wide differences in the 'standards' of adjudication which were alleged to exist between SBATs and NILTs, these tribunals 'performed' virtually identically so far as the proportion of cases decided for and against appellants was concerned.

This tends to confirm Bell's finding that, in spite of the differences in the essential criteria on which social assistance and social insurance schemes are predicated, both types of tribunal were involved in 'an exercise which is not confined to the application of objective rules and standards' (see p. 98). As a corollary to Bell's conclusion, it must be presumed that there is a mechanism at work in the process of social security appeals adjudication that is not immediately reflected in the rules and standards laid down by the benefits schemes which the tribunals purport to administer. There is, in other words, something going on within the appeals process: an unseen process which consistently rations success; an unspoken rule which consistently sustains the level at which the disciplinary authority of the social security system operates.

What is more, the consistent and relatively low success rate for social security appellants can provide no explanation of variations in the frequency with which social security claimants resort to appeal, in so far that it cannot be said that one type of tribunal has offered any more or less incentive than the other with regard to the likelihood of success.

Whilst social security appeal success rates are highly consistent overall, it should be noted that there are significant variations between the success rates experienced by different kinds of claimant. For example, retired claimants have had greater prospects of success before social security tribunals than do unemployed claimants (Dean 1988: Appendix A).

Previous research had of course detected prejudices amongst tribunal members which would tend to favour the 'deserving' elderly whilst penalising the 'undeserving' unemployed (see Lister 1974), but the variations in success rates may in fact require a more complex explanation than mere prejudice on the part of adjudicators. The point has already been made that the social security system treats different groups of recipients in different ways and one of the central tenets of this book is that the disciplinary effect of such differences lies as much in the process of distinguishing such groups (i.e. 'partitioning') as it does in the privileges or disadvantages which are accorded to the different groups thereby constituted. The different rules and criteria which are applied to different groups of claimants may, almost incidentally, provide differing opportunities for the exercise of judicial discretion. It is difficult, therefore, to draw any firm conclusions as to the relative effects of prejudice in adjudication on the one hand and the severity of the rules which adjudicators must apply upon the other. This difficulty is most clearly seen when one compares the appeals success rate of, for example, Invalid Care Allowance claimants (just 6 per cent in 1987) with the success rate of, for example, Invalidity Benefit claimants (44 per cent in 1987) (DSS 1989: Table 49.01).

The difference between success rates in these instances is likely to have much more to do with the characteristics of the particular benefits schemes in question than it does with prejudices on the part of tribunal members. Having argued therefore, as Bell does, that social security appeals adjudication is not confined to the application of objective rules and standards, it must still be recognised that the rules and standards imposed by the various distinct schemes of benefit will inevitably set certain parameters within which the tribunals operate.

Studying the success or failure rates of social security appellants does tell us something about the appeals adjudication process, but in view of the relatively small proportion of social security recipients who become appellants in the first place and the even smaller proportion who go on to 'win' their appeals, it is evident that the significance of the adjudication process is not to be understood simply in terms of the power which tribunals have to uphold or reject the appeals which come before them.

Different types of appeal

The social security claimant who appeals to a tribunal does so because s/he is in dispute with the state agency responsible for the administration of benefit. The terrain for such a dispute may be fashioned by the general nature of the benefit scheme in question and by the particular rules of that scheme, but in so far that there is an issue of contention between the parties, the grounds or the subject of the appeal provides evidence concerning some real effect of such a scheme.

Unfortunately, the limited nature of the evidence which is available, concerning the grounds of appeals to the various social security tribunals at the various stages of their history, provides a view of the social security system that is far from complete. To the extent, however, that official records have been kept, these are interesting as much for what has been regarded as worthy of compilation as for any statistical trends revealed by such records. Although no rigorous account is possible, sufficient data exists to enable shifts to be detected and, in particular, a diversification in the preoccupations of appellants, tribunals and the state benefit administering agencies.

In 1913, during the first year of operation of the Courts of Referees, 92 per cent of the cases heard revolved around issues associated with *labour discipline* (56 per cent concerned claimants alleged to have left employment without just cause, 29 per cent concerned claimants alleged to have been dismissed for misconduct, 4 per cent concerned claimants who had allegedly failed to prove their inability to obtain suitable employment and 3 per cent concerned claimants alleged to be involved in a trade dispute) (Board of Trade 1913). By 1923, this picture had not changed and some 94 per cent of the cases heard by Courts of Referees were concerned with issues of labour discipline (Ministry of Labour 1923).

In 1935 the UAT entered the field and, during its first year of operation, 99 per cent of the cases heard were expressed in the Unemployment Assistance Board's first Annual Report to be 'appeals against determinations' (UAB 1935): the remaining 1 per cent were 'Scope Appeals'. Three years later, in 1938 (when three times as many appeals were heard by the UAT), the percentage of appeals expressed to be 'against determinations' had settled down to 79 per cent, whereas 20 per cent were 'Scope Appeals' (UAB 1938). In the same year, of the cases heard and disallowed by the Unemployment Insurance Tribunal (which had succeeded the Court of Referees), the percentage of labour discipline cases had declined to 64 per cent (Ministry of Labour 1938). Clearly then, in the fifteen years since 1923 important qualitative changes had begun to overtake the expanding sphere of social security appeals adjudication, in so far that the issues at stake became and were seen to have become more diverse.

Of the Scope Appeals heard by the UAT (or rather by UAT chairpersons sitting alone) a small number (less than 1 per cent in 1938) concerned claimants alleged to be disentitled by reason of their involvement in a trade dispute, but the remainder concerned the status of claimants: did they have a 'normal occupation'? (80 per cent of Scope Appeals in 1938); were they capable of and/or available for work and were they of employable age? (19 per cent of Scope Appeals in 1938). Similarly some 10 per cent of the cases disallowed by the UIT concerned claimants who were deemed either not to be unemployed or to be incapable of or unavailable for employment. In addition therefore to the question of penalties for alleged misdemeanours in the employment sphere, the social security adjudication process now began to encompass the determination of *productive status*.

Within the all embracing category, 'appeals against determinations', which the UAT adopted, several different types of appeal are submerged. None the less, the choice of terminology is significant since at the root of social assistance benefit administration lies the business of assessing the 'needs' or the 'requirements' of claimants. Thus an appeal is essentially a challenge to a state agency's determination of the claimant's need. That challenge, however, and therefore the focus of the adjudication process, can be directed at different aspects of the state agency's determination: it can be directed to the *particularity or exceptionality* of the claimant's needs; it can be directed to *technical or legal* aspects of the determination of the claimant's need or entitlement; it can be directed to the claimant's *dependency status* and the extent to which her/his needs are met by or must include the needs of other family or household members.

Issues of particularity/exceptionality both mediate and are invested by the disciplinary technique of the 'case approach'. Technical/legal issues mediate and are invested by the disciplinary technique of 'legalisation'. The issue of dependency status, with the issue of productive status, together constitute a complex which mediates and is invested by the disciplinary technique of 'partitioning'. These issues, as well as issues of a penal nature – such as labour discipline (see p. 127) and administrative discipline (see p. 129) – all come to be encompassed within the adjudicative process.

Unfortunately it is not possible to chart the development of the adjudication process in any detail between the Second World War and the 1970s. So far as social insurance tribunals are concerned, no records appear to exist from which to determine the grounds of appeals heard. So far as social assistance tribunals are concerned, little detail had ever been recorded until the upsurge of interest in the SBAT which occurred in the 1970s and which appears to have spurred the DHSS into compiling statistics. The National Assistance Board, until its demise in 1966, did publish a few figures, which classified the vast majority of tribunal cases as 'appeals against rates' (94 per cent in 1953 and 97 per cent in 1963, NAB 1953 and 1963), but the remainder of cases were shown to relate either to labour discipline (e.g. claimants directed to attend re-establishment centres) or else to issues concerning either, the recovery of benefit allegedly overpaid, or the payment of benefit in kind or to third parties.

The latter issues are examples of what might be called *administrative discipline*; they involve elements of compulsion of the individual by the state and they are aimed either at enforcing claimants' compliance with rules and procedures, or at the direct management of claimants' personal expenditure. Administrative discipline, however, is often inescapably bound up with issues which are in themselves of an inherently technical or legal nature: many of the rules concerning the time and manner in which claims for benefit must be lodged and all means test rules regarding the treatment of requirements and resources are legal in form, but administrative in their disciplinary effect.

From 1973 until 1983 certain data is available with regard to the subject or grounds of appeals heard by the SBAT and, to the extent that this exists in a form which makes year by year comparison possible, a selective presentation of these figures is made in Table 1. It is to be regretted that the Supplementary Benefits Commission and the DHSS, who compiled the original data, were not consistent in their categorisation of subjects of appeal and this limits our ability to conduct a thoroughgoing analysis. The figures do seem to show that a substantial and increasing proportion of Supplementary Benefit appeals were ostensibly related to issues of 'particularity/ exceptionality'; that is to say to questions concerning Exceptional Needs Payments and Exceptional Circumstances Additions under the 1966 Supplementary Benefits Scheme, or Single Payments and Additional Requirements under the more rule-bound 1980 Scheme. It is not surprising that such appeals enjoyed a relatively high success rate prior to the introduction of the 1980 scheme, but that that success rate thereafter declined.

Table 1 Supplementary Benefit appeals – subjects of appeal

Appeals heard	1973		1978		1983	
	as %age of all appeals	success rate (%)	as %age of all appeals	success rate (%)	as %age of all appeals	success rate (%)
SUBJECT OF APPEAL						
Exceptional Needs Payments and Exceptional Circumstances Additions/Single Payments and Additional Requirements	32	32	46	30	52	24
Recovery of Overpayments (inc. National Insurance and Emergency Payments)	4	6	4	6	9	21
Payments to third parties and benefits in kind	0.2	17	0.8	14	0.5	11
Cohabitation / 'Living together as husband and wife'	1.3	19	1.2	22	1.8	31
Allowance for rent/housing requirements	0.8	38	0.3	32	1.7	22
Condition of registration	1.2	14	0.3	14	0.6	11
Trade dispute	1.5	4	5	7	0.1	7
Other appeals	59		44		35	
	(100%) n=24,486		(100%) n=62,308		(100%) n=60,567	

Source: Dean 1980, 191)

The recovery of overpayments would seem to have become an increasingly important issue for SBATs, as is no doubt consistent with the particular preoccupation with 'fraud and abuse' which followed in the wake of the Conservatives' General Election victory of 1979 (Squires 1985; Smith 1985). The incidence of appeals relating to trade dispute disqualifications (in spite of the contentiousness of the issue) does not appear to feature particularly prominently and is almost certainly more related to the fluctuating incidence of strikes themselves than to any other factor; although it should be noted that appellants' success rates are consistently below average in such appeals. The incidence of appeals in cohabitation or 'living together as husband and wife' cases appears to have remained consistent, if relatively low, although it may be noted that appellants' success rates in such cases seemed to improve significantly following the introduction of the 1980 Supplementary Benefit scheme (indicating perhaps a rather more rigorously judicial approach to dependency status issues, turning, as they often do, on evidence of a tenuous nature).

Since the creation of the SSAT in 1984, data of this nature, in relation to Supplementary Benefit appeals, was no longer compiled and the only distinction made in DHSS statistics was between Single Payments appeals and 'other' appeals. Such statistics show, however, that prior to 1988 a substantial majority of Supplementary Benefit appeals related to Single Payments and, therefore, ostensibly to issues of particularity/exceptionality.

Comparative data for the NILT, with which a picture of social security appeals adjudication prior to the creation of the SSAT might otherwise have been completed, is not available. It is clear that, while Unemployment Benefit appeals in 1983 still accounted (narrowly) for a majority of the appeals heard by the NILT (see Dean 1988: 185), only a minority of NILT appeals could have related to labour discipline and that the remainder would have been concerned largely with productive status issues, with administrative discipline and with technical/legal issues.

The adjudication process inherited by the SSAT was therefore considerably more complex and diverse than that which was instigated by the first tribunals. Through the expansion of the social security system a vast new range of claimants had come within the tribunal's potential jurisdiction. The reach and pertinency of the disciplinary techniques inherent in the adjudication process had thus become not only more widely applicable, but also more specific to the circumstances of many different kinds of claimant. Through the window which the tribunals provide we can thus observe the development of social policy/social control as it relates to the social security system itself.

CONCLUSIONS

This chapter considers three levels of social control in relation to the development of the social security system. The controls which are generated at the level of political settlement and those generated at the level of penality are consolidated at a third level: the level of individualised discipline. Implicit perhaps in such an analysis is a suggestion of a shift over time; a sense in which, as social policy/social control has developed, the first two levels of control, without becoming submerged, have none the less gravitated towards the third level; a sense in which, without eclipsing the first two levels of control, it is the third which has attained ascendancy.

The original Courts of Referees and the UATs were concerned exclusively with the unemployed: a group of claimants who were distanced from the proletariat only by the (temporary) incapacity of the labour market to accommodate them. In constituting these tribunals the state quite explicitly mediated a political settlement between the interests of capital and labour by providing a 'safety valve' for the unemployed and by the limited co-option of workers' representatives. Once created, the adjudication process focused its attention principally upon issues of labour discipline; upon the administration of penalties and sanctions so as to protect the integrity of the unemployed proletarian against the mere idler, against the negligent or incompetent worker and even against the striker.

Gradually, however, the adjudication process became enlarged so as to encompass issues other than labour discipline and mechanisms other than penalties and sanctions. The UAT, in particular, concerned itself with the minute assessment of the particular or exceptional needs of individual appellants. Both the UAT and the UIT became concerned with technical and legal aspects of the claims pursued by appellants as juridical subjects. The tribunal began to engage in a process of distinguishing appellants according to their productive and/or their dependency status.

In the post-Beveridge era tribunals were no longer concerned solely with the unemployed. The unemployed became merely one group of appellants amongst several; although perhaps a particularly 'dangerous' group and one which the social security system treats less favourably than any other. Chapter 4 argued that 'modern' poverty and the 'modern' poor are specific creations of the social security system since it is through the distributive mechanism of modern social security that the unproductive section of the population is marked off from the productive working-class. In the thirty years which followed the Second World War, the sustained decline in the appeals activity rates of unemployed claimants can thus be seen as an indicator of the extent to which the unemployed became 'deproletarianised' in that period; of the extent to which they came to conform to the characteristics of other disciplinary groups amongst what Jordan (1973) would call a wider 'claiming class', but which I have chosen to call the 'modern' poor. In the sphere of social policy/social control both the bargaining power of labour and the cutting edge of penal sanctions had been blunted and the technique of disciplinary partitioning now established itself as a means of isolating, ordering and examining all those who (whether temporarily or permanently) were excluded from the labour market and from productive relations.

The post-Beveridge era was also characterised by a relentless increase in social assistance appeals activity rates, compared with a decline in social insurance activity rates. Not only had social assistance come to play a more massive role than was ever envisaged for it by Beveridge, but the underlying effectiveness of social assistance benefit administration, as a component in a wider disciplinary strategy, is surely reflected in the growth in social assistance appeals activity. It is social assistance rather than social insurance which can be invested, at an administrative level, by the disciplinary technique of the 'case approach' and it is the case approach which is mediated by the adjudicative issues which pertain to the particularity/exceptionality of individual need. The growing preponderance of appeals relating to particularity/exceptionality issues would seem to account, in part, for the shift in appeals activity into the social assistance sphere. What is more, if the incidence of particularity/exceptionality issues as subjects of appeal provides a barometer of the extent to which the case approach technique bears upon social security claimants, then it is clear that this was enhanced rather than diminished by the legalisation of the Supplementary Benefit scheme.

This illustrates therefore that the categories evinced in the analysis so far are not simple, mutually exclusive categories. It also illustrates that these categories relate not to overlapping analytical constructs (as would Weberian 'ideal types') but to palpable techniques which, when they intersect, produce strategic effects.

Appeals under the early social insurance schemes had turned upon questions of labour discipline, but the strategic objective of the modern social security system is much wider. Thus, within the adjudication process, issues relating to productive status are now more evident than are issues relating to labour discipline. The social security system, whilst still concerned about 'offences' committed within the employment sphere, is just as much or rather more concerned with each claimant's specific relationship to the material productive process: the system distinguishes between claimants according to the circumstances and the degree of permanence of their exclusion from the employment market. Chapter 4 argued that, by the technique of disciplinary partitioning, the modern poor are systematically dispossessed from the 'productive' working-class. One of the keys to the effectiveness of partitioning is (once again) legalisation, since it is the construction of the claimant as a subject with a legal relationship to the state which distinguishes and distances her/him from the employee with her/his legal relationship to an employer. The legalisation of social assistance in 1980 therefore meant that both types of social security tribunal then in operation had thereafter to address every appellant as an individual whose productive status was not an incidental circumstance, but a formal and an integral part of the appellant's legal identity for the purposes of adjudication.

Disciplinary partitioning, however, by distinguishing claimants in accordance with productive status is concerned as much with relations of reproduction as with relations of production. It is concerned to distinguish, not only the able-bodied unemployed, but all claimants with a specific productive potential – such as students or the temporarily sick; it is concerned to distinguish those whose productive potential is impaired or spent, such as the disabled or the elderly; and it is also concerned to distinguish those who are engaged in caring both for children (as a future productive generation) and for the infirm (as an impediment upon productive capacity).

Disciplinary partitioning and the social security system invade the sphere of reproductive social relations even further when it comes to questions of dependency status. Dependency status-related social security appeals represented a relatively small proportion of the appeals heard by the SBAT. However, their appearance upon the social security tribunal scene and the evident controversy which has surrounded, for example, 'leaving home' cases in the 1930s and 'cohabitation' (or 'living together as husband and wife') cases in the 1970s (see Fairbairns 1985) demonstrates that dependency status issues have continuing significance within the social security system. Social security and social control may be understood not only in terms of the subjection of labour by capital but also in terms of the subjection of women by men.

It is now necessary, however, to move on to consider the adjudication process, not only as a 'window' onto the system as a whole, but also as a disciplinary mechanism in its own right. This is the subject of the next chapter.

Chapter Six

THE EMERGENCE OF THE DISCIPLINARY EXAMINATION

> Tribunals are not just safeguarding mechanisms for welfare benefits.... We need to build institutions which foster civic competence, personal responsibility and active involvement rather than over-dependency on professionals and a belief that people are not able to cope. Tribunals should be that kind of institution.
>
> (Bell 1982: 146–147)

This book has argued that the social security system generates both rewards and punishments and that these are consolidated at the level of individual discipline. The particular proposition contained in Chapter 5 has been that the unique form of the SSAT lends it to that process of consolidation and that the disciplinary techniques of the *case approach*, *legalisation* and *partitioning* operate within the SSAT. What is unique about social security tribunals is that they combine judicial form with a process which Foucault has defined as 'disciplinary examination'. Such a combination is peculiarly apt to a conception of law and social policy within the utilitarian tradition.

THE FORM OF THE TRIBUNAL

The spatial arrangement of the tribunal may be described as follows:

> A table, and behind this table, which distances them from the two litigants, the 'third party', that is, the judges. Their position indicates firstly that they are neutral with respect to each

litigant, and second this implies that their decision is not already arrived at in advance, that it will be made after an aural investigation of the two parties, on the basis of a certain conception of truth and a certain number of ideas concerning what is just and unjust, and third that they have the authority to enforce their decision. This is ultimately the meaning of this simple arrangement.

(Foucault 1981a: 8)

This description, by Foucault, was invoked to depict the basic elements of the form of the court or tribunal; a form which in his contention necessarily constitutes or is dependent upon a form of political state apparatus. Whereas in the Middle Ages the parties to a dispute or a private battle might refer their case to some form of *ad hoc* arbitration, the rise of permanent and well-defined adjudicative institutions was a feature of the development of the modern state. Judicial apparatuses were erected upon the same foundations as were tax gathering operations and the creation of a state monopoly upon the use of armed force. In the process, says Foucault, the operation of 'justice' became inverted: justice was no longer the right of those to whom it was by consent applied and no longer the duty of the wise and prestigious to whom such disputants turned for judgement; justice had become a right for those in power and an obligation for those who had to submit to it. The judicial form of the court or tribunal is an ideological as much as a repressive imposition in so far that its condition precedent is a requirement or an implication 'that there are categories which are common to the parties present (penal categories such as theft, fraud; moral categories such as honesty and dishonesty) and that the parties to the dispute agree to submit to them' (Foucault: 27).

The adaptation of the judicial form

The judicial form can be adapted, as Donzelot (1980) has shown in his analysis of the juvenile court. Just as the legislators have provided for a smaller scale and more intimate form of court arrangement for juveniles, separate from the ordinary judicial process, so they have provided for a less formal adjudicative forum for social security claimants, separate from the ordinary courts. In both cases, the specialisation and private nature of the proceedings has not so much protected juveniles and social security claimants as isolated them from their peers and from the outside world (cf. Rose 1975). The insinuation of a judicial authority has served to obliterate distinctions between penal and assistancial forms of intervention with children and to coordinate these into a unified approach. At the same time it has helped to obscure the competing discourses within social security and to provide a spurious sense of cogency to the chaotic administration of social security benefits. Just as the spatial arrangement of the judge, the prosecutor and the educators/social workers in the juvenile court (in France) symbolises the conspiratorial encirclement of the child and his/her family (Donzelot 1980: 99–117), so the arrangement of the tribunal members, the clerk and the departmental Presenting Officer in the SSAT might be seen to symbolise a kind of encirclement of the claimant.

It would be a mistake to regard the SSAT simply as a judicial appendage of the social security system or as an incidental phenomenon which serves on occasions to legitimate the functioning of the system. Although the SSAT does not adjudicate upon every claim for benefit, its jurisdiction is such that it is in fact a direct extension or development of the system. Social security tribunals have been empowered since their inception to reach any decision which it is open to the designated officials of the relevant state agency to take (under present arrangements, any decision open to an Adjudication Officer of either the DSS or the Department of Employment). The judicial form of the tribunal can be seen as permitting an intensification of the disciplinary examination to which social security claimants are in any event subject.

Foucault has attached specific meaning to the expression 'disciplinary examination'. The disciplinary examination is both a technique in itself and it is the summation of his other techniques or 'disciplines': surveillance and normalization. The examination may be seen as having had particular significance in the development of medicine and education, but to Foucault it also symbolises a procedure or technique of general significance and universal application. The examination, he says

> is a normalizing gaze, a surveillance that makes it possible to qualify, to classify and to punish. It establishes over individuals

a visibility through which one differentiates them and judges them. That is why in all the mechanisms of discipline, the examination is highly ritualised. In it are combined the ceremony of power and the form of the experiment, the deployment of force and the establishment of truth. At the heart of the procedures of discipline, it manifests the subjection of those who are perceived as objects and the objectification of those who are subjected.

(Foucault 1977: 184–185).

The daily administration of social security benefits does not afford the same opportunities for examination as are available to doctors and school teachers, but the SSAT provides the opportunity for a ritualised adjudication; a disciplinary examination to which the claimant, by appealing, submits him/herself.

Utilitarianism and justice

Chapter 3 showed that the workhouse test which underpinned the Poor Law Amendment Act of 1834 represented an essentially utilitarian device. The relief of the honest poor and the needy became a matter of rational self-interest rather than moral duty and necessitated a device which would enforce a distinction between paupers and the rest of the proletariat. As such a device, the workhouse test required a pauper to submit, not to an examination, but to the 'less eligible' treatment which the workhouse supposedly afforded. The workhouse test was seldom rigorously applied and did not in fact rigorously embody the form of social discipline envisaged within the utilitarian/philanthropic/self-help discourse discussed in Chapter 3.

Before considering the relevance of the utilitarian discourse to social security tribunals and the unique form which these have taken, it is worth discussing the particular approach taken by the utilitarian philosopher, Jeremy Bentham, to the question of law and social legislation. Upon the face of things he was highly critical of judicial formulations. He wrote:

Power and right and the whole tribe of fictitious entities of this stamp are all of them, in the sense which belongs to them in a book on jurisprudence, the results of some manifestation or other of the legislator's will with respect to such an act. Now every manifestation is either a prohibition, a command, or their respective negations.

(Bentham 1970: 206)

The object of legislation, Bentham argued, was to ensure security through constraint, but he also advocated forms of 'indirect legislation' necessary to establish an elaborate system of social discipline:

Indirect means, then, are those which, without having the character of punishments, act upon a man physically or morally to dispose him to obey the laws, to shield him from the temptations, to govern him by his inclinations and his knowledge.

(quoted in Annette 1979: 68).

The introduction, in place of the clumsy workhouse test, of an appeal mechanism coupled to a disciplinary examination represented an advance within the terms of this utilitarian discourse. The appeal was not so much a 'right' as an administrative device contrived by legislators by which, under an elaborately rule-bound scheme of relief, claimants who had been refused relief in the first instance, could then submit themselves for test. Whilst possessing judicial form, the Courts of Referees and their successors in the world of social security were essentially a means of disciplinary examination; a means by which the ordinary surveillance and the day to day normalising effects of the social security system could be consolidated; a means whereby, without compulsion, the objects of government could be subjected. Within the utilitarian discourse, the social security tribunal may be seen as an infinitely more sophisticated device than the workhouse test and as a forum before which a proper balance could be struck between policy on the one hand, and law on the other.

As noted in Chapter 5, one of the grounds upon which the SBATs in particular came under attack in the 1960s and '70s was that they seemed to their observers to be incapable of distinguishing between policy and law (Bell 1975; Burkeman 1975). SBATs were criticised for following SBC policy, rather than applying and interpreting the law and such criticism provided both fuel and a focal point for a debate between those who advocated a social security system based on discretion and those who advocated a system based on entitlement (Lister 1980; Donnison 1982). Within this debate, the SBAT and its predecessors were characterised as representing a discretion-based model (operating in the manner of a 'case committee'), whereas the NILT and its predecessors were characterised as representing an entitlement-based model (operating more in the manner of an 'adjudicative body'). Neither characterisation was entirely accurate. Social security tribunals had embodied two distinguishable traditions or discourses corresponding to two concrete and distinct disciplinary techniques, namely the case approach and legalisation.

The 'discretion vs entitlement' debate was premised upon an entirely false dichotomy, since these competing ideals merely represent the opposite sides of the same coin. Alternatively, Dworkin's (1977) more imaginative analogy acknowledges that administrative institutions in advanced capitalist states function with a kind of discretionary 'void' surrounded, like the 'hole in a doughnut', by legal rules and principles. The point is that even the most unfettered discretion must be exercised within administratively created parameters, whilst the application of even the strictest rule must involve discretion in the interpretation of that rule and of the circumstances of its application. This is not to deny that the opposition between discretion and entitlement reflects a deeper contradiction: discretion is an instrument of social regulation or administration, whereas entitlement is an abstract concept based on possessive individual right. Each may be seen as a negation of or as a constraint upon the other. However, both the exercise of discretion and the making/enforcing of rules of entitlement represent sources of *power* (cf. Bankowski and Nelken 1981). Discretion and entitlement can only therefore be understood in the total context of a complex 'web' of class powers and as complementary means of social control. The debate discloses key features of the disciplinary techniques so far identified.

The 'discretion lobby' in the debate founded their case upon a 'social rights' argument, which owed much to the concept of the essentially benevolent welfare state envisaged for example by T.H. Marshall. Marshall (1963) had contended that it was through 'social rights' that the democratic state could balance collective and individual interests. It was in this vein that Titmuss (1971) argued against the strictly 'proportional justice' sought by the entitlement lobby, and in favour of 'creative' or 'individualised' justice. Unnecessary elements of discretionary power, Titmuss conceded, should be removed from the social security system (and hence from the tribunals), but discretion was ultimately an indispensible tool for the attainment of a flexible and responsive form of justice, capable of meeting individual needs and circumstances. The appeals system was seen as an essential means of quality control and as a safeguard against the abuse of discretion by officials; as an element within the system which, like Thomas Chalmers' philanthropy (see Chapter 3), would operate at the level of the individual 'habits and economies' of the poor so as to determine the nature and the justice of their need.

The 'entitlement lobby' on the other hand founded their argument, not on a form of Diceyism, but upon a 'new property' approach typical of radical welfare reform discourse both in the USA (in the 1960s) and in the UK (in the 1970s). It was Charles Reich (1964) who had first argued that the distribution of wealth through the state in the form of welfare benefits, subsidies, grants, education, jobs, contracts, licences, etc. should be seen as a new form of property, which might properly be subject to the same rules of law as pertained to private property. Such forms of 'government largesse' should therefore be regarded as falling into the same (bourgeois) legal category as any other form of property and it ought to be subject to rules protecting the rights of recipients and limiting the powers of bureaucrats. It was in this vein that CPAG and others argued for the abolition of discretion in social security and the creation of rights subject to clearly defined procedures: rights to benefit and the rules which governed them should be legally enforcible and subject to formal adjudication. Once again, the appeals system was seen as essential, but because the benefits scheme envisaged depended upon the juridicalisation of the claimant and the imposition of self-regulating rules.

At the level of discourse, both sides in the debate none the less shared a common concern, 'equity'. Those who advocated flexibility and discretion in social security did so because they believed that in a complex and changing world it was the only way to guarantee equity of treatment. This essential objective, according to a senior civil servant at that time, had two aspects: 'equity as between one supplementary benefit claimant and another; and equity as between claimants and their neighbours' (Wilding 1975: 58).

Thus, in the pursuit of fairness to claimants, it is necessary always to weigh their needs against the demands of equity. For example, it is unfair to those claimants who have struggled and 'managed' to live on basic benefit rates to give exceptional payments to claimants who have failed to 'manage'. It is unfair to other low income groups to meet the needs of claimants to a standard that remains beyond the reach of their neighbours. It was the same concern, differently expressed, which motivated the advocates of uniformity and entitlement: a prescriptive framework of rights was seen as the only way to ensure equity and fairness of treatment.

At the level of practice, the 'case approach' technique (as the corollary of the discretion lobby's discourse) functioned so as to make each claimant a unique case; and each case 'at one and the same time constitutes an object for a branch of knowledge and a hold for a branch of power' (Foucault 1977: 191). In the cause of equity, a tribunal could by a process of 'sympathetic' inquiry fashion each individual appearing before it as a 'deserving' or as an 'undeserving' case. It could identify and categorise each individual in accordance with criteria of 'fairness' and 'need'. On the other hand, the 'legalisation' technique (as the corollary of the entitlement lobby's discourse) functioned so as to make each individual a legal subject; and the capacities and actions of each subject could therefore be judged in accordance with rules which were not of his/her own making. In the cause of equity, a tribunal could by a process of 'impartial' adjudication define each individual appearing before it as the bearer of a right or as a subject without a right; as entitled or as not entitled; or even as 'genuine' or 'fraudulent'.

Ultimately, the two techniques served the same ends: to make visible, to judge and to classify. The merger of the SBAT and the NILT to become the SSAT has in a sense merely given expression to a tendency in social security adjudication that had already been evident, since the disciplinary techniques of the case approach and legalisation have functioned in an increasingly unified manner and have enabled a third, more highly refined technique to emerge, 'partitioning'.

Partitioning and the SSAT

Chapter 4 argued that 'partitioning' enabled the division and 'branding' of social security claimants to be extended to an almost infinite degree. The disciplinary examination made possible by the form of the SSAT embodies the ultimate application of the partitioning technique. Each appellant as a 'case' and a 'legal subject' may be examined in full light; s/he may be differentiated and assigned a status; s/he may be placed and partitioned in accordance with his/her individual circumstances and in compliance with the rules.

Earlier chapters have already discussed ways in which the social security system partitions claimants; how it decides what kind of 'case' each claimant represents and how benefits are paid in accordance with a meticulous classification and gradation of a claimant's status. Although the SSAT is comparatively rarely involved in the process, it must still be understood as the culmination of the techniques in operation. A social security appeal is not and cannot be an appeal to be free from the partitions which the social security system imposes (as an inmate's appeal is an appeal to be free from the walls of his/her prison, asylum or workhouse). It is an appeal, voluntarily made, for containment merely by a different set of partitions, a different identity, a different legal status.

Jeffrey Jowell has defined 'adjudication' as 'the technique of decision-making that guarantees participation to parties affected, though a number of procedural devices' (1975: 26). In warning of the limits of the adjudicative approach, Jowell identified 'the danger of passing off as meaningful participation that which is largely ritual' (1973: 220). The thrust of the argument in this chapter is that the tribunal adjudication process now constituted in the SSAT does not so much guarantee as compel degrees of 'participation' which are indeed 'largely ritual'. What Jowell perceived as a danger of the adjudication process we have identified as its constitutive disciplinary element.

EXPOSURE TO DISCIPLINARY EXAMINATION

According to Foucault (1977), there are three essential elements to any disciplinary examination: the maximum visibility of the subject; the documentation of the individual subject; and the objectification of the subject as an individual 'case'. The tribunal hearing and the preparations which lead up to it constitute such an examination; an examination which ritualises the disciplinary techniques inherent within the social security system itself, but which, as the antithesis of mediaeval forms of ritual or ceremony, may be characterised as a clear expression of '... a modality of power for which individual *difference* is relevant' [emphasis added] (ibid.: 192).

The pre-hearing process

For the vast majority of social security recipients, the decisions upon their claims to benefit and the assessment or surveillance of their circumstances is effected by state officials and administrators who remain largely unseen. To appeal against the determinations of such officialdom is to invite further scrutiny. Even if it is only a minority of appellants who appear in the full light of a tribunal hearing, in the act of appealing every appellant submits her/himself for examination.

At the beginning of the 1970s attention was drawn by Coleman (1970) to the practice by the Supplementary Benefits Commission of conducting an internal administrative review in respect of all first instance decisions in Supplementary Benefit appeal cases and of diverting a certain proportion of such appeals. Of the appeals which never reached the tribunal, a certain number were 'superseded' by a revision to the decision appealed from; some were simply not admitted and not passed on to the tribunal upon the grounds that the appellant's challenge was inappropriate or outside the tribunal's jurisdiction; and some would be voluntarily withdrawn by appellants after officials of the Supplementary Benefits Commission had taken the opportunity of discussing or explaining their original decisions to the appellants concerned.

Comparable information in relation to social insurance appeals prior to the institution of the SSAT is not available. Since 1984 published statistics show what proportions of all social security appeals have been diverted in this way and that indeed over a half of all appeals cleared (approximately 58 per cent in 1987 – see DSS 1989: Table 49.01) do not reach a hearing before a tribunal. The first point to emerge from this is that the growth in the 'true' rate of appeals activity is considerably underestimated by data which is confined to the numbers of appeals actually heard by the tribunals. Second, the issues which come finally for adjudication before the tribunals are fashioned not only at the instigation of appellants themselves, but in substantial measure through intervention and sifting by state officials.

Appellants whose appeals do not reach the tribunal are not subject to the same degree of visibility as they would otherwise experience, but they are none the less enmeshed in a process of administrative examination. This process is not so much a negotiation as an exercise in quality control on the part of the benefit-administering agencies. This is made especially clear in the Annual Report of the Chief Adjudication Officer for 1985/86 which emphasises that 'The process of review is of great value where the making of an appeal produces fresh evidence', but which expresses concern about the high 'revision rate' (i.e. the frequency with which original decisions are changed as a result of such a process). Such concern appears to be essentially twofold: first, that it 'must cast doubts upon the standards of first-tier adjudication'; second, that some appeals may be unnecessarily diverted. The Chief Adjudication Officer enjoins his senior staff to be 'alive to the possibility of pressure having been put on claimants to withdraw or, indeed, for sound decisions to be changed in order to abort the appeal' (CAO 1987: Part VII).

The importance of what Coleman described as 'the Pre-Hearing Process' should not be underestimated, since it represents a stage within the technique of the disciplinary examination at which appellants may be accommodated within the strategic objectives of the social security system. This may be done either by way of persuasion (sometimes at a face to face interview), or more frequently, by administrative review (as a result of a more thorough scrutiny of the appellant and her/his circumstances). It is clear that the process which was more or less covert when identified by Coleman is now formally recognised and indeed 'valued'. This is not because it reduces the number of cases actually heard by the tribunals, nor even because it helps to conceal the administrative shortcomings of the DSS, but because it enhances the scrutiny to which a select number of individual cases may be subjected and because it can provide a continuous check upon the standards and rigour with which the every day scrutiny of claimants is conducted.

The hearing process

Of those appeals which do proceed to a tribunal hearing, not all will result in a 'full' disciplinary examination of the appellant, since not all appellants attend the hearing. It will be seen from Table 2 that the proportion of appellants attending Supplementary Benefit appeal hearings prior to 1984 had been increasing, although more recently that proportion has declined again to just less than a half (47 per cent in 1987 see DSS 1989: Table 49.3). It is significant (but hardly surprising) that the success rates of those appellants who make no appearance before the tribunal (either in person or by a representative) is consistently low (of the 49 per cent of appellants who neither attended nor were represented before the SSAT in 1987, only 10 per cent were successful with their appeals). At one level this illustrates that successful litigation in this sphere like any other depends upon effective oral argument, but more importantly it emphasises that a full disciplinary examination depends upon the full visibility of the subject in order meaningfully to function.

In spite of the interest which social security tribunals attracted in the 1970s, much of the research which was then conducted was concerned with the tribunals themselves, with tribunal members, with procedure and administration and with the 'quality' of adjudication: very little research was conducted upon social security appellants. Kathleen Bell's investigation of the NILT and the SBAT resulted in the interviewing of 272 National Insurance appellants and 235 Supplementary Benefit appellants respectively (Bell *et al.* 1974, 1975; Bell 1975). An investigation by the Legal Advice Research Unit of the Nuffield Foundation into the SBAT, the NILT and the Rent Tribunal resulted in the interviewing of 94 National Insurance appellants and 96 Supplementary Benefit appellants (Milton 1975; Frost and Howard 1977). Finally, Julian Fulbrook's study of the SBAT resulted in the interviewing of just 38 appellants (Fulbrook 1975). The common preoccupations of these research projects were essentially twofold: first, the competence of appellants to 'handle' the appeals process; second, the extent to which appellants considered the tribunal hearing and the appeals process to be 'fair'.

Upon the question of appellants' competence, there was some measure of agreement between the researchers' findings,

Table 2 Attendance and representation at appeal hearings

	Supplementary benefit appeals only							All appeals and referrals			
	1973		1978		1983		1985		1987	
APPELLANT	as %age of all appellants	success rate (%)	as %age of all appellants	success rate (%)	as %age of all appellants	success rate (%)	as %age of all appellants	success rate (%)	as %age of all appellants	success rate (%)
Attended and was represented	18	39	20	40	24	35	18	48	17	51
Attended but was not represented	28	27	29	27	35	21	34	29	30	32
Did not attend but was represented	4	36	4	35	4	31	4	35	4	36
Did not attend and was not represented	50	7	47	7	37	7	44	8	49	10
	(100%) n=24,486		(100%) n=62,308		(100%) n=60,567		(100%) n=114,550		(100%) n=165,307	

Sources: based on reworked figures from Social Security Statistics 1973, 1980, 1983, 1986 and 1988, London, HMSO

although a significant divergence as to the extent and the emphasis accorded to such findings. Bell found, for example, that 31 per cent of NILT appellants and 22 per cent of SBAT appellants admitted having difficulty in understanding the appeal papers (i.e. the formal documentation used at the hearing and containing the departmental reply to the appeal). In the case of NILT appellants a further 10 per cent who claimed to have understood the papers were found to have manifestly failed to do so from answers given during their interviews and, in the case of SBAT appellants, about 56 per cent of those who attended their tribunal hearing said they experienced some kind of difficulty coping in the course of that hearing. So far as SBAT appellants in particular were concerned, whilst Bell was at pains to point out that she had found no evidence of appeals being lodged irresponsibly or purely habitually, at least 30 per cent of appellants had not properly understood what they were setting in motion when they lodged their appeal.

Coral Milton, upon the other hand, reporting upon the findings of the Nuffield study, made a more sweeping statement, claiming that a 'large proportion' of appellants were 'baffled' by the tribunal process, whilst Supplementary Benefit appellants in particular '... suffer educational, social and financial deprivation, which together with a nervous attitude to appearing before tribunals seriously affects their competence to deal with the situation they encounter at the hearing' (Milton 1975: 137).

Most sweeping of all, however, was the conclusion advanced by Fulbrook, who claimed that the 'overwhelming feature' of appellants' responses was 'the obvious bewilderment at the whole tribunal process and what it involved' (Fulbrook 1975: 14). Many appellants, he reported, had not realised that a letter written in protest in response to a decision of the Supplementary Benefits Commission would be funnelled into the tribunal process and result in a hearing before a formally constituted review body. Misconceptions about the nature of the tribunal itself, alleged Fulbrook, were 'rife', whilst thirty-one out of thirty-eight appellants admitted no knowledge of the legal rules.

In spite of the inconsistent quality of this evidence, it clearly brings into question the idea of the appellant as the competent subject exercising upon reasoned grounds a consciously valued right of appeal. The picture that is suggested is that, from the moment the appellant declares her/himself, the initiative is seized from her/him and the appeals process presents as something beyond the appellant's sphere of experience and which bears in or impinges upon her/him as a more or less incompetent object. Indeed, as Bell put it, for many appellants, 'the whole business was a significant experience in their lives' (Bell 1975: 14) and was hardly something which could be taken lightly or as a matter of course.

Upon the question of the 'fairness' of tribunal hearings, the three main pieces of research on appellants' attitudes are hopelessly conflicting. Bell found that, of the NILT appellants who attend their appeal hearings, 61 per cent said they had had a fair hearing, even though only 35 per cent said they thought the tribunal's decision was fair: of the SBAT appellants who attended their hearings, almost two thirds felt the hearing was fair (74 per cent of successful appellants and 62 per cent of unsuccessful appellants), although overall only 19 per cent of appellants interviewed were satisfied with the tribunal decision.

Milton's conclusions were much less clear. She found that 'positive responses to the tribunal system' were most frequent from those appellants whose appeals had been successful and were only 'occasionally' forthcoming from those who had been unsuccessful. Her overall finding was that the level of dissatisfaction was greater than the level of satisfaction.

The arguably less rigorous empiricism of Fulbrook's research evinced a conclusion even more at odds with Bell's findings. Fulbrook claims that the attitude of appellants who appeared at their tribunal hearings was 'largely condemnatory': only one respondent (out of thirty-eight in the study) felt that the tribunal had been 'sympathetic and understanding' and only one considered that tribunals were a satisfactory method of dealing with the sort of 'problem' they had had. Fulbrook observed that

> Even when making allowance for feelings of bitterness caused by other factors such as the initial refusal of benefit and the social and economic circumstances of many claimants, the hostility displayed towards the tribunal process and towards the Commission made it clear that the right to appeal does not inspire confidence in the minds of most appellants.
> (Fulbrook 1975: 14).

It is simply not possible adequately to reconcile the views expressed above within a single theoretical framework. These questions will be addressed below upon the basis of new evidence. None the less, two tentative observations are possible at this stage, one in relation to Bell's findings and the other in relation to Fulbrook's conclusions. First, if Bell is right, then the tribunal process appears to enjoy a surprisingly high degree of legitimacy amongst appellants and its potential as a technique for accommodating resistance is in part at least already established. Second, the question which Julian Fulbrook should perhaps have addressed was not 'Does a right of appeal inspire confidence?', but 'Does a right of appeal instil discipline?': had he asked a different question, he might have arrived at a different answer.

If, however, the adjudication process is seen as a form of disciplinary examination, the 'competence' of appellants as legal subjects and appellants' perceptions of the 'fairness' of tribunal hearings are relatively incidental to the substantive effects of the process. The central feature is a process which constitutes the appellant as object rather than subject and which subjects appellants to its own and not the appellant's criteria of fairness or equity. It is the adjudication process itself which defines (or redefines) the issues of each appeal and, within that process, there may be several stages.

The representation process

One such stage is the pre-hearing process. For a certain number of appellants there is a further stage which may begin before the hearing and may intersect with the hearing stage itself: that is the stage of seeking representation. It may be seen from Table 2 (see p. 148) that in 1983 some 28 per cent of Supplementary Benefit appellants were represented at the hearing of their appeal. Of these, as may be seen from Table 3 (see p. 152), 55 per cent were represented by a friend or relative, but some 45 per cent consulted a person in some professional capacity for assistance with the presentation of their appeal.

The likelihood of appellants succeeding with their appeals, as may be seen from Table 2 (p. 148), is significantly enhanced by representation at the hearing and this suggests that representatives themselves play a significant part in the process of

Table 3 Types of representative appearing at Supplementary Benefit appeal hearings

Appeals heard	1973		1978		1983	
	as %age of all appellants	success rate (%)	as %age of all appellants	success rate (%)	as %age of all appellants	success rate (%)
TYPE OF REPRESENTATIVE						
Friend or relative	66	34	65	32	55	25
Trade Union Official	2	29	2	26	1	32
Solicitor	3	44	2	39	4	40
Social Worker	11	53	17	52	19	47
CPAG	2	57	1	58	—	—
Claimants Union	12	44	4	42	4	43
Other	4	50	9	49	17	47
	(100%) n=24,486		(100%) n=62,308		(100%) n=60,567	

Source: Dean 1988: 216

defining or redefining the issues under appeal. The success rates of the few appellants who, although they were represented did not actually appear before the tribunal, have in some years been not much lower than the success rates of those who both were represented and themselves appeared. In such cases, it could be argued, the examination of the appellant had already been conducted by the representative, rather than by the tribunal. In any event, representation, where it occurs, must be regarded as a part of the adjudication process.

Although Table 3 shows that the majority of persons appearing at SBAT hearings as representatives are described as friends or relatives of the appellant, this proportion appears to have been diminishing, whilst the 'effectiveness' of such representatives – in terms of the success rates of the appellants – also appears to have been in decline. This no doubt reflects the far more technical/legal nature of the Supplementary Benefit scheme after 1980, which plainly limited the capacity of persons lacking fairly specific knowledge to influence the adjudication process. The representatives who seem to be most 'effective' and to be appearing before tribunals more frequently as time goes on are described as 'social workers' and 'other' representatives – which latter category must be taken to include specialist welfare rights and advice workers. Although these representatives have been marginally less effective since the 1980 Supplementary Benefit reforms than they were before, they also figure more prominently than they did before and their significance to the adjudication process was underlined in the report of a survey by the DHSS on Supplementary Benefit Appeals presentation (CAO 1985: Appendix 7).

The survey, a study of seventy-eight Supplementary Benefit appeals, was instigated out of 'concern' about the increased levels of representation by 'welfare rights officers [sic]' and, of the twenty-one appeals in which the appellant was represented, in eighteen of them (86 per cent) the representative was classified by the DHSS as a 'welfare rights worker', one as a Probation Officer, one as a solicitor and one as the appellant's son. In view of the small sample size, the value of these findings may be limited, but the shift in official discourse represented by the reclassification of representatives is highly revealing. It is not clear whether the term 'welfare rights worker' included specialist local authority workers as well as voluntary sector advice workers, but what is clear is the recognition on the part of the DHSS of an emerging 'breed' of professional representative.

Once again, unfortunately, comparable data upon social insurance tribunals is virtually non-existent, with the notable exception of Bell's study of the NILT (Bell *et al.* 1974 and 1975). Bell found that about 20 per cent of NILT appellants were then represented at their appeal hearings and, of these, 75 per cent were represented by trade union officials. This is suggestive of a degree of 'proletarianisation' amongst social insurance appellants that was and is absent amongst social assistance appellants, although it must also be noted that trade union representation was only really commonplace in appeals relating to the Industrial Injuries scheme, since in Unemployment Benefit and Sickness Benefit cases, for example, only 7 per cent and 12 per cent of appellants respectively were represented by trade union officials. It is notable none the less that only two out of 1,538 representatives in Bell's sample were social workers and 85 per cent of tribunal chairpersons interviewed had never encountered a social worker at a tribunal hearing. Bell's findings point quite clearly, therefore, to the difference in character between the social insurance and the social assistance tribunals which existed at that time: the social insurance tribunals were more amenable to the adversarial approach of the trade union representative, whilst the assistance tribunals were more amenable to the 'case approach' of the social worker.

In this context, the increase in the numbers of representatives described in DHSS statistics as 'social workers' and appearing at Supplementary Benefit appeal hearings might appear strange in view of the far more technical/legal nature of the Supplementary Benefit scheme since 1980. However, the disciplinary techniques embodied in the case approach and legalisation are not incompatible and they intersect in such a manner as to elicit an enhanced disciplinary effect. It is not therefore surprising to find social case-workers participating in proceedings of a 'judicial' nature since this in fact underlines the unique nature of the social security tribunal hearing as a disciplinary examination.

In spite of the confusions which exist within the available statistical data with regard to the categorisation of representatives, a new breed of professional representative – the welfare rights worker – appears to have emerged: a professional whose 'calling' is fashioned partly in the social case-worker's tradition, but partly also out of the discourse of the welfare rights and legal services movements. The simple distance in terms of knowledge and legal skills between the providers and the consumers of welfare rights and legal services is not necessarily sufficient to explain the authority which invests the provider as a 'professional' and the dependency which invests the consumer as 'client'. However, the disciplinary implications of such authority are clear.

The social security appeal, as a project in disciplinary examination, constitutes the appellant within intersecting relations of power; as the 'claimant' of the social security system; and as the 'client' of her/his professional representative. Adjudicative issues – issues lying between the individual and the state – are thus furnished upon the terrain of the social security system and by a discourse of needs, of claims and of statuses furnished (for some) by professional representatives, or (for others) by the tribunal itself, or by both.

The definition of adjudicative issues

This leads to the question of the definition of adjudicative issues. Bell, in her study of Supplementary Benefit appellants, concluded that, because 38 per cent of her respondents had received no reasons for the decision against which they were appealing, then '... for these at least there must be doubt about whether the appeal was lodged with understanding of the facts and issues in dispute' (Bell 1975: 14).

Commenting upon the same phenomenon, Fulbrook puts it another way:

> From the written appeals on the hearing papers from other appellants, it was also possible to see the same kind of reaction [i.e. bewilderment]: 'I have wife and 3 children – please help'; 'I just cannot afford to live on this'. In the majority of cases it was impossible to define the precise nature of the appeal.
> (Fulbrook 1975: 13)

For the social security tribunals, and indeed for both these researchers, the 'real' adjudicative issues can be defined only in terms of the rules of the state benefits scheme. The issues, if they do not appear on the face of the appeal, are to be inferred from what the appellant says. The appellant's definition of the issues must be modified and moulded so that it can be accommodated within the tribunal's jurisdiction and within the kinds of needs, claims and statuses generated by and through the social security system. During the pre-hearing process, social security officials and professional representatives may contribute to this process of redefinition, but, in the last instance, it will be the tribunal which imposes a definition.

The moulding of definitions is a central and constitutive feature of the adjudication process. An illustrative analogy may be drawn between the disciplinary effect of tribunals upon social security claimants and the effects of formalised state courts upon Mexican Indians as observed by Hunt and Hunt (1969). The customs and perceptions of the subordinated Indian community became deformed and subverted when they were obliged reluctantly to take matters before the Mexican state courts. Thus, an action brought against a witch who failed to bring rain, when paid to do so, was recast by the court as a case of fraud, and an application to the court for protection against charges of witchcraft was accommodated as a case of libel. In neither case would the court concede to Indian social reality (encompassing the power of witchcraft) and in neither case was the result satisfactory to the Indian litigants: regardless of whether the Indians 'won' or 'lost', it was the reality of the bourgeois Mexican state which prevailed.

In the case of social security appeals, the grounds for the appeal appearing upon the face of the documentary record need not correspond with the purposes of the appellant in appealing. The outcome of the appeal as it appears upon the face of the documentary record, need not correspond with the effects of the appeal process upon the appellant. That failure of correspondence is not the result of a failing in the adjudication process. It springs from the essence of the process as a disciplinary examination. It represents precisely the target of discipline and the purpose of examination.

PERFORMANCE OF THE TRIBUNALS

As has been seen, several writers have assessed the extent to which social security tribunals have measured up to the procedural and judicial standards set for them. This book, however, addresses the issue of 'performance' more in the theatrical sense of that word and judges the tribunal's 'act' for its coherence as an exercise in disciplinary examination.

The SSAT in action: an empirical study

The discussion which follows is based on an empirical study of some 127 substantive SSAT hearings and interviews with some fifty individual appellants conducted between October 1986 and March 1987 (see Dean 1988 for full details). The hearings observed and the appellants interviewed formed a reasonably representative sample and the subject matter and the outcomes of the appeals concerned were quite typical in relation to prevailing statistical norms.

It was found that the vast majority of appeals arose essentially out of four broad areas of dispute between the individual and the state. First, there were disputes about the special needs claimed by appellants to be peculiar to them. These disputes arose because the levels of basic provision made by the social security system are insufficient to encompass certain needs which are deemed explicitly to be over and above the 'normal' or the 'ordinary'; (around 35 per cent of the appeals observed fell into this category). Second, there were disputes about the application of administrative rules. These disputes arose because of the restrictive parameters of the social security system and their punitive consequences; (around 29 per cent of the appeals observed fell into this category). Third, there were disputes about the dependency status attributed to appellants. These disputes arose because of the social security system's preoccupation with the 'norms' of family or household dependency (around 16 per cent of the appeals observed fell into this category). Finally, there were disputes about the productive status attributed to appellants and/or the application of rules of labour discipline. These disputes arose because of the social security system's preoccupation with the 'norms' of the labour market (around 20 per cent of the appeals observed fell into this category). Each of these areas of dispute could also be characterised as or reduced to a legal or technical area of dispute in which the parties were subject to arbitrary rules and abstract principles.

While appellants themselves would usually identify the purposes of their appeals in terms of the specific departmental decisions which they disputed, the logic and the dissatisfaction to which they gave expression by appealing were often more broadly founded than were the departmental decisions themselves. An analysis of what appellants said about their own appeals suggested that, at an implicit or discursive level, appellants accepted or in some measure subscribed – to notions of protest, to perceptions of punishment, to the ethos of the 'case approach', to the 'legalisation' of welfare provision, and/or to the 'partitioning' of claimants according to category or status. In particular, there was some evidence to suggest that the experience of appealing had some effect in modifying appellants' perceptions. For example, the punitive aspects of social security law were sometimes seen to have been legitimised as a consequence of the appeal process, and the technical or legal character of the social security system and of the citizen's claims upon it were often more fully accepted by claimants as a result of their experience of appealing.

Characteristics of the tribunal process

Having thus reinforced the general theoretical claims of this book, the study considered the manner in which the tribunal itself functions. In this respect there were three immediately observable characteristics which appeared to be both problematic for the tribunal process and yet which, at this historical conjuncture, are constitutive of that process:

1. the ambiguity of the tribunal process arising from the unresolved tension between its adversarial and inquisitorial aspects;
2. the isolated spheres of competence of the actors engaged in the process;
3. the dependence of the process on the role of the chairperson as its principal actor.

Chapter 5 considered at some length the 'participatory' model to which the modern SSAT aspires and the compromise which this entails between the adversarial and inquisitorial traditions of adjudication. Observation of the tribunals reveals just how uneasy a compromise this represents and yet how effective a synthesis between such traditions can be in the management of appellants.

At every hearing attended by an appellant, it is customary for the chairperson to embark upon an introductory discourse, the length and detail of which may vary, but which is plainly designed to impress upon the appellant the 'participatory' nature of the proceedings. How the proceedings proceed from this point then depends upon the appellant's response and the extent to which s/he elects, whether explicitly or implicitly, to play a hostile or a submissive role.

The chairperson's introductory speech usually contains an explicit invitation to the appellant to choose whether to speak first or to allow the departmental Presenting Officer to open the proceedings, but the speech often contains a more subtle invitation. If the appellant responds with any measure of aggression, the proceedings tend thereafter towards the adversarial and the structuring of the explanation and disputation of the various facts and issues. If, however, the appellant responds with any degree of deference, the proceedings then tend towards the inquisitorial and a more fluid orchestration of questions and answers.

Apellants who come prepared with arguments may be managed by subjecting them to the rules of adversarial procedure, whilst appellants who come unprepared may be managed by subjecting them to the processes of inquisitorial procedure. Either way, the tribunal succeeds (apparently quite unconsciously) in protecting the integrity of the social security system from challenge on anything other than terms set by the system itself. The appellant, as instigator of the process, is constituted and subjected as an object of that process.

The second problematic characteristic to emerge relates to the highly specific nature of the tribunal's jurisdiction and, as a corollary, the distinctly limited competencies of those involved in the tribunal process. In the course of their introductory preamble, most chairpersons make some reference to the fact that the tribunal is bound by the rules and regulations of the social security scheme and has no power to change them. Some make clear that the tribunal is not there to apologise for the social security system but to ensure that its rules are properly applied and interpreted. Others, in emphasising that the rules are not of the tribunal's own making, go so far as to admit that they would sometimes *wish* to change those rules. It was observed that, in explaining to appellants the reasons why they had lost or were likely to lose their appeals, several chairpersons and lay members did in effect apologise for the social security system and for the restrictive rules which the tribunal was obliged to observe. They would express their sympathy for the appellant and bemoan the fact that 'our hands are tied'.

This clog upon the capacity of the tribunal to offer the substantive relief sought by the appellant would often raise in the minds of tribunal members and appellants alike the hope that some alternative form of relief might yet be available. However, a number of obstacles would inevitably intervene to constrain such hope and to preserve the distance between the appellant, as object of examination, and the tribunal, as his/her examiners. The tribunal's jurisdiction of course was confined to the consideration of the particular decision under appeal and any fresh claim for the same or some other form of benefit would have to be processed by the relevant office or department. The tribunal was only competent to hear appeals and, whilst it might informally advise appellants what else they might do, it was not really the proper authority. Although the tribunal was competent to consider detailed and highly technical matters of social security law, it was not necessarily very familiar with every aspect of a vastly complex social security system, still less with any other aspect of welfare law or welfare provision.

The tribunal, like any other examiner (and even like the mediaeval executioner) can bear no responsibility for the circumstances and political context in which it exercises the highly particular technique that is its preserve and, even if it is not required of the tribunal, it is likely that it will abstain from any extraneous involvement with those whom it must subject and that it will be largely ignorant of the matters which are beyond its sphere of responsibility.

The final observation to be drawn from having watched the SSAT in action is the centrality of the role played by the chairperson. Plainly, the chairperson of any tribunal is a central figure, but certain factors seem to be investing the chairpersons of the SSAT with a very peculiar role. First, the less adversarial role promoted for and largely adopted by departmental Presenting Officers since the creation of the Presidential system has cast additional functions and responsibilities upon the tribunal chairperson. It is usually s/he who must, for example, conduct most, if not all, cross-examination and who must if necessary reformulate or explain the Department's case in terms which the appellant might understand. Second, the new emphasis upon legal qualification and upon appointment through the independent Presidential system has clearly brought a new 'breed' and a new style of chairperson and even a new sense of prestige.

The effect is in many ways striking. Donzelot's (1980) application of the concept of 'encirclement' to the court room situation describes at best a partial encirclement by distinct and individual actors. It is perhaps not too fanciful to suggest that the role now being fashioned by many SSAT chairpersons is such as to provide a focal point around which the roles of the individual actors on the tribunal stage may be concerted, giving a greater strength and completeness to the appellant's 'encirclement'. The appellant will always be seated directly opposite the chairperson and the chairperson instantly becomes – first, host and guide for the appellant (introducing everybody in the room and explaining what will happen); then master of ceremonies (directing the order of proceedings); and later chief interrogator. Often, the chairperson also becomes chief apologist if an adverse decision must be handed down. The chairperson never leaves the centre stage and the parts played out by the surrounding actors tend to become supporting acts to complement a plot dictated from the chair.

It would be wrong to suggest that this scenario always functions perfectly, but the point being made is that the process is increasingly dependent upon the chairperson. Certainly, in those instances where the chairperson fails to hold centre stage in the course of a hearing, the hearing tends to become, not necessarily chaotic, but aimless. Interestingly, Jackson *et al.* (1987a and 1987b) report that, in their recent research, they observed a small number of hearings at which an inexperienced chairperson and an experienced lay tribunal member effectively reversed their respective roles, so that the most experienced tribunal member assumed the part of principal actor (1987b). However, the main thrust of the findings by Jackson *et al.* was that lay tribunal members continue by and large to play a secondary role. The overwhelming impression which one receives is that the performance required of lay members is indeed primarily a formal one. Their participation at hearings is ordinarily a matter of ritual. They tend to play 'walk on' parts. Whilst clearly they are not to be ignored as mere 'extras', the role they generally fulfil is that of a necessary 'supporting cast'.

The construction of records and the exercise of discretion

The responsibility for recording evidence and submissions given in the course of each tribunal hearing rests with the chairperson. Chairpersons seldom, if ever, take verbatim notes and some are very much more selective than others in what they choose to write down. Inevitably (and most particularly with the more loquacious appellants), chairpersons undertake some sifting of the evidence and the submissions they hear. In determining what it is necessary for them to record, chairpersons are often making discernible judgements as to what is relevant. Thus, at more than half of the hearings observed in the author's study, things which were said by the appellant in the clear belief that they were relevant were not included in the record of proceedings. In a small but significant number of cases the discrepancies between the researcher's notes and the tribunal's official record of proceedings were such as to indicate that the chairperson had gone beyond the point of sifting out apparent irrelevancies and had missed out or misconstrued things which were palpably essential to the issues under adjudication (Dean 1988: 262–3).

It should be emphasised that an analysis of the records of proceedings was conducted not as commentary upon the competence of tribunal personnel but for the light it cast on the adjudication process. The tribunal process is capable of literally rewriting the experience of appellants and of reconstructing their perception of what is or is not relevant. For example, the detailed explanation given by one Supplementary Benefit claimant with regard to her children's need for clothing was largely omitted from the record of the appeal proceedings because the explanation related to circumstances which arose after the date upon which the claim for assistance with the costs of such clothing, had been made and which were therefore deemed immaterial (see Regulation 3 Supplementary Benefit (Single Payments) Regulations 1981 and RSB 26/83). In such circumstances, the negation by the tribunal of explanations offered by the appellants may be seen as an essential (albeit of course unintended) component of a process of disciplinary examination.

Closely associated with the discretionary process by which the tribunal organises or reconstructs the evidence and submissions before it is the discretion it exercises in the interpretation of such evidence and submissions. I have alluded earlier to the question of discretion in adjudication, but it is worth recalling that the concern of some commentators has been that the increasing legality and hostility of the social security system has reduced the capacity of tribunals to exercise discretion and may therefore undermine the credibility of the appeals system (Partington 1986a). For that reason, in the author's study the various sets of appeal papers were studied to determine in how many instances the tribunals concerned had clearly exercised some measure of discretion in reaching their decisions. Had they, for example, been concerned to ascertain what was 'reasonable' or 'sufficient', or with whether there had been 'good cause' or 'due care'? Had they been required to weigh conflicting evidence in order to reach a conclusion or to choose between conflicting interpretations of the law?

The findings were largely consistent with those of Bell *et al.* (1974), namely that there is a great deal more scope for discretionary decision-making by tribunals than might be supposed having regard to the increasingly rule-bound nature of the social security system. Discretion appeared to have been exercised at the vast majority (92 per cent) of the hearings which had had a successful or partly successful outcome and in almost half (45 per cent) of those with an unsuccessful outcome. Discretion, therefore, is not yet dead and appears still to play an essential part in the tribunal adjudication process (Dean 1988: 265).

Appellant's perceptions

Finally, appellants were asked questions about the outcome of their appeals. First, they were asked to say what they thought about the result of their appeal. 36 per cent appellants expressed satisfaction or some positive sentiments in response to this question, while 64 per cent expressed dissatisfaction or negative sentiments. Understandably, appellants whose hearings had been successful or partly successful were more likely to express satisfaction, although several successful appellants still expressed dissatisfaction. Conversely, appellants whose hearings had been unsuccessful were much more likely to express dissatisfaction and very few unsuccessful appellants expressed satisfaction with the outcome.

Appellants were then asked whether the results of their appeals were 'fair'. 42 per cent of appellants said 'yes', whilst 58 per cent said 'no' or 'not really'. Hardly surprisingly, appellants whose hearings had been successful or partly successful were more likely to consider the result to be fair and, conversely, appellants who had lost their appeals were more likely to consider the result unfair. It is important, however, to note that this tendency was not universal and that, indeed, there were a few appellants (just three out of fifty) who, having expressed dissatisfaction with the outcome of their appeal, none the less accepted that it was 'fair' (Dean 1988: 281–4).

The questions put to appellants were of course concerned solely with the outcome of their appeals and not with more problematic or global considerations regarding the tribunal hearing or the tribunal process, but the findings go some way towards clarifying the conflicting accounts given by previous researchers. Appellants' perceptions of the substantive outcomes of their appeals is largely but not entirely related to whether they win or lose. Certainly the fact that more appellants express dissatisfaction than satisfaction is a direct reflection of the fact that more people lose than win, but the story does not end there. A small but significant minority of appellants are capable of making certain distinctions between their liking for a tribunal decision and the propriety of that decision. This attribute of the appeals process may be regarded as a disciplinary effect, and one which may be more clearly understood if we go on to consider who or what it is that appellants blame if indeed they do not consider the results of their appeals to be fair.

The appellants who said the results of their appeals were unfair were each asked who or what was to blame. Comparatively few appellants blamed the tribunal itself for the unfairness of its decision. Rather more appellants blamed the government department or the Adjudication Officer responsible for the original decision which the tribunal had upheld and, naturally enough, some appellants attributed some measure of blame to the way in which their appeals had been presented. But most of these appellants (83 per cent) blamed in whole or in part the government and/or the rules of the social security system itself.

To summarise, nearly three-fifths of the appellants interviewed considered the tribunal's decision to be unfair, but most of these were prepared to blame the government or the social security system in preference to blaming the 'independent' tribunal. While it may not be particularly effective in quelling the dissatisfaction of appellants with the workings of the social security system, the tribunal is on the whole very effective in deflecting the grievances of appellants. The disciplinary effect of the tribunal process lies not so much in its capacity to convince appellants that the decisions it imposes are fair or just, but in its capacity to impose decisions with reference to a source of power that is remote and unassailable. The tribunal hearing, as a disciplinary examination, does not operate at the level of persuasion, but at the level of compulsion. In so doing, the tribunal preserves its distance from the appellant across the table, whilst still drawing him/her towards the focus of attention. It manages the conduct of the appellant during each hearing and, in its process of examination and deliberation, is capable of reconstituting each appellant as a 'case' intelligible to the tribunal's own terms of reference. Appellants who are subjected to such an examination may not be 'reformed' by the experience, but they are none the less exposed as the impotent objects of a state social security system whose power, mediated through the impartiality of the tribunal, is demonstrated to be unanswerable.

The final picture

The picture of the SSAT which emerges is, of course, far from straightforward. We remain confronted with a situation in which up to four-fifths (on a national average) of the claimants who appeal to a tribunal reap no material advantage from doing so. Yet claimants continue to appeal in increasing numbers. Tribunals have a quite limited jurisdiction, they review a very small proportion of all social security benefit claims and they have no power at all to influence the direction of social policy. Yet the state has been prepared to legislate for an increasingly sophisticated and costly structure for such tribunals.

Clearly then, this ritualised form of adjudication is invested with some particular significance and it is to the very nature of such ritual that this chapter has been looking.

Chapter 2 presented three general levels of social control and related these to three levels of discourse through which the modern social security system has been constituted. The SSAT provides a commentary upon the workings of the social security system and the last two chapters have examined such levels of control and discourse through the window which the tribunal provides.

At the first level, the ritual of formalised adjudication at a tribunal hearing provides a 'safety valve'. At the level of political settlement, the right of appeal forms a part of the social wage; it is a part of the price paid by capital to labour to secure social order. At the level of paternalistic/humanitarian/pro-populationist discourse, the tribunal provides a participatory setting through which dissent may be resolved. Whether the appellant wins or loses, the tribunal's ritual can provide a response to protest – even if it is merely to dissipate such protest through a gradual process of attrition.

At the second level, the tribunal's ritual offers a legalistic exercise in 'due process'. At the level of sanctions and penality, the right of appeal is a procedural device; a safeguard perhaps to the individual, but thereby a guarantee of legitimacy to the state. At the level of repressive/Malthusian/anti-populationist discourse, the tribunal's ritual can provide a theatre in which the alleged deficiencies of the ineligible claimant may be paraded.

At the third level, the tribunal's ritual contains a process of examination. At the level of individualised disciplinary techniques, the right of appeal represents a 'test' to which the claimant must voluntarily submit if they are to assert a claim to benefit. At the level of utilitarian/philanthropic/'self-help' discourse, the tribunal's ritual can provide the means to constitute the appellant as a 'case', as a legal subject, or as an object belonging to a specific class or category. The triumvirate of disciplinary techniques specifically identified in this book (the case approach, legalisation and partitioning) are thus incorporated and surmounted within the ritualistic character of a disciplinary examination.

Inscribed within the ritual processes of the SSAT, therefore, we may see underlying relations of power. Relations in which the tribunal itself is only an incidental apparatus. The source of that power is a post-industrial capitalist state and the object is individualised labour. The vehicle of that power is the social security system and the outcome which is constituted through the exercise of such power is the process of class subjection characterised in Chapter 4 as 'modern poverty'.

CONSEQUENCES OF SOCIAL SECURITY REFORM FOR THE SSAT

It is clear that, in spite of the real or imagined designs of the Thatcher governments, the substantive changes they have made to the British social security system in the 1980s have not resulted in a purely 'residual' welfare state. Indeed the changes have retained if not intensified many of the preoccupations of the pre-existing social security system. Since the principal areas of conflict between the individual claimant and the welfare state have not in themselves been radically transformed by the changes to the system, it seems unlikely that the role of the SSAT will be greatly changed.

The Social Fund

However, certain changes were inevitable and there was one major change brought about in 1988 by the Social Security Act 1986. That Act provided that the system of loans and discretionary grants now available from the Social Fund in place of single payments under the old Supplementary Benefits scheme are not subject to any right of appeal to the SSAT. The only exception is claims for non-discretionary grants for maternity and funeral expenses, where the right of appeal is retained.

Prior to the change, a substantial and growing proportion of appeals heard by the SSAT had related to claims for single payments of Supplementary Benefit (58 per cent in 1987 – see DSS 1989: Table 49.01 – although this figure undoubtedly resulted from a last-minute 'rush' to claim such payments). It is therefore clear that the tribunal has lost jurisdiction over many of the disputes upon which it previously adjudicated. In considering the significance of this important change, it is also clear that the loss of such jurisdiction, together with those changes in the Act specifically related to adjudication, ought not in themselves to affect the general role and fundamental character of the tribunals. Indeed, had the SSAT been given jurisdiction to hear appeals against discretionary Social Fund decisions, then the tribunal itself might well have been forced to undergo a fairly radical reorientation.

In order to explain this observation, it is first necessary to say a little more about the way in which the new Social Fund operates. Applications for assistance from the discretionary Social Fund may be made by claimants already in receipt of Income Support. Decisions upon such applications are made by Social Fund Officers of the DSS who are subject to 'direction and guidance' by the Secretary of State (DHSS 1987b). The overriding consideration to which Social Fund Officers must have regard is a budgetary one, in so far that no local DSS office is allowed to exceed its Social Fund budget for the current financial year. Within this limitation, Social Fund Officers have discretion to make 'budgetary loans', 'crisis loans' (both of which are fully repayable by the claimant) or 'community care grants' (which are restricted to specific situations such as that of people moving out of institutional care into the community). Such discretion, however, is constrained by a complex set of rules based, not on conventional adjudicative principles, but on a scheme of 'priorities' by which officers establish which claimants and which needs are most deserving of assistance. The guidance candidly states: 'Social Fund Officers will sometimes be obliged to refuse applications in order to meet higher priorities in the budget' (DHSS 1987b: para. 3024).

Whilst clearly this has elements of the 'case approach' once employed by Poor Law officials and the Charity Organisation Society, it is concerned too blatantly with the rationing of relief to be consistent with the more sophisticated case approach techniques observed to be immanent within the practices of the modern social security tribunal. The retreat to a crude regime of administrative discretion is a reversal of the trend to 'legalisation' and entitlement which had been evident within the 1980 reform of the Supplementary Benefit system and which was decisive in shaping the subsequent refinements of the tribunal system.

The government perceived, no doubt, that the SSAT could not, with any degree of credibility, operate within the budgetary constraints to be imposed upon the Social Fund, but that to allow the SSAT to award payments which might exceed local office budgets would dilute the intentionally punitive impact of the Social Fund. The only right of redress therefore allowed to claimants is to a internal departmental review by a DSS-appointed Social Fund Inspector.

There is barely the pretence of independence for the Social Fund review procedure, since all that has been provided is a somewhat elaborate framework for the administrative oversight of the officials charged with decision making. Presented by the government to its critics as a concession, the review procedure was insufficient to silence the protests from the welfare rights lobby about the absence of a right of appeal, nor a continuing debate upon the issue (see Partington 1986b: 10).

Critics of the government have remarked how 'strange' it is that: 'having only recently rationalised the social security adjudication structure, the Government should now be seeking to remove an important element of the system from its jurisdiction' (Lambeth 1985: para. 10.11), but none of these critics seem to have grasped that the Social Fund, as a very blunt instrument of social control, could not be tempered by the tribunal and is simply not compatible with a 'rationalised' adjudication structure. The tribunal process is intelligible as a process of 'disciplinary examination' before which the individual claimant is subjected as a 'case' and through which the remote and unassailable power of the state is mediated. It is the claimant as an individual who is centre stage before the tribunal. In contrast, the process envisaged by the Social Fund involves a cruder relationship between state and individual in which the claimant is brought into a direct confrontation with budgetary criteria which are dictated by the state and which are quite extraneous to the claimant's individuality. Because the Social Fund places state authority rather than the individual at centre stage, and because it is not essentially preoccupied with the constitution of individuals as claimants, it is a system beyond the pale of the pre-existing strategy of social control, as indeed the recipients of Social Fund largesse are, in a sense, placed beyond the pale of the general body of claimants. The Social Fund is a strategically separate project to the other schemes and benefits over which the SSAT has continued jurisdiction.

Family Credit and Income Support

Furthermore, because means testing and its associated complexities are to play a greater part in the reformed social security system, it is likely that the work-load lost to the tribunals, by the abolition of the single payments scheme, will in time be compensated for by increasing numbers of appeals relating to Income Support and Family Credit. Prior to 1988, if appeals relating to Supplementary Benefit single payments are excluded, just over a half the remaining appeals dealt with by the SSAT related to means-tested benefits (i.e. Supplementary Benefit and FIS) (DSS 1989). That proportion seems set to increase.

Because the levels of Child Benefit, as a universal non-means-tested benefit, are to be allowed to fall in real terms (so as to give priority in funding terms to the new Family Credit scheme (Social Security Consortium 1986: 12)), more low income families ought to be brought within the ambit of means testing and its associated areas of dispute than might otherwise have been the case. It should also be noted that the proportion of appeals relating to Family Credit, the benefit which succeeded FIS, is likely to be much higher than the relatively low percentage of appeals which at present relate to FIS (less than 1 per cent of all appeals in 1987 (DSS 1989)). This arises because, for example, under the new scheme, if either partner of a married or cohabiting couple should work more than twenty-four hours per week, neither is eligible for Income Support and, if they have children, they are obliged to claim Family Credit instead. What is more, Family Credit entitlement rules are more detailed than those of the old FIS scheme, added to which assessments take place twice rather than once every year. These factors can only increase the number of appeals against assessments.

The claim made by the government (e.g. DHSS 1985b) for the means test upon which the Income Support scheme, and in turn the Family Credit and Housing Benefit schemes, are based, is that its rules are simpler and require less interpretation by Adjudication Officers and tribunals alike. Certainly, there have been significant changes to the rules, which shift the terrain upon which disputes are likely to occur, but the new scheme has in fact discarded very few of the complexities which characterised Supplementary Benefit. The scope which existed for tribunals to exercise discretion in adjudication was far greater under the post-1980 Supplementary Benefit scheme than might have been supposed from the rule-bound nature of that scheme and, in all probability, so far as the new Income Support and Family Credit schemes are concerned, the tribunals will exercise their discretion in a similar manner.

In order to predict the changes in the subject matter and in the substance of the appeals which the tribunals will now be hearing, it is first necessary to examine in rather more detail how the basic Income Support means test works. The basis of entitlement is still a 'requirements less resources' calculation, but there are important changes in the way in which 'requirements' in particular are calculated. 'Normal' and 'additional' requirements have been replaced by 'personal allowances' and 'client group premiums': in other words, long-term and householder rates, heating, dietary, laundry additions, etc. have all been abolished and instead there are weekly personal allowances which have been set at four levels: one level for single persons over 24 years of age and single parents over 18 years of age; a higher level for couples; and two lower levels for single persons aged 18–24 and 16–17 respectively. The personal allowance is deemed sufficient for claimants to meet all day to day needs, including water rates, home maintenance and insurance, and 20 per cent of general rates (or poll tax). The 'client group premiums' are additional set weekly amounts allowable to specific groups of people: to families with children; pensioners; the disabled; single parents. Additions for dependent children and for mortgage interest (or part thereof) continue as under Supplementary Benefit and, subject to certain modifications with regard to savings and earnings disregards, the treatment of resources remains largely the same as under Supplementary Benefit.

The most fundamental change to what has been confirmed as the most important part of the social security system has little to do with 'simplicity' or 'effectiveness'. It is a shift at the level of discourse from definitions based on individual need to definitions based on individual status. Individual circumstances are to be interpreted less in terms of the specifics of personal or domestic experience and more in terms of the characteristics of a claimant's socio-economic 'station'.

General shifts

The issues upon which the SSAT is now being called upon to adjudicate must therefore be undergoing some changes. The tribunals, of course, no longer consider appeals relating to Supplementary Benefit single payments, but neither will they consider appeals relating to Supplementary Benefit additional requirements. Thus questions of special need will have effectively disappeared from before the tribunal.

Because the distinction between householders and non-householders no longer affects scale rates, certain issues relating to household status will no longer come before tribunals, but, because the 'aggregation' of requirements and resources are dealt with in the same way as before, issues relating to household composition and dependency will continue to be important. Similarly, disputes over the treatment or determination of income, capital and liabilities will continue and may indeed be exacerbated under the new system.

Questions relating to claimants' productive capacity and to their recent or current employment will have become increasingly prominent as issues to be determined by tribunals. This is partly because of the new emphasis in the Income Support scheme upon 'client groups' and the necessity for membership of legitimately unproductive groups to be established in order to qualify for the new 'premiums': in the area of sickness and disability, this may incidentally be reflected in greater appeals activity in relation for example to (the non-medical aspects of) Severe Disablement, Attendance and Mobility Allowances, since eligibility for such non-means-tested benefits has been made a condition precedent of eligibility for certain Income Support premiums. Also, however, questions of productive capacity and employment are likely to have become particularly important because of changes in conditions of entitlement (which now define full-time employment as twenty-four hours or more per week, rather than thirty hours per week, and will so disqualify some claimants from benefit altogether) and because of the extension of the voluntary unemployment/misconduct disqualification period and the more rigorous application of availability for work tests which affect both Income Support and Unemployment Benefit claimants.

Finally, questions relating to late claims, the backdating of benefits, overpayments, etc. will continue to be dealt with by the SSAT as before, but the rules on overpayments in particular are harsher than in the past and this in itself may generate more appeals.

The main change to the underlying substance of social security appeals will be a shift away from 'particularity/exceptionality'

THE DISCIPLINARY EXAMINATION

issues and towards 'productive status', 'dependency status' and 'labour discipline' issues. Issues relating to 'administrative discipline' and 'technical/legal' issues will continue to permeate appeals as before, although some of the rule changes with regard to the administration of benefits and adjudication may add to the amount of technicality which tribunals and appellants must face.

At one level these changes will assist the tribunal in clarifying its role and enhancing its coherence as a project of disciplinary examination. The ambiguity inherent in tribunal procedure and the tension between inquisitorial and adversarial styles were in the past exacerbated by the way in which the 'case approach' and 'legalisation' techniques respectively inherited by the SSAT were sometimes conflated rather than concerted. To explain this more concretely, those appeals which in the past revolved around pleas by claimants for special treatment from the social security system were increasingly disposed of by recourse to tighter and tighter legal regulation of the system to restrict the grounds upon which such pleas might succeed. The new system, however, does not so much continue this process as close off the possibility of certain such pleas being made. Appellants are therefore rather less likely to make the kind of pleas for sympathetic consideration which can only be answered by conspicuously obstructive legalism.

Appellants will still be able to plead for sympathetic consideration, but such pleas are bound increasingly to be framed as pleas to be considered as a unique and integral 'case' – as claims not to *exceptionality* but to *conformity* with legal regulations and/or with the characteristics of a particular 'client group'. Before the forum of the tribunal, the essential concept of entitlement will become at the same time less abstract and philosophically subjective and more technical and legally precise. A preoccupation with status categorisation will become increasingly central, thus further consolidating the disciplinary effect defined here as 'partitioning'. The techniques of the case approach, legalisation and partitioning will thus continue to be concerted in the tribunal setting so as to perpetuate an effective process of disciplinary examination.

At the same time, the tribunal is likely to be increasingly concerned with issues of penality and the administration of sanctions, most particularly in the area of labour discipline. Increased penalties for voluntary unemployment and dismissal through misconduct are being imposed through the social security system.

Entitlement to benefits for the unemployed will be increasingly dependent upon claimants being prepared to accept placements on temporary training schemes, etc. At a more general level, the entire tenor of the new scheme is such as to penalise, not only the unemployed, but most especially young people who are unemployed. Indeed, it seems probable that young people will come to constitute an even greater proportion of the appellants who resort to the SSAT with their grievances than has been the case in the past. What is more, the tightening of administrative rules relating to benefit overpayments can clearly be seen to have punitive consequences for claimants; consequences which will be reflected in the substance of at least some of the appeals which come before the tribunals.

There remains the fact that, in part at least, the jurisdiction of the SSAT has been curtailed by the SSA'86. The abolition and restriction of certain benefits represents an inroad into the value of the social wage, while the limitation of rights of appeal and the legal rigidities of parts of the new social security system amount to a diminution of claimants' avenues of protest. The SSAT is to survive, none the less, both as a symbolic guarantee which underpins a leaner, meaner but no less pervasive social security system and as the embodiment of a sophisticated form of individualised discipline.

The SSAT, as an institution in the mould idealised by the quotation at the very beginning of this chapter, is, in fact, very much in tune with the Thatcherite values which have informed the latest social security reforms.

Chapter Seven

STRATEGIES FOR SOCIAL CONTROL

> Strategic objectives ... do not so much explain power relations as render them intelligible in terms of a macro-pattern or a general aim. They may be intentional: embodied in programmes, declamations attributable to a specific locus of decision-making; or alternatively, they may be 'unintentional': that is 'the logic is perfectly clear, the aim decipherable and yet it is often the case that no one is there to have invented them, and few who can be said to have formulated them'.
> (Coussins and Hussain 1984: 247–8 (paraphrasing and quoting Michel Foucault))

This final chapter considers the 'strategic objectives' implicit within the latest social security reforms. It reflects upon the future of social security, the constraints of the state/claimant relationship, and the possibility of resistance to social control.

First, however, it might be helpful to recapitulate the main themes and arguments of the preceding chapters.

REPRISE

This book has attempted to show that the form of the state which distributes social security benefits, and the social construction of the individual claimant to whom such benefits are directed, are each ultimately contingent upon the capital/labour relation.

To this end I have sought to marry Marxist (or, perhaps more particularly, Poulantzian) and Foucauldian theoretical frameworks in a manner which will doubtless appear heretical to the purist disciples of either school. The attempt may be considered in some respects crude, but it has facilitated an explanation of both the source and the exercise of the power of the welfare state under capitalism. I have attempted to show the sense in which the state/claimant relationship is both economically determined and discursively constituted; in which the class forces incarnate in the apparatuses of the welfare state operate, not mysteriously or by magic, but through palpable disciplinary mechanisms.

In furthering this analysis, it has been necessary to resuscitate the much overworked expression, 'social control'. Under capitalist social relations, that which we call 'social policy' may be regarded and is perhaps better understood in terms of 'social control'. Under capitalism, the necessary regulation of our social lives is not so much a matter of policy (let alone 'social' policy), as a matter of untheorised and often unintended strategies of domination. Following a line of argument stemming partly from Pashukanis and partly out of the so-called State Derivation debate, I have contended that those aspects of life which the welfare state purports to regulate are ultimately fashioned and constrained by the internal dynamic of capitalism itself. The superintendent, juridical and administrative relationships between the welfare state and the welfare subject necessarily assume, in their essential form, the same character as the subordinating, individuating and exploitative relationships sustained by capital over wage labour.

To this abstract theory of the state's form, must be added an account of the concrete substance of the state's day to day operations (whether or not these conform to any declared 'policy'!). We must account for what Poulantzas calls the 'institutional materiality' of the state. Achieving this, requires a new, pragmatic concept of social control that is not merely a substitute term for 'class domination' or 'hegemony', but which refers to specific and tangible processes of subjection which occur through the welfare state. In place of crude instrumentalist theories of state welfare functions, we need to develop an understanding of the complex, subtle and ambiguous mechanisms of power through which such functions are invested: we require, in fact, a relational theory of power such as that offered by Foucault. If Marxist epistemological theory may be developed into a science of power relations within any given social formation, then post-structuralist or Foucauldian theory may be regarded as furnishing the necessary technological account of how those power relations can work. The notion of social control which is used in this book has therefore been constructed at the point where two quite different theoretical traditions meet.

Social control may be understood to operate at three distinct but overlapping levels: first, at the level of political settlement and rewards; second, at the level of penality and sanctions; third, at the level of the individual and of discipline. The historical emergence of the modern social security system can be interpreted as a story of development at each of these three levels of social control.

First, the development of social security may be understood as a story of change in which the begging bowl has at last been replaced by the 'social wage'. Central to this story of change is a discourse or philosophical tradition with elements of paternalism, humanitarianism and a positive view of population. The so-called social wage is a ransom paid by capital to labour through the state in a bid to secure social order. It is a form of compensation paid to society's lower orders for the adverse consequences or 'diswelfares' of capitalist development. It is an investment in the reproduction of a productive, or potentially productive, population.

Second, the history of the social security system is equally intelligible as a story of change from the spectacular and violent punishments once visited upon beggars and vagrants to a more subtle system of pecuniary sanctions and disincentives. Central to this story of change is a repressive discursive tradition, with elements of Malthusianism or anti-populationism. The social security system, whilst more sophisticated than the Poor Laws which preceded it, is similarly principally directed towards the non-productive population and several of the system's key features are calculated to repress and to deter that population.

Third, the evolution of social security provision is a story of emerging 'disciplinary techniques'. The multitude of rewards and punishments generated at the first two levels of social control are consolidated and translated into a coherent project of individualised discipline. Central to this story of change is a discourse and tradition emanating from philanthropy, utilitarianism and the 'self-help' ideal. Our complex system of social security provision has emerged through the refinement of techniques of surveillance and normalisation once directed against the mendicant and destitute. The argument identifies and defines three such disciplinary techniques: the 'case approach', by which the individual may be constituted as a 'case' and an object of state intervention; 'legalisation', by which the individual may be constituted as a juridical subject having a voluntaristic, rule-bound relationship to the state; and 'partitioning', by which the individual may be constituted as a victim of poverty and assigned to a particular class or category.

Moreover, poverty in advanced capitalist countries like the UK, is in effect a unique creation of the welfare state. Just as Foucault and others have argued that the techniques developed by the penal system have constituted criminality as a field of knowledge and as a problem to be managed, so the techniques of the social security system have constituted the phenomenon of 'modern' poverty. The modern poor are at one and the same time a discursive construction of social policy and a real target of the specific disciplinary techniques by which they are identified, accommodated and 'partitioned'. If the incidence of poverty is to be regarded as a measure of the effectiveness of social policy, then the evidence suggests that the modern welfare state has demonstrably failed us. However, the social security system is better understood for the successful manner in which it sustains poverty both as a regulated or manageable 'problem' and as a process of subjection: social policy interventions calculated to prevent or to relieve poverty have in fact contributed effectively to a strategy of social control.

In pursuit of this analysis, the argument has traced the history of social security tribunals since 1911, using such tribunals as a 'window' on to the social security system and as a 'case-study' in social security development. Because the form of the tribunal interpellates the form of the state/claimant relationship it has been possible to use an empirical study of the tribunal process to interpellate the social security system as a project in social control. This has served, incidentally, to illuminate a fertile area for further study of the conjuctions between administrative law and social policy; conjunctions such as exist where specialist tribunals adjudicate disputes and therefore provide a commentary upon the often obscure relations of power between the welfare state upon the one hand, and the 'consumer', 'client' or 'claimant' upon the other.

In the case of the modern Social Security Appeal Tribunal ('the SSAT'), its emergence in 1984 as a single tribunal followed an intensive period of consolidation in social security adjudiction: a process which plainly embodied a 'strategic objective' in the Foucauldian sense. The final unification of social insurance and social assistance tribunals reflected the superimposition of a legalised framework (with its discourse of individual rights) upon the case approach orientation of social assistance (with its discourse of individual needs). It served thereby generically to reconstruct the social security claimant, by investing her/him both as an individual 'case' (i.e. as an object of scrutiny) and as an individual 'subject'. Such a reconstruction, although it had a decipherable aim in terms of social discipline, could not be attributed to any specific locus of decision-making, since it emerged almost independently if not actually in spite of the intentions of either the government or its critics. The latest reforms to the social security system are intelligible in a similar way.

THE GREAT SOCIAL SECURITY DEBATE

The process of legislative 'reform' which reached its high point with the enactment and implementation of the Social Security Act 1986 ('SSA'86') began towards the end of 1983 when Norman Fowler, then Secretary of State for Health and Social Security, announced a series of reviews on various aspects of social security: on pensions, Housing Benefit, benefits for children and young people and on Supplementary Benefit. Mr Fowler claimed that 'Taken together, the various reviews I have set in hand constitute the most substantial examination of the social security system since the Beveridge Report 40 years ago' (House of Commons Hansard 2/4/84, Cols. 252–60).

The evidence submitted to the reviews was not published, nor were the reports of all but one of the various review teams (see Bennet 1985), but in mid-1985 the government did publish a Green Paper containing detailed proposals for the 'Reform of Social Security' (DHSS 1985b), which started from the premise that 'To be blunt, the British social security system has lost its way' (ibid.: para. 1.1). The government's proposals, however, were 'not based on a grand design for a new state system, but on a view of social security which allows important roles for both the state and individual provision' (ibid.: para. 1.14).

These proposals, fundamentally unaltered by public consultation, were republished at the end of 1985 as a White Paper (DHSS 1985c), in which Mr Fowler asserted on behalf of the government that:

Our aims ... remain the same. We want to see a simpler system of social security. We want to see more effective help going to those who most need it. We want to see a system which is financially secure. And we want to see more people looking forward to greater independence in retirement.

(DHSS 1985b: Preface)

Legislation based on this White Paper was introduced in 1986 and enacted later that year as the SSA'86. The conspicuous flourish with which the government had sought to prepare and introduce the new Act implied that it portended a root and branch reform of the social security system. However, the substance of the legislation and the single-minded determination with which the government initiated, framed and then defended its own proposals would seem to indicate more limited objectives and that the government had been guided by what Ward (1985) has characterised as certain 'secret agendas'.

First, it has been suggested, there was an agenda set by the DHSS itself, faced as it was by the impossibility of administering an arcane and crumbling benefit system. Second, there was an agenda set by the Treasury, which demanded far reaching cuts in public spending. Third, there was an agenda set by right-wing ideologues within the Conservative Party who wished to see a 'withering away' (see Boyson 1978) of the welfare state.

The outcome does not properly satisfy the dictates of any of these agendas, although at the level of social control it did portend:

1. a degree of retrenchment at the level of political settlement, in the sense that the value of the social wage has in several respects been diminished;
2. a shift in certain parts of the social security system towards greater penality and more explicit sanctions against claimants;
3. a refinement of certain of the disciplinary mechanisms inherent within benefits administration.

The question arises, therefore, whether a root and branch reform of the social security system itself is, in fact, possible within the parameters set by advanced capitalism. Certainly there have been demands for root and branch reform, but would the alternatives proposed radically change the social control effects of the social security system?

The great 1980s debate about the future of social security is conventionally regarded as a contest between, on the one hand, the 'New Right' approach and, upon the other, an established tradition of welfare liberalism. The debate has been said to mark the end of a post-war 'consensus' in relation to social security policy (e.g. Mack and Lansley 1985: ch. 8). Reverting, however, to the theoretical arguments outlined above, this latest debate has been rather more complex than that and, at the level of discourse, many pivotal areas of 'consensus' remain unrecognised and undisturbed. The debate has been pitched in several different registers. These registers seldom harmonise, but often elide or coincide with each other and are in themselves 'locked in' to the same discursive traditions which were identified in Chapter 3. Three such registers will be discussed: one in relation to each of the three levels of social control identified in this book.

The political settlement

The first of the registers in which debate occurred was concerned with the level of political settlement and, most crucially, whether social security's proper role lies in preventing or in merely relieving poverty; whether the adequacy of benefit levels should be assessed with reference to a 'participation' standard or merely a 'subsistence' standard. This debate was in essence a contest between the pro- and anti-populationist discursive traditions; between humanitarian and repressive discourse. At an intellectual level, the debate is a long-running one and it will continue, but the contest has for the time being been resolved by a fairly decisive retrenchment at the level of political settlement, reflected by a shift towards greater selectivity in social security. The SSA'86 may be seen as a bare reassertion of capital's domination over labour and a devaluation of the social wage but, to those enmeshed within their discursive traditions, it was a defeat for the welfare liberals and the welfare rights lobby. This is illustrated by the anger of organisations such as the Child Poverty Action Group, towards the government's manipulation of the social security reviews.

In particular, CPAG complained, groups giving evidence to the review of benefits for children and young persons were wrongfooted by having questions sprung upon them as to the role of the welfare state: is it to relieve poverty? is it to redistribute income?

The narrowly framed consultation documents issued to witnesses before the hearings had given no clue that such broad and fundamental questions might be asked and, remarking upon the unfairness of this tactic, Fran Bennet has protested:

> It is hard to see the value of any conclusion drawn from the various off the cuff answers to this crucial question, directed at individuals who had not been warned in advance.... However, it was increasingly evident from the reactions of the review team members that the 'correct' answer, so far as they were concerned, was that the overriding aim of the welfare state must be the relief of poverty ... [M]any groups giving the 'correct' answer may find they have unwittingly lent their support to government moves towards greater selectivity in the social security system, via an extension of means testing. For, while the 'relief of poverty' may at first sight seem a laudable goal, it demonstrates a distressingly narrow view of the various functions of social security provision. If such an aim were to be seen as the only justification for spending on social security benefits, it would mean ... declaring that the *prevention* of poverty had been struck from the list of desirable objectives.
> (Bennet 1985: 137; emphasis in original)

Similarly, while welfare liberals argued that benefits should be paid at levels which would allow all claimants to participate in the life of the community, the authors of the government's Green Paper on social security reform astutely evaded the question by emphasising the importance of correctly identifying those claimants whose needs are greatest (DHSS 1985b: para. 4.6). Instead, the government chose to interpret the Beveridge Report of forty years before as authority for the payment of subsistence standard benefits, whilst permitting or encouraging individuals to provide, so far as possible, for their own needs independently from the state (ibid.: paras. 1.8 and 6.6; DHSS 1985c: para. 1.7). So it was that elements of a philanthropic/self-help discourse elided with and obscured the competing pro- and anti-populationist discourses.

Incentives and disincentives

The second of the registers in which debate occurred was

concerned at the level of penality and sanctions, or more particularly, with 'incentives' and 'disincentives'. Underpinning the New Right ideal of minimal state intervention and competitive individualism has been a very old preoccupation with work incentives; a preoccupation which owes as much to a tradition of repressive/anti-populationist discourse as it does to any emboldened intellectual appeal to the efficacy of free market forces. Within such discourse, 'incentives' underwrite the fitness of the individual to survive; compulsion is the proper guarantee of productivity and independence; punishment is the proper reproach to idleness and dependency.

One of the articles of New Right faith has been that the social security system 'creates barriers to the creation of jobs, to job mobility or to people rejoining the labour force' and allows people at least to 'believe themselves better off out of work than in work' (DHSS 1985b: para. 1.12). Clearly then, the government wished to restore incentives by reducing assistance and increasing controls for unemployed claimants. In advancing specific proposals, however, the government was, for the most part, quite circumspect, not merely because of the vocal objections of humanitarians and welfare liberals, but because of a constraining consensus within the utilitarian/self-help tradition; a consensus in favour of inner compulsion and self-discipline rather than external compulsion and penality; a consensus in favour of vigilant regulation rather than indiscriminate sanctions.

The issue of 'incentives' was addressed by several of the participants in the 1980s debate, particularly in relation to the phenomena severally called the 'Poverty Trap' and the 'Unemployment Trap', or collectively called the 'Disincentive Trap' (see, for example, House of Commons 1982). Arguments against the New Right view have been characterised, on the one hand, by an emphasis upon the supposedly inherent satisfactions of being employed (i.e. over and above the level of remuneration) and, on the other hand, by arguments which bear upon structural factors, the so-called 'skills gap', and the need for re-training programmes (ibid.).

In the event, the immediate outcome in legislative terms was one which did penalise the unemployed to a greater extent, although, with one exception, in much the same way as before. The most significant area of change has been the shift towards the particular repression of young unemployed people. Errol Lawrence has perceptively observed that 'The idea of 'youth' ... , like that of 'retirement', is not simply a reference to some objective natural state of being, it is a social construction which has its origins in the capitalist division of labour' (Lawrence 1982: 55).

'Youth', as a potentially dangerous stage between the states of 'childhood' and 'adulthood', has been curiously problematised during the 1980s. Even before the SSA'86, cuts and changes in Supplementary Benefits for school leavers and other young people, the notorious Board and Lodging Allowance regulations, the introduction of the Youth Training Scheme and the rules associated with it (Allbeson 1985), all centred upon an obsessive ambivalence towards youth. The government repeatedly professed a desire to restore a role for the family and quite clearly implied that young people should ideally remain dependent upon their families rather than the state, at least until they achieve independence or adulthood. In particular, Margaret Thatcher insisted that unemployment 'should not be an option' for young people and that in essence they must either be dependent (as pupils or trainees) or independent (as wage earners) (Allbeson 1985). In effect, adulthood has been made synonymous with independence and childhood with dependence. The unemployed youth, belonging to neither category, constitutes both a threat and a scapegoat and, particularly within the structure of the new Income Support scheme and under the rules associated with the Youth Training, the (now defunct) Job Training and now the Employment Training Schemes (see Chapman and Tooze 1987; NATFHE 1984), it is young people of under 25 who are subjected to the severest of sanctions or disincentives. It is young people, therefore, who have borne the brunt of the ascendancy of a discourse within the repressive/anti-populationist tradition.

The individual claimant

The third register in which debate has occurred is concerned at the level of the individual claimant; it is concerned about the 'dignity' of claimants, the 'genuineness' of their needs and the 'clarity' of their entitlements. The discourse within this register of the debate belongs, of course, to the philanthropic/utilitarian/self-help tradition and, even when it contests with other discourses, it is a discourse which tends to carry consensus with it. New

Right reformers and welfare liberals alike were concerned about the 'efficiency' of the social security system. If all sides agreed that the system could be more efficient, there were different understandings and different emphases being given to the matter. For the government, and certain others, there was the question of benefits going where they ought not to go and their obsessive preoccupations with 'fraud and abuse'. For the welfare liberals, there was the question of low take-up rates (e.g. Bradshaw 1985) and their long-standing preoccupation with the stigma and humiliation associated with claiming benefits. What has enabled these divergent discourses to converge, however, has been the shared concern for efficiency and a shared and unquestioned conception of the individual as claimant in relation to the state.

This has perhaps most clearly emerged in the contributions to debate made by the National Consumer Council (1984). The NCC sought to assess the provision of social security in terms of a check list of criteria based on 'consumer principles': these included access, information, redress, etc., but drawing particularly on the Meade Report (1978), they included such criteria as 'adequacy' and 'dignity'. NCC took the view that claiming and receiving means-tested benefits was endemically undignified and argued with Meade that benefits should be provided not only at an adequate and guaranteed minimum level, but 'with dignity, so that the recipient perceives no loss of social esteem' (NCC 1984: para. 1.14).

Dignity is regarded as a fundamental attribute of citizenship and individuality. To confer such an attribute upon social security claimants is to cast them as consumers and to cast the state as the suppliers of a service. Just as the formal bourgeois concept of 'freedom' mystifies and conceals the disparities of power between wage labourer and employer, so the ideal concept of 'dignity' would mystify and conceal the disparities of power between the social security claimant and the state.

For its part, the government would not seem to have anywhere used the word 'dignity' in relation to claimants, but they do, none the less, speak of individual 'responsibility' and 'independence' (DHSS 1985b: para. 1.14). They claim to seek a 'partnership between the individual and the state'. The government's intention was to reduce the provision of state benefits in favour of private provision but, at the level of rhetoric, they still project a relationship based on dignity between individual and state: relations of power are reduced to formal responsibility and illusory independence. These emphases, recurrent throughout the debate, upon dignity, self-sufficiency and individuality are vital elements to the disciplinary technique which we have called the 'case approach'; a technique which uniquely constitutes the individual as a claimant.

Another of the consumer principles advocated by the NCC is the criterion of 'simplicity', and another of the deficiencies of the social security system upon which all participants in the debate were agreed related to the complexity of the system. One of the government's main objectives was stated to be that 'the social security system must be simpler to understand and easier to administer' (DHSS 1985b: para. 1.12). Regardless of whether such an objective has been achieved (and it has already been argued that by and large it has not), official government discourse makes the claim that the reforms to income-related benefits are such that 'claimants will no longer need detailed knowledge of the system to claim their full rights' (DHSS 1985c: para. 1.29).

This claim must be regarded, not as an intention which has failed, but as a further statement of the discursively constituted relationship between the claimant as consumer/citizen/juridical subject and the state. The substance of that relationship and the relations of power which underpin it are obscured by a bid for formal simplicity. The supposed clarity of the entitlements bestowed upon the individual claimant lies, not in the technical substance of such entitlements, but in a formal global conception of claimants' 'full rights'. Throughout the discourse of debate, therefore, persists this strand which bears upon the disciplinary technique which we have called 'legalisation'; a technique which constitutes the claimant as a juridical subject.

Another of the government's stated objectives for the social security system was that it 'must be capable of meeting genuine need' (DHSS 1985b: para. 1.12); words which struck a chord – albeit for different reasons – with opposite ends of the political spectrum. For CPAG, for example, meeting genuine needs is a question of redistributing income to particular groups in society or to particular people at particular stages of their lives – to families with children, the sick and disabled, the unemployed, etc. (Lister 1987). For the Adam Smith Institute, however, the failing of the existing social security system was that it 'in fact hurts the poor by spending valuable resources on those who do not really need them' (Omega Report 1984: 4).

Implicit in each of these conflicting arguments is a view that there are certain people or groups with 'real' needs and others with no such needs. Each argument embraces in its own way that original Lutheran injunction – that everybody should 'know their own paupers' and assist only them (see Chapter 3). None of the participants in the debate, whether they argued for the prevention or merely the relief of poverty, would have dissociated themselves unequivocally from the government's stated ambition – 'to see more effective help going to those who most need it' (DHSS 1985c: Preface). The 'targeting' of social security benefits has thus become a matter of consensus, in spite of wide ranging disagreements as to the selection and identification of 'targets'. As already observed, this acceptance of targeting as common currency within social policy discourse has given fillip to the disciplinary technique here called 'partitioning' – a technique which constitutes each claimant as a member of a highly specific group or status category.

Counterproposals for reform

Injected into this complex debate were certain very specific counterproposals for the reform of social security. There were essentially three such proposals and, while each was in reality a development of theoretical approaches which pre-dated the particular schemes presented and each enjoyed support from quarters other than the groups who made the actual presentations, they have become associated with the respective names of the three organisations who submitted them. First there was the National Council for Voluntary Organisations' scheme, based on the concept of a Basic Income Guarantee or Social Dividend (Ashby 1984). Second, there was the Institute of Fiscal Studies' scheme, based on the concept of Tax Credits (and having elements in common with earlier ideas of a Negative Income Tax) (Dilnot et al. 1984). Finally, there was the National Consumer Council scheme, which urged a return to the original intentions of the Beveridge scheme by revitalising contributory benefits, but with relaxed contribution conditions and reduced means-tested supplementation (NCC 1984).

This is not the place for a full exposition or critique of these various hypothetical schemes, but in order to conclude the theoretical project contained within this book, it is necessary to draw out key strands from each scheme in order to show that even the most radical alternative proposals for social security reform are in reality 'locked in' to the same discursive traditions.

The concept of a Basic Income (as NCVO call it) or Social Dividend gives ultimate expression to the notion of the 'social wage' and Peter Ashby of the NCVO has acknowledged that this 'would mean that society would have to make a decisive break in the historic link between employment and income' (Ashby 1984: 20).

What is clear, however, is that even those who advocate a Basic Income do not propose to break the relationship between capital and labour, only to obscure it behind the individual relationships of claimants to the state. Their object is to give every individual a 'positive stake in the economy' by distributing the benefits of growth in Gross National Product through the social security system, rather than through the wage packet. But crucial to this project remains a bourgeois concept of the individual subject and the questions of individual 'incentives', 'choice' and 'dignity'; words which are prominent within the NCVO's argument. Intersecting the paternalistic/humanitarian/pro-populationist discourse of the Social Dividend advocates there are elements from other discourses which limit the focus of attention to the individual claimant or recipient. Even a fully developed Basic Income scheme, according to NCVO, would require that additional help be given for 'cases of exceptional need, for example, single parent families' (Ashby 1984: 14). Claimants would still be 'cases' and certain such cases would still be partitioned off as needing particular attention. The writer's own view is that a Social Dividend scheme would almost certainly represent a necessary component to any means of distribution under socialist relations of production, but as a social policy intervention under capitalism, it would inevitably be formed or deformed as a vehicle for social control. This contention, however, will be more fully discussed below when Bill Jordan's more recent work on this subject is considered.

The underlying principle of the IFS Tax Credit scheme, of earlier Negative Income Tax proposals, and even of proposals such as those advanced by the Social Democratic Party (1983), is the extension of means testing to every individual in society. This would make possible what Dilnot *et al.* describe as 'a savage but selective, retrenchment of the benefit system' (1984: 5). Their belief, which is very much in tune with the New Tory approach, is that 'Benefits do not go to those who are entitled to them, and do go to those who are not entitled to them or who should not be entitled to them' (Dilnot *et al.* 1984: 2).

The IFS scheme provides for a combined and cost-efficient tax and social security system resting on the principle that, for most households, 'provision for children, old age, dependent spouses and other contingencies is a matter for these households rather than the state' (ibid.: 5).

But this scheme, whilst clearly within the repressive/anti-populationist discursive tradition, was none the less dependent upon a massive extension of surveillance and enquiry into individual household circumstances. The use of computers and new technology, it was argued, would make such enquiry 'less demeaning', but the impersonal and all-pervasive surveillance thereby entailed would amount to a radical enhancement of disciplinary technique.

The principle which underlies the calls made, not just by the NCC, but by organisations such as the Society of Civil and Public Servants (1985), was for a return to insurance principles and this book has already discussed the significance of the social insurance principle in relation to the philanthropic/utilitarian/self-help discursive tradition. The insurance principle embodies notions of responsibility and self-help; of individual rights and legal status; of claims based on contingencies that are related to a priori definitions and statuses.

These, however, have not been the only alternative proposals for the reform of social security, although they serve to illustrate the parameters within which the 'great debate' took place. Other influential participants in the debate, like CPAG, have refrained from putting forward comprehensive alternative schemes, but continue to advocate piecemeal reforms, building upon the 'best elements of the present system' (Lister 1987) and remaining therefore essentially within the framework upon which the present system is founded. Also, outside the mainstream of the debate, there have been proposals such as the explicitly 'left-wing' reforms proposed by Esam *et al.* (1985).

Esam *et al.*'s 'socialist radicalism', as might be expected, is invested with elements of a humanitarian/pro-populationist discourse but, unlike proposals for Basic Income or Social Dividend schemes, lays emphasis (as has the Labour Party since its 1986 Annual Conference) upon the need for a Statutory Minimum Wage. Such a device would ensure a more direct or obvious relationship between social welfare and the costs which capital must bear. Additionally, there are elements of utilitarian/self-help discourse evidenced in Esam *et al.*'s emphasis upon individual 'rights', which are seen as encompassing issues such as privacy, dignity (once again !) and confidentiality, and to extend to an 'adequate right of redress' (from which, a continuing role for tribunals might be assumed) (Esam *et al.* 1985: 38). Esam *et al.*'s scheme, however, demonstrates, with commendable clarity, the fundamental objectives which must be reconciled by the welfare state under capitalist social relations, since it proposes just two distinct kinds of state benefit: 'positional benefits' for those without wages for reasons such as caring responsibilities, sickness or unemployment; and 'cost-related' benefits for those with 'exceptional' costs caused for example by high rents or disablement.

In essence, this left-wing analysis makes the same theoretical distinction as one which is contained in the essentially right-wing IFS analysis; a distinction between 'contingent' and 'income related' benefits (Dilnot *et al.* 1984: ch. 3). Esam *et al.*, on the one hand, and Dilnott *et al.*, upon the other, approach the distinction referred to from different directions and they propose very different ways of achieving, within an integrated system, two basic goals. But they are the same two goals which they identify: 'positional' or 'contingency' provision according to the claimant's position or standing within the relations of production and reproduction; 'cost-related' or 'income-related' provision according to the personal 'needs' of the individual claimant.

Only at the extremities of the 'great debate' has this distinction been made in these particular terms and yet, even here, the fundamental criteria, once understood, are never challenged. The acceptance of such goals constitutes the basis of the state/claimant relationship as a relation of power which derives (i) from the *wage relation* which determines the modality of claimants' positions in relation both to productive or 'economic' and reproductive or 'social' processes; and (ii) from the *commodity form* which determines the modality of claimants' 'needs'.

The wage-relation and the commodity form

To explain this further, it is necessary to return to arguments raised in Chapter 2, which contended that the form of the state and of welfare provision is derived from the form of the wage-relation. The wage-relation may be understood readily enough as a form which constitutes the relationship between the 'free' labourer and capital. The 'dull compulsion' of this fetishised form can thus constitute the individual, at a more general level, in relation both to the means of production at large and the means of his/her own subsistence. The states of employment and unemployment; of youth and retirement; of disablement and able-bodiedness are all socially constructed and comprehended with reference to the wage-relation. The power that is vested in the state as provider assumes the same form as the power wielded by capital (as employer) over labour (as workers), although it is incarnated and exercised by means of concrete and specific disciplinary techniques, such as legalisation and partitioning by which the 'positional' identity of each social security claimant is established.

Similarly, the commodity form may be understood as constituting the relationships between individuals as legal subjects and, most particularly, between the providers and consumers of goods and services. The individual may thus be constituted, not merely as a legal subject and consumer of commodities, but as a client or claimant in relation to a state having power to define, as much as to satisfy, the individual's 'needs'. Because the needs related to personal subsistence are 'commodified', they become specific to the individual as consumer, as client, as claimant, or as a 'case'. Needs are dictated by the commodity form, and the power that is vested in the state as provider assumes the same form as the distributive power that is wielded by capital (as owners of the means of production) over labour (as mass consumers of essential produce). That power, moreover, is incarnated and exercised by means of concrete and specific disciplinary techniques, such as legalisation (once again) and the 'case approach'.

This then is the sense in which social security is about social control.

This is not to say that different approaches to social security could not produce quite different effects in terms of social control, but the contention of this book is that social control will be implicit in any social security system which operates within capitalist social relations. Social policy, as a discursively constituted field of debate, is 'locked in' to a continuing series of dilemmas or contradictions perpetuated through a number of continuing discursive traditions. Ultimately, however, social policy is constrained to be a vehicle for the disciplinary mechanisms by which state power may be exercised.

SOCIAL SECURITY AND 'NEW TIMES'

This book has demonstrated that the developing strategic objectives of apparatuses, like the social security system, exhibit an extraordinary degree of historical continuity and it is therefore misleading to analyse the reforms of the 1980s solely in terms of the effects of the economic, political and cultural phenomena that have characterised the 1980s. None the less, it is important to consider the relevance and the influence of 'post-Fordism', 'Thatcherism' and 'post-modernity'; it is useful to apply the analysis of 'New Times' (see in particular Hall 1988 and Campbell *et al.* 1989) to our understanding of the social security system.

The 'modern' age of mass production has been supplanted by a new age in which industrial production can now be decentralised and made increasingly flexible, whilst control over such processes can be concentrated around fewer and less visible global sources of power. Conventional and constitutional forms of political resistance have been paralysed by the ascendancy of elective dictatorship, the emasculation of local and corporate state provision and the burgeoning of a more secretive and authoritarian central state. The immense diversity in goods and services produced is reflected in a contrived diversity in tastes and life-styles, a fragmentation of social life and a brand of consumer individualism which is nurtured, managed and paradoxically unified through expanded means of mass communication.

Discovering the underclass

Part and parcel of this process of restructuring, claim the proponents of the 'New Times' analysis, is the creation of a 'one-third/two-thirds society', of a 'new chasm in society between the excluded one-third and a more prosperous but highly differentiated two-thirds' (Campbell *et al.* 1989: 11). Certainly, statistics show that, in 1985, 29 per cent of the UK population had incomes which did not exceed 140 per cent of the prevailing level of Supplementary Benefit and who, on one definition, could be said to be 'in or on the margins of poverty' (Oppenheim 1988: 5) (and see discussion in Chapter 4). The argument of Dahrendorf (1987), for example, (to which we referred in Chapter 1) is that there is a sizeable 'underclass' which is being cut adrift from the life-style and opportunities of the more prosperous 'overclass'. The process may in some senses be even further advanced in the USA but, while proponents of the idea can be accused of running ahead of the evidence (see Pahl 1988: 258–9), the notion that a British underclass is emerging is gaining ground (see, for example, Field 1989).

The growth in 'New Times' of a modern underclass may be attributed in part to the structural and technological transformation of industrial production, and in part to underlying demographic changes which have expanded that proportion of the population that is not of 'working age'. The extent to which such an 'underclass' is marginalised from the 'overclass' or from the 'productive working-class', is attributed variously to prejudice, stigma and/or the effects of low income. The argument here is that what distinguishes and marks off the members of the posited 'underclass' is not the mere fact of their exclusion from 'work' or from productive relations, but the effects of the disciplinary partitioning mechanism identified in the preceding pages of this book. This mechanism identifies the grounds on which any individual is excluded from supposedly 'normal' productive relations. It assigns meanings to such grounds and constitutes a particular identity for the excluded.

Thus the social security system of 'New Times' is not distinguished merely by its parsimony or its preoccupation with fraud and abuse, but by the extent to which it continues increasingly to afford quite different and distinctive treatment to the various categories of claimant which it creates; to retirement pensioners, to single parents, to the sick and disabled, to the unemployed, etc. All these categories may be partitioned and sub-partitioned with reference to criteria pertaining to age, gender, dependency, health, aptitude and so forth. These criteria pertain to the precise circumstances, standing and potential of the claimant in relation to the formal sphere of economic production and social reproduction. In this way, the so-called 'underclass' may be minutely partitioned, not only from some other class or classes, but within itself, and the mechanism by which this is achieved is far more palpable than 'prejudice' or 'stigma', yet far more subtle than the oppressive consequences of 'relative material deprivation'.

The term 'underclass' is therefore a misnomer. There is no homogeneous, anonymous mass existing beneath the margins, but a highly heterogeneous and precisely identified population of more or less regular social security claimants. One of the principal means by which such a population may be constituted, ordered and sustained is that here described as 'partitioning'. In an age when there are no longer any simple class distinctions to be drawn between the 'haves' and the 'have nots', partitioning can shoulder class aside and create a more immediate dimension of subjection.

The term 'overclass' is equally a misnomer. Whilst the majority of the population may enjoy a tolerable or even comfortable existence and indeed a degree of illusory freedom, the Thatcherite principles on which popular capitalism is founded deny people the basis for any collective identity. Indeed, Margaret Thatcher has claimed (in an interview for 'Women's Own' magazine in October 1987) that 'there is no such thing as society'. However, the allure of popular capitalism lies, not just in the chances it offers for personal self-enrichment, but also in the illusions it creates about consumer sovereignty and about ownership and self-interest. Consumer choice, home ownership and share ownership are presented and seen as means of empowering the ordinary citizen, in so far that these things now fall potentially within the spending power of up to two-thirds of the population.

Discovering citizenship

Just as society has been restructured, so has the basis of citizenship. Margaret Thatcher and former Home Secretary, Douglas Hurd, sought in the late 1980s to promote the concept of the responsible and neighbourly 'active citizen'. Their view of citizenship was founded on property, in so far that without property, as Ignatieff puts it, 'the citizen is passive, a ward of the state, a dependent on the benefit cheque, the social services and the council housing department' (Ignatieff 1989: 34).

Concepts of citizenship have thus become central to the politics of 'New Times'. The New Right's attempt to forge a citizenship based on exclusion has been mirrored by attempts, in several quite disparate quarters, to recapture a more ancient concept of democratic citizenship as an idealised basis for social unity and inclusionary politics; a citizenship based on prescriptive values, rather than property (e.g. Keane 1988; Labour Party 1988 and the campaign, 'Charter 88', launched in December 1988 by the magazine *New Statesman and Society*). To the extent that 'welfare rights' (and therefore social security benefit entitlements) are seen explicitly as a component of citizenship, the old discursive consensus remains undisturbed. The foundations of the disciplinary technique, here called legalisation, remain unseen and intact and the social security claimant, as a formally free and equal citizen, must none the less be subject to rules of entitlement which will inevitably remain to some extent conditional upon behaviour (see Plant 1988: 15).

The new individualism of 'New Times' has not, however, signalled the death of altruism. Social attitude surveys and opinion polls show consistently that most people are essentially altruistic; they still value the caring and sharing principles of the 'traditional' welfare state (Taylor-Gooby 1985). The most tangible testimony to the survival of altruism has been the resurgence of charity in the 1980s, with spectacular media events such as 'Band Aid' concerts and 'Telethon' appeals. What is significant is that, by and large, the anonymous recipients of the charity of 'New Times' are not the modern poor, but distant or symbolic objects of need or pity, such as the famine victims of Africa or 'Children in Need'. And, in spite of its professed belief in the values of welfarism, the UK electorate throughout the 1980s has rejected the images of a 'caring society' projected by the Labour Party, the Liberal Party and the SDP. The reason for this rejection, as Ignatieff (1989) points out, is that such images have come to imply an overweaning, overprofessionalised 'nanny state' which neglects the demands of the individual for 'justice'.

The consensus of 'New Times' has thus been for a retreat from statism and, while Thatcherism has projected its version of this consensus, the Labour Party (1989) has responded belatedly with its own. Within the context of its new vision of 'supply side socialism', the Labour Party has none the less retreated, not only to such established concepts as 'social insurance', but to a discourse which counterposes poverty with independence: the way to combat poverty is for individuals to realise independence and the task of government is therefore to create 'pathways out of poverty' (Labour Party 1989: 29). It is a discourse which, while allowing for an expansion of state social security provision, is anxious to emphasise the 'enabling' role of the state and to speak in terms of opening doors to those who have been denied opportunity and of the nurturing of individual talent. It is a discourse very much in tune with 'New Times', but which is, in some respects, strangely reminiscent of the discourse of nineteenth-century philanthropy and the Charity Organisation Society. It is a discourse which preserves the foundations of the disciplinary technique, which has here been called the case approach, and which, while espousing minimal intervention, is preoccupied with the habits and economies of the poor and with directing each 'case' along prescribed or appropriate 'pathways'.

The Basic Income proposal

Perhaps the most radical and detailed design for an alternative social security system, and one that might constitute an apt response to the nature of 'New Times', has been that furnished by Bill Jordan (1985 and 1987). It is a version of a Basic Income or Social Dividend scheme such as we have already discussed and as is supported, for example, by the Green Party (1988: 73). Jordan's 'design' is an important, if flawed, attempt to envisage a welfare state based upon the same principles of sharing and co-operation which characterise every-day informal human interactions between family, relatives and friends. The attempt is important because it touches upon key issues relating to social control; it is flawed because it never quite transcends fetishised concepts of 'fairness' and 'autonomy' and because it ommits any effective analysis of power relations.

> The fundamental idea of my proposal is that individual citizens should have their basic needs guaranteed before they enter the labour market or the family, so that they have security of income support as well as health care as a precondition of co- operation and fairness. So, instead of trying to compensate individuals for

economic or domestic disadvantages through redistribution, the state should provide a basis of equality for all spheres of co-operation, and allow people to enter them or withdraw from them as they choose, secure in the knowledge that in the long run they will seek fairness in sharing their product, at the same time as seeking their own individual welfare.

(Jordan 1987: 216)

Such a design, says Jordan, would work in a capitalist market economy as well as in a socialist planned economy, and indeed he analyses, in some detail, both the attractions of the scheme to free market liberals (because of the 'freedom' it offers the individual) and the limitations to which the scheme would be subject under capitalism (because basic guaranteed incomes would remain at or below subsistence levels and other social services would be provided principally through the market rather than the state). But even under capitalism, the claim made by Jordan for such a scheme is that it would dispense with the 'unpleasantness of state coercion and surveillance' (Jordan 1985: 293). In practice, however, a Basic Income Guarantee scheme would require various forms of benefit supplementation (including means-tested assistance with housing costs). It would still leave the state in control of the final incomes and living standards of a very substantial proportion of the population. In actual practice, most versions of the Basic Income/Social Dividend concept begin to bear an uncanny resemblance to the more practicable versions of the Negative Income Tax/Tax Credit concept. The more they are scrutinised, just as in the final scene of George Orwell's *Animal Farm*, the more the pigs begin to look like men and the men begin to look like pigs! Far from expanding the co-operative capacities of ordinary people, such a scheme leaves capital in command of both wage structure (and thereby the size of the tax base) and the market (and thereby the cost of subsistence), leaving the state in the same mediating and distributive role and with the same powers of coercion and surveillance.

The value of Jordan's contribution, however, lies in his portrayal of a concept of 'fairness' based on co-operation, reciprocity and consent. This portrayal gives substance to a popular approach to welfare founded, not upon moral fetishes, but upon what Pashukanis (1978) once called 'the clear and simple concepts of harm and advantage'. Sadly, ideas expressed with clarity in one breath, Jordan muddies in the next with references to fairness based on bourgeois notions of equity, compensation and equivalence. These are fetishised concepts which derive from the commodity form and the competitive sphere of market relations. Jordan correctly identifies the importance of the recurring preoccupations of both social policy makers and popular opinion with the 'problem' of the 'free rider' or cheat, but he incorrectly attributes the phenomenon to a mere failure of trust. He fails to detect that the fetishist nature of such preoccupations is traceable or derivable from the form of the wage-relation. If the source of all income, including the tax revenues for social security transfers, is perceived to be the wage-relation, then even the 'social' wage is a matter of what capital will pay and/or what labour can extract. Mutual support and provision for social needs, instead of being the purpose or object of material production, becomes an incumberance upon the productive process and the subject of struggle. In this way, all social security spending may be regarded as a 'burden' (cf. Esam *et al.* 1985: 148) and each net beneficiary must have some justification for receiving the fruits of others' sacrifice. So long as the wage-relation is preserved intact, the question of trust does not and indeed cannot enter into it.

It is Jordan's view that the provision of a guaranteed basic minimum for all would ensure individual autonomy and remove all elements of compulsion. This, of course, is to misunderstand the nature of power. The state, if it is to exist at all, cannot be neutral. Even within the most democratic socialist society, the capacities and the power of the people would be vested in specific regulative and decision-making agencies (cf. Hirst 1980). Equally, the individual, if s/he is to have a social existence, cannot be entirely autonomous: the elusive goal of autonomy is a fiction generated by the bourgeois doctrine of rights. Where Jordan is right, however, is in suggesting that 'welfare' need not be a matter of paternalistic or bureaucratic service delivery, but that it could stem from everyday 'laws of co-operation'. Just as the influence of Adam Smith's imaginary 'invisible hand' depends upon the socially constructed compulsion to acquire or accumulate, so Jordan posits the possibility of a 'hidden hand of welfare' arising out of a socially constructed compulsion to co-operate and to share. But, says Jordan, 'the hidden hand of welfare does not work, as Smith claims the market does, without the conscious intention of human agents' (Smith 1987: 214). And here Jordan is in effect making the same distinction as this book has sought to make between social control (which may be largely unseen and unintended) and social policy (which would give expression to popular experience).

A Basic Income or Social Dividend could constitute the basis of a distributive social policy, but not if it is to be ensnared within a state form which specifically and necessarily mediates the power of capital over labour. There is purpose in generating alternative social policy programmes in response to 'New Times', but only if they can be linked to an entirely new theoretical and discursive tradition and founded in a form of popular resistance to social control.

BEYOND SOCIAL CONTROL

The seemingly impossible challenge for the modern poor, for 'the left', for anti-poverty campaigners and for those, for example, in the welfare rights and advice centre movement who engage with the social control effects of the social security system, is to conceive an effective counter-strategy.

By the close of the 1980s, public debate about poverty in the UK had descended to the level of pantomime ritual. While the poverty lobby continued vigorously to assert that poverty still exists, John Moore, then Secretary of State for Social Security, cried, 'Oh no it doesn't' (see Chapter 4). 'Oh yes it does', the poverty lobby retorted, and so it went on. What is significant about John Moore's attempts to deny the existence of poverty is that he was not so much dispossessing the poor, as enjoining the poor to dispossess themselves. To the extent that the subjective experience of poverty may be associated with the objective act of claiming social security, that act is constituted as an act of self-abasement, as an exercise in self-discipline.

It is no longer an answer to claim that social security claimants must assert themselves as citizens, when they must thereby define and defend themselves as the victims of poverty. It is no longer enough to seek for social security claimants a guarantee of 'normal' consumption, if they must still justify a conditional right to a comfortable survival. It is no longer possible to pretend that social security claimants may identify themselves with labour in class terms, when they are identified and individually constituted in terms of their exclusion from labour.

The struggle of the modern poor and of the social security claimant must be constituted as a movement in its own right, addressing a very particular dimension of oppression, just as the women's movement and the black people's and anti-racist movements have been constituted. It must be constituted, at the level of popular discourse, as something which transcends the formal contest between individual and state (such as is theatrically played out before the SSAT) but which engages with the substantive nature of the social control to which social security claimants are subject. It must be a struggle through which the poor become unmanageable; a struggle, not fostered through compassion, but born out of anger; a struggle founded upon resistance to social control.

Foucault has argued that 'where there is power there is resistance' (1981b: 95). The SSAT, for example, is capable of accommodating the resistance of social security claimants to the power of the welfare state, but the tribunal is none the less a site of resistance. Foucault contends that resistance can never be external to power relationships. Resistance does not intrude upon such relationships, but on the contrary plays the role of 'adversary, target, support or handle'. The very existence of power relationships depends upon a multiplicity of points of resistance and it is only 'the strategic codification of these points of resistance which makes a revolution possible' (ibid.: 96).

The latter proposition seems to imply that popular resistance can make power, like the tide, flow in the opposite direction, but Poulantzas has challenged Foucault's conceptions, saying

> For if power is already there, if every power situation is immanent in itself, *why should there ever be resistance? From where* would such resistance come and *how would it ever be possible?*
>
> (Poulantzas 1980: 149; emphasis in original)

For Poulantzas, resistance is a matter of popular struggle. But, like Foucault, he argues that such struggles cannot be autonomous or external to the state, rather he says they are 'inscribed' within the apparatuses of the state. The democratic road to socialism would consist, not of seizing and modifying state power, but:

in the spreading, development, reinforcement, co-ordination and direction of those diffuse centres of resistance which the masses always possess within the State networks, in such a way that they become the real centres of power on the strategic terrain of the State.

(Poulantzas: 258).

From Foucault's anarchic concept of resistance, Poulantzas returns to the necessity of struggle, as informed human action.

What we can perhaps, therefore, begin to see is the possibility that the state and the social security system as relations of power may be confronted, not 'head on', nor even piecemeal by scattered acts of resistance, but by constructing a popular resistance based on a knowledge of the social security system as a vehicle for social control, rather than as the product of 'good' or 'bad' social policy. We cannot rewrite social policy effectively unless and until social security claimants, and other 'clients' of the welfare state, begin to resist what is here defined as social control. It is in such resistance, and resistances like it, that alternatives to the wage-relation and the commodity form may come to be popularly understood.

The basis for such alternatives may, as Jordan suggests, already exist in many of our daily reciprocal and co-operative human transactions, but the key to such understanding will lie, not in passively generated intellectual insights, but in an active process which will empower ordinary people and encode their demands at the level of popular discourse. The precise nature of such a process cannot perhaps be predicted in advance but, if indeed such a process is to occur at all, it is clear that the social security system should be one of its key targets or sites.

The necessary counter-strategy must therefore be one which disrupts the binary opposition between dependence and independence; a strategy which propogates a new 'resistance culture' as an alternative and an antidote to the 'dependency culture' posited by John Moore to characterise the world of the social security claimant. Such a resistance culture would subvert the common-sense notion that social security claimants must aspire to an impossible normality in which real people are supposed to be 'consumers' in search of 'choice', and would instead portray claimants as people in search of survival and control over their own lives. This resistance culture would accord new status and meaning to being non-employed; new value to the 'work' performed by parents, carers, friends, neighbours and community activists; new substance to the creativity of labour beyond the 'workplace'; new assurance and determination to those with practical needs associated with sickness or disability. Resistance culture would found a logic running contrary to that of the rules on which the social security system is based; a logic which, by transcending the formal basis of that system, would necessarily confront the system's underlying strategy of social control.

REFERENCES

Abel, R. (ed.) (1983) *The Politics of Informal Justice*, Vol. 1, New York, Academic Press.
Abel-Smith, B. & Stevens, R. (1967) *Lawyers and the Courts*, London, Heinemann.
Adler, M., Burns, E. & Johnson, R. (1975) 'The Conduct of Tribunal Hearings' in Adler, M. & Bradley, A. (eds) *Justice, Discretion & Poverty*, Abingdon, Oxon., Professional Books.
Alcock, P. (1985) 'Welfare State: Safety Net or Poverty Trap', *Marxism Today* Vol. 29 No. 7.
Allbeson, J. (1985) 'Seen but not heard: Young People' in Ward, S. (ed.) *DHSS in Crisis*, London, Child Poverty Action Group.
Allbeson, J. & Smith, R. (1984) *We Don't Give Clothing Grants Any More: The 1980 Supplementary Benefit Scheme*, London, Child Poverty Action Group.
Althusser, L. (1971) 'Ideology and Ideological State Apparatuses' in *Lenin and Philosophy and Other Essays*, London, New Left Books.
Annette, J. (1979) 'Bentham's Fear of Hob-goblins: Law, Political Economy and Social Discipline' in National Deviancy Conference/Conference of Socialist Economists (eds) *Capitalism and the Rule of Law*, London, Hutchinson.
Ashby, P. (1984) *Social Security After Beveridge – What Next?* London, Bedford Square Press/NCVO.
Atkinson, A.B. & Micklewright, J. (1988) *Turning the Screw: Benefits for the Unemployed 1979–1988*, Suntory-Toyota International Centre for Economics and Related Disciplines, London, London School of Economics.
Bankowski, Z. & Mungham, G. (1976) *Images of Law*, London, Routledge and Kegan Paul.
Bankowski, Z. & Nelken, D. (1981) 'Discretion as a Social Problem' in Adler, M. & Asquith, S. (eds) *Discretion and Welfare*, London, Heinemann.
Banks, M.H. & Ullah, P. (1986) *Youth Unemployment: Social and*

REFERENCES

Psychological Perspectives, London, Department of Employment Research Paper No. 61.

Bell, K. (1969) *Tribunals in the Social Services*, London, Routledge & Kegan Paul.

—— (1970) 'Administrative Tribunals since Franks', *Social & Economic Administration*, Vol. 4 No. 4.

—— (1973) *Disequilibrium in Welfare*, Inaugural Lecture, University of Newcastle upon Tyne.

—— (1975) *Research Study on Supplementary Benefit Appeal Tribunals: Review of Main Findings: Conclusions: Recommendations*, London, HMSO.

—— (1982) 'Social Security Tribunals – A General Perspective', *Northern Ireland Legal Quarterly*, Vol. 33 No. 2.

Bell, K., Collison, P., Turner, S. & Webber, S. (1974) 'National Insurance Local Tribunals: A Research Study – Part I', *Journal of Social Policy*, Vol. 3 No. 4.

—— (1975) 'National Insurance Local Tribunals: A Research Study – Part II', *Journal of Social Policy*, Vol. 4 No. 1.

Bennet, F. (1985) 'Closed doors and closing options' in Ward, S. (ed.) *DHSS in Crisis*, London, Child Poverty Action Group.

Bentham, J. (1970) *An Introduction to the Principles of Morals and Legislation*, (Burns, J.H. & Hart, H.L.A.), London, Athlone Press.

Bevan, A. (1978) *In Place of Fear*, London, Quartet.

Beveridge, W. (1942) *Social Insurance and Allied Services* ('The Beveridge Report') Cmd. 6404, London, HMSO.

Board of Trade (1913) *Report on Unemployment Insurance*, Cd. 6965, London, HMSO.

Booth, C. (1888) 'Conditions and Occupations of the People of East London and Hackney, 1887', *Journal of the Royal Statistical Society*, Vol. 80 No. 1.

Bosanquet, N. (1983) 'Poverty under Thatcher' in Loney, M., Boswell, D. & Clarke, J. (eds) *Social Policy and Social Welfare*, Milton Keynes, Open University Press.

Boyson, R. (1978) *Centre Forward*, London, Temple Smith.

Bradley, A. (1975) 'National Assistance Tribunals and the Franks Report' in Adler, M. & Bradley, A. (eds) *Justice, Discretion & Poverty*, Abingdon, Oxon., Professional Books.

Bradshaw, J. (1985) 'Tried and Found Wanting: the Take-Up of Means-Tested Benefits' in Ward, S. (ed.) *DHSS in Crisis*, London, Child Poverty Action Group.

Burkeman, S. (1975) 'We Go by the Law Here' in Adler, M. & Bradley, A. (eds) *Justice, Discretion & Poverty*, Abingdon, Oxon., Professional Books.

Burton, J. (1987) *Would Workfare Work? A Feasibility Study of the Workfare System to Replace Long-Term Unemployment in the UK*, University of Buckingham, Employment Research Centre.

Campaign Against Poverty (1989) *Decade of Despair*, Manchester, Campaign Against Poverty.

REFERENCES

Campbell, B., Darke, M., Davis, T., Green, D., DeGroot, J., Halverson, R., Hart, S., Jacques, M., Leadbeater, C., Pearce, B., Rodrigues, J., Stewart, M. & Temple, N. (1989) *Manifesto for New Times – A Communist Strategy for the 1990s*, London, Marxism Today.

Campbell, D. & Connor, S. (1987) *On the Record: Surveillance, Computers and Privacy – The Inside Story*, London, Michael Joseph.

CAO (Chief Adjudication Officer) (1985) *Annual Report for 1984/85*, London, HMSO.

—— (1987) *Annual Report for 1985/86*, London, HMSO.

Chapman, P. & Tooze, M. (1987) *The Youth Training Scheme in the UK*, Aldershot, Avebury.

Coates, K. & Silburn, R. (1970) *Poverty: the Forgotten Englishmen*, Harmondsworth, Penguin.

Cohen, J.L. (1921) *Insurance Against Unemployment*, London, King & Son.

Cohen, R. & Lakhani, B. (1986) 'Board and Lodging Supplement' (issued February 1986) to the *National Welfare Benefits Handbook – 15th. Edition (1985)*, London, Child Poverty Action Group.

Cohen, S. (1985) *Visions of Social Control*, Oxford, Polity Press.

Cohen, S. & Scull, A. (1985) 'Introduction: Social Control in History and Sociology' in Cohen, S. & Scull, A. (eds) *Social Control and the State*, Oxford, Basil Blackwell.

Coleman, R.J. (1970) *Supplementary Benefit and the Administrative Review of Administrative Action*, 'Poverty' pamphlet No. 7, London, Child Poverty Action Group.

Commission of Inquiry into the Poor Laws (1834) 'Report of His Majesty's Commissioners into the Administration and Practical Operation of the Poor Laws' published by order of the House of Commons (44) xxvii Session 1834, reproduced (1970) in *British Parliamentary Papers – Poor Law 8*, Shannon, Irish University Press.

Coussins, M. & Hussain, A. (1984) *Michel Foucault*, London, Macmillan.

CPAG (Child Poverty Action Group Staff) (1989) 'One year on ....', *Poverty* No. 72.

Crosland, C.A.R. (1956) *The Future of Socialism*, London, Jonathan Cape.

Dahrendorf, R. (1987) *The Underclass and the Future of Britain*, St. George's House Tenth Annual Lecture, Windsor Castle, 27 April 1987.

Davies, C. (1987) 'JTS: Towards Workfare?' *Welfare Rights Bulletin*, No. 80.

Dean, H. (1988) *Social Security, Social Control and the Tribunal Process*, Ph.D. Thesis, University of Kent at Canterbury.

DHSS (Department of Health and Social Security) (1985a) *Social Security Appeal Tribunals: A Guide to Procedure*, London, HMSO.

—— (1985b) Green Paper, *The Reform of Social Security*, Vol. 1, Cmnd. 9517, London, HMSO.

—— (1985c) White Paper, *Reform of Social Security: Programme for Action*, Cmnd. 9691, London, HMSO.

—— (1987a) *Social Security Statistics 1986*, London, HMSO.

REFERENCES

—— (1987b) *Social Fund Manual*, London, HMSO.
Dilnot, A.W., Kay, J.A. & Morris, C.N. (1984) *The Reform of Social Security*, Oxford, Institute of Fiscal Studies/Oxford University Press.
Donnison, D. (1982) *The Politics of Poverty*, Oxford, Martin Robertson.
Donzelot, J. (1980) *The Policing of Families*, London, Hutchinson.
DSS (Department of Social Security) (1989) *Social Security Statistics 1988*, London, HMSO.
Durkheim, E. (1964a) *The Division of Labour*, New York, Free Press.
—— (1964b) *The Rules of Sociological Method*, New York, Free Press.
Dworkin, R. (1977) *Taking Rights Seriously*, Duckworth.
Esam, P., Good, R. & Middleton, R. (1985) *Who's to Benefit: A Radical View of the Social Security System*, London, Verso.
Fairbairns, Z. (1985) 'The Cohabitation Rule: Why it Makes Sense' in Ungerson, C. (ed.) *Women and Social Policy*, London, Macmillan.
Field, F. (1972) 'Poor People's Courts', *New Law Journal*.
—— (1975) *Unequal Britain*, London, Arrow.
—— (1981) *Inequality in Britain: Freedom, Welfare and the State*, London, Fontana.
—— (1989) *Losing Out: The Emergence of Britain's Underclass*, Oxford, Basil Blackwell.
Fischer, E. (1963) *The Necessity of Art: A Marxist Approach*, Harmondsworth, Penguin.
Foster, J. (1976) 'Imperialism and the Labour Aristocracy' in Skelley, J. (ed.) *The General Strike*, London, Lawrence & Wishart.
Foucault, M. (1977) *Discipline and Punish*, Harmondsworth, Penguin.
—— (1981a) 'On Popular Justice: A Discussion with Maoists' in Gordon, C. (ed.) *Power/Knowledge*, Brighton, Harvester.
—— (1981b) *History of Sexuality*, Vol. 1: An Introduction, Harmondsworth, Penguin.
Franks, O. (1957) *Report of the Committee on Administrative Tribunals and Enquiries* ('The Franks Report'), Cmnd. 218, London, HMSO.
Frost, J. & Howard, C. (1977) *Representation and Administrative Tribunals*, London, Routledge & Kegan Paul.
Fulbrook, J. (1975) *The Appellant and His Case: The Appellant's View of Supplementary Benefit Appeal Tribunals*, London, Child Poverty Action Group.
Ganz, G. (1974) *Administrative Procedures*, London, Sweet & Maxwell.
Garland, D. (1981) 'The Birth of the Welfare Sanction', *British Journal of Law & Society*, Vol. 8 No. 1.
George, V. (1973) *Social Security and Society*, London, Routledge & Kegan Paul.
George, V. & Wilding, P. (1985) *Ideology and Social Welfare*, London, Routledge & Kegan Paul.
Gilbert, B. (1966) *The Evolution of National Insurance in Great Britain*, London, Michael Joseph.
—— (1970) *British Social Policy 1914–1939*, London, Batsford.
Ginsberg, N. (1979) *Class, Capital and Social Policy*, London, Macmillan.

REFERENCES

Gough, I. (1979) *The Political Economy of the Welfare State*, London, Macmillan.
Gramsci, A. (1971) *Prison Notebooks*, London, Lawrence & Wishart.
Green Party (1988) *Manifesto for a Sustainable Society*, London, Green Party.
Gueron, J. (1986) *Work Initiatives for Welfare Recipients*, New York, Manpower Demonstration Research Corporation.
Haines, H. (1979) 'Cognitive Claims-making, Enclosure and the Depoliticisation of Social Problems', *Sociological Quarterly*, Vol. 20 No. 1.
Hall, S. (1988) 'Brave New World', *Marxism Today*, Vol. 32 No. 10.
Hammond, J.L. & Hammond, B. (1936) 'The Village Labourer' 4th. ed., London, Longman.
Harlow, C. (1981) 'Discretion, Social Security & Computers', *Modern Law Review*, Vol. 44 No. 5.
Harris, N. (1983) 'The Reform of the Supplementary Benefit Appeal System', *Journal of Social Welfare Law*, [1983] pp. 212–27.
Hay, D. (1975) *Albion's Fatal Tree*, London, Allen Lane.
Hay, J.R. (1978) 'Employers' Attitudes to Social Policy and the Concept of "Social Control" 1900–1920' in Thane, P. (ed.) *Origins of British Social Policy*, Beckenham, Croom Helm.
Herman, M. (1972) *Administrative Justice and Supplementary Benefits*, London, Occasional Papers on Social Administration No. 47.
Higgins, J. (1980) 'Social Control Theories of Social Policy', *Journal of Social Policy*, Vol. 9 No. 1.
Hirsch, J. (1978) 'The State Apparatus and Social Reproduction: Elements of a Theory of the Bourgeois State' in Holloway, J. & Picciotto, S. (eds) *State and Capital: A Marxist Debate*, London, Edward Arnold.
Hirst, P. (1980) 'Law, Socialism and Rights' in Carlen, P. & Collison, M. (eds) *Radical Issues in Criminology*, Oxford, Martin Robertson.
Hobsbawm, E.J. (1962) *The Age of Revolution 1789–1848*, New York, Mentor.
Holloway, J. & Picciotto, S. (eds) (1978) *State and Capital: A Marxist Debate*, London, Edward Arnold.
Holman, R. (1978) *Poverty*, Oxford, Martin Robertson.
House of Commons (1982) Report and Minutes of Evidence of the Treasury and Civil Service Committee Sub-Committee ('The Meacher Report') *The Structure of Personal Income Taxation and Income Support*, London, HMSO.
Hunt, E. & Hunt, R. (1969) 'The Role of Courts in Rural Mexico' in Bock, P. (ed.) *Peasants in the Modern World*, University of New Mexico Press.
Ignatieff, M. (1978) *A Just Measure of Pain*, New York Pantheon.
—— (1985) 'State, Civil Society and Total Institutions: A Critique of Recent Social Histories of Punishment' in Cohen, S. & Scull, A. (eds) *Social Control and the State*, Oxford, Basil Blackwell.

REFERENCES

—— (1989) 'Caring Just Isn't Enough', *New Statesman and Society*, 3 February 1989.
Illich, I. (1973) *Tools for Conviviality*, London, Calder & Boyars.
Jackson, M., Stewart, H. & Bland, R. (1987a) 'Appeal Tribunals on Supplementary Benefit', *Social Policy & Administration*, Vol. 21 No. 1.
—— (1987b) 'Tribunals Hearing Supplementary Benefit Appeals: The Members' Role', *Policy & Politics*, Vol. 15 No. 4.
Janowitz, M. (1975) 'Sociological Theory and Social Control' *American Journal of Sociology*, Vol. 81 No. 1.
Jordan, B. (1973) *Paupers: the Making of the Claiming Class*, London, Routledge & Kegan Paul.
—— (1981) *Automatic Poverty*, London, Routledge & Kegan Paul.
—— (1985) *The State: Authority and Autonomy*, Oxford, Basil Blackwell.
—— (1987) *Rethinking Welfare*, Oxford, Basil Blackwell.
Jowell, J. (1973) 'The Legal Control of Administrative Discretion' Public Law [1973] pp. 178–220.
—— (1975) *Law and Bureaucracy: Administrative Discretion and the Limits of Legal Action*, New York, Dunellan.
Keane, J. (1988) *Democracy and Civil Society*, London, Verso.
Kincaid, J.C. (1975) *Poverty and Equality in Britain: A Study of Social Security and Taxation*, Harmondsworth, Penguin.
Labour Party (1988) *Democratic Socialist Aims and Values*, London, Labour Party.
—— (1989) *Meet the Challenge Make the Change: Final Report of the Labour Party Policy Review for the 1990s*, London, Labour Party.
Lambeth (London Borough of) (1985) *The Social Security Reviews: Lambeth's Response*, London, London Borough of Lambeth.
Land, H. (1975) 'The Introduction of Family Allowances' in Hall, R., Land, H., Parker, R. & Webb, A. (eds) *Change, Choice and Conflict in Social Policy*, London, Heinemann.
Lawrence, E. (1982) 'Just plain common sense: the "roots" of racism' in Centre for Contemporary Cultural Studies (eds) *The Empire Strikes Back*, London, Hutchinson.
Lea, J. (1979) 'Discipline and Capitalist Development' in National Deviancy Conference/Conference of Socialist Economists (eds) *Capitalism and the Rule of Law*, London, Hutchinson.
Le Grand, J. (1982) *The Strategy of Equality*, London, Allen & Unwin.
Lenin, V. (1965) *State and Revolution*, Moscow, Progress.
Lis, C. & Soly, H. (1979) *Poverty and Capitalism in Pre-Industrial Europe*, Brighton, Harvester.
Lister, R. (1974) *Justice for the Claimant: A Study of Supplementary Benefit Appeal Tribunals*, Poverty Research Series 4, London, Child Poverty Action Group.
—— (1980) 'Discretion – Getting it Right' in Coussins (ed.) *Dear SSAC Poverty Pamphlet No. 49*, London, Child Poverty Action Group.
—— (1987) *There is an Alternative: Reforming Social Security*, London, Child Poverty Action Group.
Lukács, G. (1971) *History and Class Consciousness*, London, Merlin Press.

REFERENCES

Lukes, S. (1974) *Power: A Radical View*, London, Macmillan.

Lynes, T. (1975) 'Unemployment Assistance Tribunals in the 1930s' in Adler, M. & Bradley, A. (eds) *Justice, Discretion & Poverty*, Abingdon, Oxon., Professional Books.

Mack, J. & Lansley, S. (1985) *Poor Britain*, London, Allen & Unwin.

Manning, N. (1985) 'Reconstructing Social Problems: Policy Failure, Ideology and Social Knowledge' in Manning (ed.) *Social Problems and Welfare Ideology*, London, Gower.

Marcuse, H. (1964) *One Dimensional Man*, London, Routledge & Kegan Paul.

Marshall, T.H. (1963) 'Citizenship and Social Class' in *Sociology at the Crossroads and Other Essays*, London, Heinemann.

Marx, K. (1969) 'Preface to a Contribution to the Critique of Political Economy' in *Marx & Engels Selected Works*, Vol. I, Moscow, Progress.

—— (1970a) *Capital*, Vol. I, London, Lawrence & Wishart.

—— (1970b) *Capital*, Vol. III, London, Lawrence & Wishart.

—— (1975) 'The Critique of Hegel's Philosophy of Right' in *Marx – Early Writings*, Harmondsworth, Penguin.

—— (1976) 'The German Ideology' in *Marx & Engels Selected Works*, Vol. V, London, Lawrence & Wishart.

Marx, K. & Engels, F. (1970) *Communist Manifesto*, New York, Merit Pamphlet.

Mayer, J. (1985) 'Notes Towards a Working Definition of Social Control in Historical Analysis' in Cohen, S. & Scull, A. (eds) *Social Control and the State*, Oxford, Basil Blackwell.

Meade, J.E. (1978) *The Structure and Reform of Direct Taxation* ('The Meade Report'), London, Allen & Unwin for the Institute of Fiscal Studies.

Melossi, D. (1979) 'Institutions of Social Control and Capitalist Organisation of Work' in National Deviancy Conference/Conference of Socialist Economists (eds) *Capitalism and the Rule of Law*, London, Hutchinson.

Melossi, D. & Pavarini, M. (1981) *The Prison and the Factory*, London, Macmillan.

Miliband, R. (1969) *The State in Capitalist Society*, London, Wiedenfield & Nicolson.

Milton, C. (1975) 'Appellants' Perceptions of the Tribunal Process' in Adler, M. & Bradley, A. (eds) *Justice, Discretion & Poverty*, Abingdon, Oxon., Professional Books.

Ministry of Labour (1923) *Report on National Unemployment Insurance to July 1923*, London, HMSO.

—— (1938) *Annual Report 1938*, Cmd. 6016, London, HMSO.

Morris, A., Giller, H., Szwed, E. & Geach, H. (1980) *Justice for Children*, London, Macmillan.

Murray, R. (1988) 'Life After Henry (Ford)', *Marxism Today*, Vol. 32 No. 10.

NAB (National Assistance Board) (1953) *Annual Report 1953*, Cmd. 9210, London, HMSO.

REFERENCES

—— (1963) *Annual Report 1963*, Cmnd. 2386, London, HMSO.
NATFHE (National Association of Teachers in Further and Higher Education) (1984) *The Great Training Robbery: An Interim Report on the Role of Private Training Agencies within the Youth Training Scheme in the Birmingham and Solihull Area*, Birmingham, Birmingham Trade Union Resource Centre.
NCC (National Consumer Council) (1984) *Of Benefit to All: A Consumer Review of Social Security*, London, NCC.
Novak, T. (1988) *Poverty and the State*, Milton Keynes, Open University Press.
O'Connor, J. (1973) *Fiscal Crisis of the State*, New York, St Martin's Press.
Ogus, A.I. & Barendt, E.M. (1978) *The Law of Social Security* (second edition), London, Butterworth.
O'Higgins, M. (1983) 'Issues of Redistribution in State Welfare Spending' in Loney, M., Boswell, D. & Clarke, J. (eds) *Social Policy and Social Welfare*, Milton Keynes, Open University Press.
Omega Report (1984) *Social Security Policy*, London, Adam Smith Institute.
Oppenheim, C. (1988) *Poverty: The Facts* (second edition), London, Child Poverty Action Group.
Pahl, R. (1988) 'Some Remarks on Informal Work, Social Polarisation and the Social Structure', *International Journal of Urban and Regional Research*, Vol. 12 No. 2.
Paine, T. (1915) *Rights of Man*, London, Dent & Sons.
Park, R.E. & Burgess, E.W. (1924) *Introduction to the Science of Sociology*, Chicago, University Press.
Parsons, T. (1951) *The Social System*, London, Routledge & Kegan Paul.
Partington, M. (1986a) 'The Restructuring of Social Security Appeal Tribunals: A Personal View' in Harlow, C. (ed.) *Public Law and Politics*, London, Sweet & Maxwell.
—— (1986b) 'Adjudication and the Social Fund: Some Preliminary Observations', *Legal Action*, April 1986.
Pashukanis, E.B. (1978) *General Theory of Law and Marxism*, London, Ink Links.
Pasquino, P. (1980) 'Criminology: the Birth of a Special Saviour', *Ideology & Consciousness*, No. 7.
Pinker, R. (1971) *Social Theory and Social Policy*, London, Heinemann.
Piven, F. & Cloward, R. (1974) *Regulating the Poor: the functions of public welfare*, London, Tavistock.
Plant, R. (1988) *Citizenship and Social Rights Tract 531*, London, Fabian Society.
Poulantzas, N. (1973) *Political Power and Social Classes*, London, New Left Books.
—— (1980) *State, Power, Socialism*, London, Verso.
Prosser, T. (1977) 'Poverty, Ideology and Legality: Supplementary Benefit Appeal Tribunals and their Predecessors' *British Journal of Law and Society*, Vol. 4 No. 1.
—— (1983) *Test Cases for the Poor*, London, Child Poverty Action Group.

REFERENCES

Reich, C. (1964) 'The New Property', *Yale Law Journal*, Vol. 73 No. 5.
Rose, H. (1975) 'Who Can De-label the Claimant?' in Adler, M. & Bradley, A. (eds) *Justice, Discretion & Poverty*, Abingdon, Oxon., Professional Books.
Ross, E.A. (1959) *Social Control and the Foundations of Sociology* (edited by Borgetta, E. & Meyer, H.) Boston, Beacon Press.
Rothman, D. (1980) *Conscience and Convenience*, New York, Little, Brown.
Rowntree, B.S. (1902) *Poverty, a Study of Town Life*, London, Macmillan.
—— (1918) *The Human Needs of Labour*, Thomas Nelson & Sons.
—— (1937) *The Human Needs of Labour*, London, Longman.
Royal Commission on the Distribution of Income and Wealth (1976) *Report No. 6 – Lower Incomes*, Cmnd. 7175, London, HMSO.
Saville, J. (1958) 'The Welfare State: An Historical Approach', *New Reasoner*, Vol. 1 No. 3.
SBC (Supplementary Benefits Commission) (1979) *Annual Report 1979*, Cmnd. 8033, London, HMSO.
de Schweinitz, K. (1961) *England's Road to Social Security*, University of Pennsylvania, Perpetua.
Scull, A. (1977) *Decarceration: Community Treatment and the Deviant*, New Jersey, Prentice Hall.
SDP (Social Democratic Party) (1983) *Attacking Poverty*, London, Social Democratic Party.
Seabrook, J. (1985) *Landscapes of Poverty*, Oxford, Basil Blackwell.
Shragge, E. (1984) *Pensions Policy in Britain: a Socialist Analysis*, London, Routledge & Kegan Paul.
Smart, B. (1983) 'On Discipline and Social Regulation' in Garland, D. & Young, P. (eds) *The Power to Punish*, London, Heinemann.
Smith, R. (1985) 'Who's fiddling: fraud and abuse' in Ward, S. (ed.) *DHSS in Crisis*, London, Child Poverty Action Group.
Social Security Consortium (1986) *Of Little Benefit: A Critical Guide to the Social Security Act 1986*, London, Association of Metropolitan Authorities.
—— (1987) *Of Little Benefit: An Update*, London, Association of Metropolitan Authorities.
Society of Civil and Public Servants (1985) *Social Security for All the People: An Alternative to the New Poor Law*, London, Society of Civil and Public Servants.
Sohn-Rethel, A. (1978) *Intellectual and Manual Labour: A Critique of Epistemology*, London, Macmillan.
Spicker, P. (1984) *Stigma and Social Welfare*, Beckenham, Croom Helm.
Squires, P. (1985) *Pauperism, Pathology and Policing: Studies in the Criminalisation of Poverty*, PhD Thesis, Bristol University.
Stedman-Jones, G. (1985) 'Class Expression vs Social Control' in Cohen, S. & Scull, A. (eds) *Social Control and the State*, Oxford, Basil Blackwell.
Strathern, M. (1985) 'Discovering "Social Control"', *Journal of Law and Society*, Vol. 12 No. 2.

REFERENCES

Street, H. (1975) *Justice in the Welfare State*, London, Stevens & Sons.
Szasz, T. (1961) *The Myth of Mental Illness*, New York, Harper & Row.
Taylor, I. (1981) *Law and Order: Arguments for Socialism*, London, Macmillan.
Taylor-Gooby, P. (1985) *Public Opinion, Ideology and State Welfare*, London, Routledge & Kegan Paul.
Taylor-Gooby, P. & Dale, J. (1981) *Social Theory and Social Welfare*, London, Edward Arnold.
Thane, P. (1982) *The Foundations of the Welfare State*, London, Longman.
Thompson, E.P. (1968) *The Making of the English Working Class*, Harmondsworth, Penguin.
—— (1975) *Whigs and Hunters*, New York, Parthenon.
Titmuss, R. (1968) *Commitment to Welfare*, London, Allen & Unwin.
—— (1971) 'Welfare Rights, Law and Discretion', *Political Quarterly*, Vol. 42 No. 2.
—— (1973) *The Gift Relationship*, Harmondsworth, Penguin.
Townsend, P. (1979) *Poverty in the UK*, Harmondsworth, Penguin.
—— (1980) 'Social Planning and the Treasury' in Bosanquet, N. & Townsend, P. (eds) *Labour and Equality*, London, Heinemann.
Trinder, C. (1976) 'Inflation and the Social Wage' in Willmott, P. (ed.) *Poverty Report 1976*, London, Temple Smith.
UAB (Unemployment Assistance Board) (1935) *Report 1935*, Cmd. 5177, London, HMSO.
—— (1938) *Report 1938*, Cmd. 6021, London, HMSO.
Walker, A. & Walker, C. (1987) (eds) *The Growing Divide: A Social Audit 1979–1987*, London, Child Poverty Action Group.
Ward, S. (1985) 'Introduction: the Political Background' in Ward, S. (ed.) *DHSS in Crisis*, London, Child Poverty Action Group.
Webb, S. & Webb, B. (1909) *Break up of the Poor Law*, London, Fabian Society.
—— (1927) *English Poor Law History Part I*, London, Longman (1927).
Weber, M. (1949) *The Theory of Social and Economic Organisation*, Glencoe, Ill., Free Press.
White, R. (1973) 'Lawyers and the Enforcement of Rights' in Morris, P., White, R. & Lewis, N. *Social Needs and Legal Action*, Oxford, Martin Robertson.
Wilding, R. (1975) 'Discretionary Benefits' in Adler, M. & Bradley, A. (eds) *Justice, Discretion & Poverty*, Abingdon, Oxon., Professional Books.
Younghusband, E. (1964) *Social Work and Social Change*, London, Allen & Unwin.

NAME INDEX

Abel, R. 93
Abel-Smith, B. 90
Adler, M. 99
Alcock, P. 110
Allbeson, J. 6, 100, 184
Althusser, L. 21, 28, 29
Annette, J. 140
Ashby, P. 187, 188
Atkinson, A.B. 5

Bankowski, Z. 2, 141
Banks, M.H. 6
Barendt, E.M. 105, 107
Bell, K. 88, 89, 97, 98–9, 102, 125, 126, 136, 140, 147, 149, 150, 151, 154, 155, 163
Bennet, F. 86, 179, 182
Bentham, J. 30, 53, 54, 79, 81, 139–40
Bevan, A. 12
Beveridge, W. 12, 13, 41, 59, 67, 86
Blackley, W. 58
Booth, C. 67
Bosanquet, N. 68, 70
Boyson, R. 180
Bradshaw, J. 185
Burgess, E.W. 25
Burkeman, S. 140
Burton, J. 6
Butler, R. 13

Callaghan, J. 14
Campbell, B. 192, 193
Campbell, D. 63, 64
Castle, B. 38
Chadwick, E. 53, 55, 79, 81, 82
Chalmers, T. 54, 55–6, 84, 142

Chapman, P. 184
Churchill, W. 90
Cloward, R. 2, 4
Coates, K. 66
Cobbett, W. 81
Cohen, J.L. 91
Cohen, R. 110
Cohen, S. 10, 19, 20, 23, 25, 86, 101
Coleman, R.J. 145, 146
Connor, S. 63, 64
Coussins, M. 175
Crosland, C.A.R. 84

Dahrendorf, R. 7, 74, 193
Dales, J. 12, 14, 83
Darwin, C. 45
Davies, C. 5
Dean, H. 116, 124, 125, 131, 157, 162, 163, 164
Dilnot, A.W. 187, 189, 190
Disraeli, B. 47, 79
Donnison, D. 42, 67
Donzelot, J. 31, 36, 38, 137, 138, 161
Durkheim, E. 24, 25, 32
Dworkin, R. 141

Engels, F. 43
Esam, P. 189–90, 198

Fairburns, Z. 135
Field, F. 12, 59, 66, 68, 193
Fischer, E. 76
Foster, J. 92
Foucault, M. 18, 20, 22, 23, 29, 30, 31, 33, 63, 71, 76–7, 79, 85, 89, 136–7, 138–9, 143, 144, 175, 178, 200–2

NAME INDEX

Fowler, N. 179
Franks, O. 98, 96–7
Frost, J. 99, 147
Fulbrook, J. 99, 115, 147, 149, 150 151, 155

Ganz, G. 99–100
Garland, D. 69–70
George, V. 12, 13, 84
Gilbert, B. 90, 93, 109
Ginsberg, N. 16, 61
Goschen, G. 57
Gough, I. 3, 13, 16
Gramsci, A. 28
Gueron, J. 6

Haines, H. 69
Hale, M. 39
Hall, S. 192
Hammond, B. 40
Hammond, J.L. 40
Harlow, C. 60
Harris, N. 89
Hay, D. 19
Hay, J.R. 90
Herman, M. 99, 115
Higgins, J. 10
Hill, O. 56
Hirsch, J. 15
Hirst, P. 198
Hobbes, T. 53
Holloway, J. 14
Holman, R. 66
Howard, C. 99, 147
Hunt, E. 156
Hurd, D. 194
Hussain, A. 175

Ignatieff, M. 18, 20, 22, 194, 195
Illich, I. 73

Jackson, M. 161
Janowitz, M. 23–4
Jordan, B. 74, 75, 78, 133, 188, 196–9, 201
Jowell, J. 58, 144

Keane, J. 195
Keynes, J.M. 12
Kincaid, J.C. 12, 16, 67

Lakhani, B. 110
Land, H. 41

Lansley, S. 66, 67, 181
Lawrence, E. 184
Lea, J. 17
Le Grand, J. 67
Lenin, V. 21
Lis, C. 37, 51
Lister, R. 99, 100, 115, 125, 187, 189
Locke, J. 53
Lukács, G. 28
Lukes, S. 29
Luther, M. 51–2, 53
Lynes, T. 93, 94, 95, 109, 110

Mack, J. 66, 67, 181
Malthus, T.R. 45, 46
Manning, N. 69
Marcuse, H. 73
Marshall, T.H. 37–8, 80, 141
Marx, K. 14, 27, 28, 43, 52, 61–2, 74
Mayer, J. 10
Meade, J.E. 185
Melossi, D. 18, 20, 22, 33, 62
Micklewright, J. 5
Miliband, R. 14
Milton, C. 99, 147, 149, 150
Moore, J. 66, 199, 201
Morris, A. 19
Mungham, G. 92
Murray, R. 3

Nelken, D. 141
Newman, D. 64
Novak, T. 2

O'Connor, J. 13
Ogus, A.I. 105, 107
O'Higgins, M. 68
Oppenheim, C. 193
Orwell, G. 197
Owen, R. 39

Pahl, R. 193
Paine, T. 80
Park, R.E. 25
Parsons, T. 25–6, 32
Partington, M. 102–3, 163, 169
Pashukanis, E.B. 15, 176, 197
Pasquino, P. 70
Pavarini, M. 18, 20, 22
Piciotto, S. 14
Pinker, R. 37
Pitt, W. 40
Piven, F. 2, 4

214

NAME INDEX

Place, F. 81
Plant, R. 195
Poulantzas, N. 14, 21, 22, 23, 29, 30, 31, 200–1
Prosser, T. 88, 89, 94

Reich, C. 142
Roosevelt, T. 12
Rose, H. 99, 138
Ross, E.A. 25
Rothman, D. 18, 20, 61
Rowntree, B.S. 67
Rushton, B. 78, 82

Saville, J. 11
Schweinitz, K. de 37, 38, 39, 40, 46, 47, 48, 49, 52, 53, 55, 56, 82
Scott, J. 46
Scull, A. 19, 23, 25, 86
Seabrook, J. 65, 73, 78
Senior, N. 53
Shragge, E. 16–17, 50
Silburn, R. 66
Smart, B. 70, 71
Smith, A. 198
Smith, R. 100, 131
Sohn-Rethel, A. 17, 18
Soly, H. 37, 51
Spicker, P. 38, 79, 82
Squires, P. 104, 113, 114, 115, 131

Stedman-Jones, G. 10
Stevens, R. 90
Street, H. 89, 92
Szasz, T. 19

Taylor, I. 61
Taylor-Gooby, P. 12, 14, 83, 195
Thane, P. 35, 86
Thatcher, M. 4, 7, 184, 194
Thompson, E.P. 18, 39, 58, 73, 74, 78, 80, 81
Titmuss, R. 37, 141–2
Tooze, M. 184
Townsend, P. 1, 14, 65–6, 67, 68
Trinder, C. 38

Ullah, P. 6

Walker, A. 7
Walker, C. 7
Ward, S. 180
Webb, B. 52, 83–4
Webb, S. 52, 83–4
Weber, M. 21, 26–7, 32
White, R. 114
Wilding, R. 12, 84, 142
Wilson, H. 14

Younghusband, E. 56

SUBJECT INDEX

Adam Smith Institute 187
adjudication 144, 146, 151, 153, 155–6, 165, 166; *see also* tribunals
Adjudication Officer: role of 102, 115, 138, 146, 164
administrative discipline 129, 131, 173
administrative rules: disputes about 157
anti-populationist discourse 81, 110; *see also* repressive discourse
appellants: attitudes of 150, 158, 163–5; role of 159; success rate of 124–6, 147; understanding of tribunal process 149–50
Assistance Tribunals 95, 108
Attendance Allowance 172
availability for work tests 5, 172

badging 38, 79; *see also* begging
Basic Income Guarantee 187, 188, 190, 196–9
begging 37–8, 42, 44, 51, 52, 177
Beveridge Report 41, 50, 59, 95, 111, 116, 179, 182, 187; post-Beveridge era 133
Board of Trade 91, 92, 127
Boards of Guardians 49, 57

capital/labour relations: and development of welfare state 11–14, 61, 92, 188; and social sanctions 20–3, 32; and Social Security Act 1086 181; and social security system 35, 72, 76, 85, 175–9; and tribunals 132
capitalism: and poverty 3, 65, 69, 72, 73; and social control 10, 21; and social security reform 180; and the social wage 17; and technological development 74–5; and the welfare state 12, 82, 92, 176; *see also* state derivation debate
case-approach 36, 63, 133, 177–8, 191, 196; development of 55–8, 84; and the Social Fund 168; and tribunals 128, 141, 143, 158, 173; *see also* disciplinary techniques
charity: resurgence of 195
Charity Organisation Society 56–7, 168, 196
Charter 88, 195
Child Benefit 4, 6, 42, 95, 170
Child Benefit Act 1975 42
Child Poverty Action Group (CPAG) 5, 6, 97, 142, 181, 186, 189; *see also* welfare rights lobby
citizens 71, 82; and government 89; and participation 8, 67, 97; *see also* individual and the state
citizenship 7, 37–8, 42; and dignity 185–6, and Thatcher government 194–6
civil disorder 2, 11; *see also* resistance
claimants 9, 184–7; as citizens 42–3; as consumers 185; as juridical subjects 186; and resistance 199–202; and right of appeal 88, 89, 94, 166; and state 175–6, 178, 190, 191; status of 77, 82, 84–5, 199–200; and tribunals 88, 96; types of 121–4; *see also* appellants
claiming class 9, 74–6, 77, 133

216

SUBJECT INDEX

client group premiums 5, 171
cohabitation 113–14, 131, 135
Commission of Inquiry into the Poor Laws 1833–4 48, 82
commodity form 191–2, 198; *see also* wage relation
constructive household concept 110; *see also* family dependency
consumer culture: and poverty 73
Council of Tribunals 96
Courts of Referees 90–3, 94, 95, 96, 104–5, 106, 107, 108, 116, 127, 132, 140
crime 18–20
criminality 67–71

deindustrialisation: and capital 75
Department of Employment 6, 138
Department of Health and Social Security (DHSS) 5, 6, 60, 63, 64, 101–2, 111, 112, 114, 115, 129, 131, 180
Department of Social Security (DSS) 63, 111, 138, 145, 146, 168
dependency culture 7, 9
dependency status 135, 157, 201; *see also* family dependency
deprivation: material 71; and social control 11, 72; *see also* poverty
disabled people 5, 72, 193
disciplinary examination 136–74; *see also* tribunals
disciplinary mechanisms 9, 36, 64, 73, 75, 176; *see also* disciplinary techniques
disciplinary techniques 2, 22–3, 33, 35–64, 65–87, 89, 121, 131, 136, 141, 145, 154, 166, 177–8, 180, 186 187, 189, 191; *see also* case-approach; legalisation; partitioning
discretion 97, 119, 140–3; and Family Credit 170; and Income Support 170; and the Social Fund 168; and tribunals 163; *see also* welfare rights lobby disincentives 182–3; and young people 184
disqualification from benefits 104; and social assistance 108, 172; and trade disputes 106–7; *see also* suspension of benefit

Earnings Related Supplements 4

elderly 72; *see also* retirement pensioners
Elizabethan Poor Law 44–5, 79
employment training schemes (ET) 6, 111, 184
enterprise culture 7
entitlement 97, 140–3, 168; *see also* welfare rights lobby
equity 142–3; *see also* need
Exceptional Circumstances Additions 129
Exceptional Needs Payments 129

Fabian/Social Democrat school 61, 81, 83–5, 86
fairness 143, 197–8
family: dependency 109–11, 157; and social control 31; and the workhouse 82
Family Allowance 41–2, 95
Family Credit 4, 6, 41, 42, 169–70
Family Income Supplement 41, 42, 96, 170
Franks Committee 1955 96
fraud and abuse 113–14, 115, 130–1, 185, 193; *see also* misrepresentation; overpayments of benefits

Gilbert Act 1782 46
Gladstone Report 1895 19
Green Party 196

Health and Social Services and Social Security Adjudication Act 1983 101
Housing Benefit 4, 110, 170, 179
humanitarian/pro-populationist discourse 190

ideology: concept of 27–9, 33
incentives 5, 182–3
Income Support 1, 4, 5, 41, 42, 50, 51, 60, 168, 169–71, 172; suspension of 108; and young people 6, 111, 174, 184
Income Support (General) Regulations 1987 50, 51
indigence 55, 70
individual: discipline 136; and participation 7–8; and social control 23–31; and social fund 169; and social wage 18; and the state 70–1, 129, 157, 176–7, 185,

SUBJECT INDEX

186, 191; and tribunals 88–9; *see also* appellants; claimants
Industrial Injuries scheme 95
inequality 67–8; and the welfare state 12; *see also* poverty
Institute of Fiscal Studies (IFS) 187, 188–9, 190
Insurance Commissioners 91
Invalidity Benefit: and tribunals 126
Invalid Care Allowance: and tribunals 126

Job Training 184

Labour discipline 110, 111, 127, 129, 131, 132, 134, 157, 173–4; *see also* work-testing, trade disputes
Labour Party 14, 38, 77, 84, 90, 195–6; and Courts of Referees 91; and Statutory Minimum Wage 190; and Wilson/Callaghan government 14
leaving home cases 109–10, 135
legalisation 36, 58–60, 63, 84, 128, 134, 141, 143, 158, 168, 173, 178, 186, 191, 195; *see also* disciplinary techniques
less eligibility 53, 79, 80, 81–2; and the workhouse 47, 139
Liable Relatives Officers 114
Liberal Party 195
Local Government Board 49, 91
Local Government Board Act 1871 49

Meade Report (1978) 185
means-tested benefits 4, 5, 42, 60, 65–6, 91, 95–6, 170; and Speenhamland system 41; and work-testing 107–9; *see also* Meade Report
means testing 49, 50, 57, 110, 129, 169, 197; extension of 189; and the household 109–110
Metropolitan Poor Act 1867 48
Minister of Labour: and UATs 94, 95
Ministry of Health's Annual Report 1926–7 38
Ministry of Social Security 60
Ministry of Social Security Act 1966 59, 79
misrepresentation, or failure of disclose 112; *see also* overpayments; fraud; abuse
Mobility Allowance 172

National Assistance 41, 50, 96, 108
National Assistance Act 1948 59, 79, 95, 110, 111
National Assistance Board (NAB) 111, 129
National Assistance Tribunals (NAT) 95, 97, 108, 111, 119
National Consumer Council (NCC) 185, 187, 189
National Council for Voluntary Organisations (NCVO) 187–8
National Insurance Act 1911 49, 58, 90, 91, 104, 106
National Insurance Act 1916 49
National Insurance Act 1946 95
National Insurance benefits 4, 42, 50–1, 59, 116, 119, 121
National Insurance Commissioners 100, 105–6
National Insurance Local Tribunals (NILT) 95–101, 106, 107–8, 119, 124, 131, 143, 147, 149, 150, 154
need: and Basic Income 188; determination of 128, 191; and social security system 5, 6, 171–2, 186–7; and tribunals 128, 132–3, 142, 157; *see also* equity; poverty
Negative Income Tax 187, 188–9
New Poor Law 1834 40–1, 47–9, 79
New Right 181, 183, 185; and citizenship 195
New Times 192–9
normalisation 23, 30–1, 42–3, 63–4, 138, 140, 177

Old Age Pension 49, 58; and appeals 93, 95
Old Age Pension Act 1908 90–1
outdoor relief 46, 49, 55
Outdoor Relief Prohibitory Order 1844 48
overpayments of benefits 112, 114, 129, 130, 172, 174; *see also* fraud; abuse

participation 67; and benefit levels 181, 182; and tribunals 144, 159, 166; *see also* citizenship
partitioning 36, 65, 75–87, 128, 133, 134–5, 173, 178, 187, 191; and SSAT 143–4; and tribunals 109, 125–6; and the underclass 193–4;

SUBJECT INDEX

see also disciplinary techniques
paternalistic, humanitarian, pro-populationist discourse 36, 38, 39–45, 61, 62; and Basic Income 188; and development of social security 177, 181; and tribunals 84, 90, 97, 102, 103, 166
penal policy 18–20
penal theory 70, 110–111
penality 132, 177; and development of welfare 70; *see also* sanctions
Pensions Committees 91
personal social services 55
philanthropy 54, 57
Police Court Missioners 56
political settlement 11–18, 35, 89, 132, 166, 176; and future of social security 181–4; and SSA'86 180
Poor Law 39, 49, 55, 59, 60, 80, 83
Poor Law Amendment Act 1834 53, 56, 78–9, 80, 90, 110, 139
Poor Law Amendment Act 1867 48–9
Poor Law Amendment Act 1868 48–9
Poor Law Board 56
Poor Law Commissioners 48, 53
Poor Law Guardians 48
poverty: and capital accumulation 3; and criminality 67–71; definitions of 8, 66–7; in feudal times 37, 43, 68–9; and the Labour Party 196; levels of 66; measurement of 66, 193; and partitioning 65–87; and the poverty trap 183; sexuality 71; and social control 73–5; and social security 1, 2, 3, 8, 9, 67, 68, 85–6, 178, 181, 182, 187, 199; and the social wage 18, 35; and stigma 37, 75; and subjection 72–5; *see also* underclass; need
poverty lobby 7, 66, 199
power 29, 71, 60; mechanisms of 76, 84, 176–7; and poverty 68, 70; and power relations 85; and the social security sytem 3, 89, 186; sources of 141, 166–7; and the state 190–1, 198; *see also* technology of power
Presenting Officers 114–15
Public Assistance Committees 109

rationing 168
redistribution and social security 12, 68, 186
Reform Act 1832 47, 78

Relief Committee of the Board of Guardians 89
Relief Regulation Order 49
Rent tribunal 147
Report of the Commission of Inquiry into the Poor Laws 1833–4 53–4
Report by the Poor Law Commissioners 1840 48
representation: and success rate 148, 151–3; and tribunals 98, 151–5
repression 11, 35, 110; and tribunals 104, 113
repressive 'Malthusian', anti-populationist discourse 36, 40, 45–51, 61, 62, 103, 106, 109, 113–14, 166, 177, 181; and incentives 183, 184; and tax credits 189
reserve army 7, 62; *see also* underclass; capital/labour relations
resistance 175, 192, 199, 200–2; *see also* civil disorder
Restart interviews 5, 51
Retirement Pension 4, 116
Retirement pensioners 5, 76, 121–2, 193; and tribunals 125
Royal Commission on the Distribution of Income and Wealth 1976 12, 67
Royal Commission on the Poor Laws 1905–1909 49, 83; Minority Report of 83
Royal Commission on the Poor Laws of 1905–1911 58

saftey net 5, 51, 59, 96
sanctions 18–23, 36, 89, 177; development of 43–53; and SSA'86 180, 183–4; and tribunals 103, 166, 173; and young people 184
Scope Appeal 127–8
self-determination 53
self-discipline 2, 51–5, 183
self-help 55, 58, 60, 84, 189
self-partitioning 84
self-regulation 84, 110
self-sufficiency 55
Severe Disablement Allowances 172
Sickness Benefits 4
single parents 5, 72, 76, 193; and cohabitation 113–14
single payments: appeals 131, 167
social assistance 4, 57, 82, 90, 95, 107–9, 110; and overpayments

219

SUBJECT INDEX

112; and tribunals 116–19, 124–5, 128–9, 133, 154; and the work test 50
social control: concept of 2, 10–34; levels of 177; operation of 11; and physical force 11, 18; and social policy 176
Social Democratic Party 188, 195
Social Dividend 187, 188, 190
social duties 42; *see also* citizenship
Social Fund 5, 165–7; Inspector 168–9; Officers 168; and right of appeal 167
social insurance 4, 42, 49, 58–60, 63, 82, 90, 93, 104–7; and eligibility 50–1, 98; and and the Labour Party 196; and NCC 189; overpayments of 112; and tribunals 116–19, 124–5, 128–9, 133, 134, 154
social justice 82, 106
social rights 37–8, 80, 81, 82, 141; *see also* citizenship
Social Security: and control of behaviour 1–2, 7; development of 177–8; effects of 3; history of 2, 35–64; and need 1; and political behaviour of poor 2; and poverty 68–87; and stigma 37
Social Security Act 1975 50, 101
Social Security Act 1986 (SSA'86) 5, 50, 77, 87, 108, 110, 111, 112, 167, 174, 179, 180, 181, 184
Social Security Act 1988 6, 110, 111
Social Security Act 1989 108
Social Security Appeal Tribunal (SSAT) 88–135, 136–74, 178–9, 200; characteristics of 158–62; and competence 158; and discretion 163; jurisdiction of 159–60; members of 101; nature of appeals to 157; and recording 162–3; and role of chairperson 158–62; and role of lay members 161–2; and social security reform 167–74
Social Security Commissioners 100
Social Security Consortium 1987 5
Social Security and Housing Benefits Act 1982 110
social security reforms 4–9, 167–74; counter-proposals to 187–191; future of 175, 181–202; objectives of 175

social wage 11–18, 35, 37–8, 43, 92, 198; and Basic Income 188; and SSA'86 181; and tribunals 103, 166, 174, 177, 180
social work 55, 56; and representation at tribunals 153–4
socialist radicalism 189–90
Society of Civil and Public Servants 189
Special Investigators 114
Speenhamland system 39–41, 48
state derivation debate 14–16, 176
State Earnings Related Pension Scheme 4
Statute of Labourers 1349 43
stigma 37, 75, 185, 194; *see also* underclass; welfare rights lobby
strikers 108; *see also* trade disputes
subjection 72–5
subsistence standard 67, 72, 113, 181, 182; *see also* need
Supplementary Benefits 5, 41, 42, 50, 60, 66, 68, 96, 100, 108–29, 153, 170; and appeals 114, 121, 145; claims for 119; and single payments 167, 170, 171–2; and welfare rights lobby 97
Supplementary Benefit Appeal Tribunal (SBAT) 96, 97, 98, 99, 100, 101, 108, 111, 114, 119, 124, 129, 130, 135, 140, 143, 147, 149, 150, 153
Supplementary Benefit Board and Lodging Regulations 1985 110, 184
Supplementary Benefits Commission 60, 111, 114, 115, 129, 140, 145, 149
Supplementary Benefits (Single Payments) Regulations 1981 162
surveillance 4, 23, 30–1, 42, 63, 84, 138, 140, 145, 177; and Basic Income 197; and tax credit scheme 189
suspension of benefit 104–5, 106–7, 108, 111; *see also* disqualification

targeting 5, 6, 187
tax credits 187, 188–9, 197; *see also* Negative Income Tax
technology of power 29–31, 33, 68, 70, 71; *see also* power
Thatcher government: and poverty 66, 86, 199; and social security

SUBJECT INDEX

reforms 4–9, 121, 131, 167, 170, 179–81, 185–7, 189, 194–6; and the social wage 14
Thatcherism 174, 192, 194, 195
trade disputes 104, 106–7, 108, 128, 131; *see also* labour discipline; work-testing
trade union movement 17, 90, 91; and representation at tribunals 154
Transitional Allowances 41, 50, 93
tribunals 2, 88–135, 136–74, 178; adversarial and inquisitorial models of 99–100, 103, 114, 158, 159; as appellant's friend 100, 102–3; and attitudes of members 115; characteristics of 158–62; form of 136–44; hearing of 146–51; numbers of 115–21; participatory model of 99–100, 102, 103; and penalties 104–15; pre-hearing stage of 145–6; as a saftey value 94, 111, 166; success rate of 124–6, 147; and types of appeal 126–32, 157
Tribunals and Inquiries Act 1958 96

underclass 7, 9, 74, 192–3
unemployed 5, 6, 72, 121, 124; long term 113; and SSA'86 183–4; young 174, 184
unemployment 5, 75
Unemployment Assistance 41, 50, 93, 108–9
Unemployment Assistance Act 1934 93
Unemployment Assistance Board (UAB) 93, 94, 95, 96, 109, 110, 127
Unemployment Assistance Tribunal (UAT) 93–5, 96, 108, 109, 110, 116, 127, 128, 132
Unemployment Benefits 4, 5; appeals 131; eligibility for 50, 172
Unemployment Insurance 83, 90, 91, 93, 107
Unemployment Insurance Act 1920 49

Unemployment Insurance scheme 1911 104
Unemployment Insurance Tribunals (UIT) 95, 127–8, 132
Unemployment Review Officers 114
utilitarian, philanthropic, 'self-help' discourse 36, 40, 47, 52–60, 62; and the individual claimant 184–7, 189, 190; and partitioning 78–82, 84, 136, 139–40, 166, 177, 182, 183
utilitarianism 53–4; and justice 139–43

vagrancy 43

wage relation 76, 191–2, 197, 198; *see also* capital/labour relation
welfare rights lobby 77, 97, 169, 181, 185; *see also* CPAG
welfare rights officers: and representation 153, 154–5
welfare state: benefits of 3; development of 11–12, 82, 89; functions of 3, 176; growth of 35–64; and poverty 66–7; and redistribution 12; *see also* social wage
Widows, Orphans and Old Age Contributory Pensions Act 1925 49
widows pensions: and appeals 95
work-test 45, 49–51
work-testing 104–9, 172
workhouse 45–50; and partitioning 77, 79, 81–2; test 110, 139–40
working class 3, 73–4, 134; and the claiming class 75, 77; and disputes 90; formation of 78; and the social wage 12, 16–17; and tribunals 92–3
Workmen's Compensation Act 1897 90

young people: and social security system 6; *see also* family dependency; Income Support
Youth Training Scheme (YTS) 111, 184